Sarah Kane in context

edited by
Laurens De Vos
and
Graham Saunders

Manchester University Press
Manchester and New York

Distributed in the United States exclusively by Palgrave Macmillan

Published by Manchester University Press
Oxford Road, Manchester M13 9NR, UK
and Room 400, 175 Fifth Avenue, New York, NY 10010, USA
www.manchesteruniversitypress.co.uk

Distributed in the United States exclusively by
Palgrave Macmillan, 175 Fifth Avenue,
New York, NY 10010, USA

Distributed in Canada exclusively by
UBC Press, University of British Columbia, 2029 West Mall,
Vancouver, BC, Canada V6T 1Z2

British Library Cataloguing-in-Publication Data is available

Library of Congress Cataloging-in-Publication Data is available

ISBN 978 0 7190 8645 8 paperback

First published by Manchester University Press in hardback 2010

This paperback edition first published 2011

The publisher has no responsibility for the persistence or accuracy of URLs for any external or third-party internet websites referred to in this book, and does not guarantee that any content on such websites is, or will remain, accurate or appropriate.

Printed by Lightning Source

Contents

Part II: Subjectivity, responsibility and representation

Note to the text

Unless otherwise stated, all quotations from Sarah Kane's plays are taken from *Complete Plays* (London: Methuen, 2001).

Notes on contributors

Elaine Aston is Professor of Contemporary Performance at Lancaster University. Her authored studies include *Sarah Bernhardt: A French Actress on the English Stage* (Oxford University Press, 1989); *Theatre as Sign-System* (Routledge, 1991 with George Savona); *An Introduction to Feminism and Theatre* (Routledge, 1995); *Caryl Churchill* (1997, Northcote House rev. edn 2001); *Feminist Theatre Practice* (Routledge, 1999) and *Feminist Views on the English Stage* (Cambridge University Press, 2003). Her edited work includes four volumes of plays by women; *The Cambridge Companion to Modern British Women Playwrights* (Cambridge University Press, 2000, with Janelle Reinelt); *Feminist Futures: Theatre, Performance, Theory* (Palgrave, 2006, with Geraldine Harris), and *Staging International Feminisms* (Palgrave, 2007, with Sue-Ellen Case). Her most recent monograph is *Performance Practice and Process: Contemporary [Women] Practitioners* (Palgrave, 2008, with Geraldine Harris). She currently serves as editor of *Theatre Research International*.

Edward Bond is one of Britain's most significant postwar playwrights. His plays include *The Pope's Wedding* (Royal Court, 1962), *Saved* (Royal Court, 1965), *Early Morning* (Royal Court, 1968), *Lear* (Royal Court, 1971), *The Sea* (Royal Court, 1973), *The Woman* (National Theatre, 1978), *Restoration* (Royal Court, 1981), *Summer* (National Theatre, 1982), *The War Plays* (RSC, 1985), *Olly's Prison* (BBC, 1993), *In the Company of Men* (RSC, 1996), *Tuesday* (BBC, 1993), *At the Inland Sea* (Big Brum, 1995), *Coffee* (Rational Theatre Company, 1996), *The Children* (Classworks, 2000), *Chair* (BBC Radio 4, 2000). *Volumes I–IV* of his letters are published by Harwood Academic Press and Methuen have published *Selections from the Notebooks of Edward Bond* (*Volume One: 1959–1980*) and (*Volume Two 1980–1995*). Selected writings are published in *The Hidden Plot: Notes on Theatre and the State* (Methuen, 2000).

Mateusz Borowski teaches at the Drama Department at the Jagiellonian University, Kraków. In 2005 he received his PhD from Johannes-Gutenberg University in Mainz. His dissertation *In Search of the Real. New Developments of the European Playwriting of the 1990s* was devoted to the changes of the mimetic paradigm at the turn of the twenty-first century. In his research, he concentrates on the contemporary European and American drama, queer theory and translation studies. He is also active as a translator of literary and scholarly texts. Recently he co-edited a collection of essays, *Fictional Realities/Real Fictions* (Cambridge Scholars Press, 2007) as well as an anthology of Polish theatre theory in the twentieth century, *Theater spielen und denken* (Suhrkamp, 2008).

Stefani Brusberg-Kiermeier is currently professor of English literature and culture at the University of Paderborn. She has lectured in Austria, Germany, Britain, Italy, Spain and the USA. Her PhD thesis on stagings of the body in Shakespeare's history plays (*Körper-Inszenierungen in Shakespeares Historien*) was published in 1999 by Peter Lang, who also published *Shakespeare in the Media: From the Globe Theatre to the World Wide Web* (2004), which she co-edited with Jörg Helbig. The second edition is in preparation. She submitted her second thesis, *Domesticating the Grotesque: Transgression and Sublimation in Victorian Fiction*, at Potsdam University in October 2008. She continues publishing on Shakespeare and Aemilia Lanyer, on Victorian literature and culture as well as on contemporary British drama and film.

Peter A. Campbell directed the New York City premiere of Sarah Kane's *Phaedra's Love*. Recent publications include an essay on Heiner Müller's Medea plays in *Modern Drama* and a review of the US premiere of Kane's *Blasted* in *Theatre Journal*. His trilogy of remakings of Greek tragedies, *iph.then*, *Yellow Electras* and *Orestes/West*, was created with his company, red handle, at the Ontological-Hysteric Incubator in New York City. He received his MFA in Dramaturgy and his PhD in Theatre from Columbia University. He is Assistant Professor of Theatre History and Criticism at Ramapo College of New Jersey.

Hillary Chute is a Junior Fellow in literature at the Harvard Society of Fellows. Her book *Out of the Gutter: Women's Contemporary Graphic Narrative* is forthcoming from Columbia University Press. She is also Associate Editor of Art Spiegelman's forthcoming book project *MetaMaus* (Pantheon), and has published essays in *American Periodicals, Literature and Medicine, Mfs: Modern Fiction Studies, PMLA, Postmodern Culture,* and *Twentieth-Century Literature,* among others.

Laurens De Vos is a research fellow at Ghent University. He studied English and German literature at the universities of Ghent and Vienna, and literary theory in Leuven. He holds a PhD in literary theory and English literature. He has written articles on playwrights such as Sarah Kane, Mark Ravenhill, Samuel Beckett and Tom Stoppard. He is particularly interested in the legacy of Antonin Artaud in contemporary theatre practitioners and authors (e.g. Jan Fabre) and examines both drama and theatre from a psychoanalytic point of view.

Ehren Fordyce has taught performance, drama and directing at Stanford University, Freie Universität Berlin and Columbia University. He has written articles on contemporary performance and opera, dealing with the work of Reza Abdoh, Goat Island, Societas Raffaello Sanzio, Rimini Protokoll and Christoph Schlingensief, among others. He also works in documentary film and recently directed a performance piece for the Vienna/New York-based performance group Cabula6. He currently lives in Berlin.

Zina Giannopoulou is Assistant Professor of Classics at the University of California, Irvine. Her primary research interest is the intersection of literature and philosophy in Plato, and she has published articles on many of his dialogues. She is currently Fellow at the Centre for Hellenic Studies in Washington, DC, where she is completing a monograph on *Theaetetus.* A secondary interest is the reception of classical texts in modern and contemporary literature and philosophy. In that vein, she has published on appropriations of Homer (in Derek Walcott), Plato's *Symposium* (in Milan Kundera) and *Timaeus' chôra* (in Jacques Derrida). Her second book project will be a study of literary and philosophical rewritings of Platonic philosophy.

Robert I. Lublin is Assistant Professor of Theatre Arts at the University of Massachusetts Boston. He regularly publishes articles on early modern and postmodern drama, and is currently completing a book on costuming practices on the Shakespearean stage.

Annette Pankratz is professor for British Cultural Studies at the Ruhr-Universität Bochum (Germany). Her research and publications focus on the long seventeenth century, representations of death and dying, contemporary British drama, sitcoms and films.

Dan Rebellato is Professor of Contemporary Theatre at Royal Holloway, University of London. His books include *1956 and All That* (Routledge, 1999) *European Theatre Directors* (co-edited with Maria Delgado) and *Theatre & Globalization* in 2009 for the Palgrave *Theatre&* series he edits with Jen Harvie. He has written widely on British theatre including essays on David Greig, Suspect Culture, Sarah Kane, Caryl Churchill, David Hare, globalisation, mental imagery, and violence. In 2009, he wrote and presented the documentary *Blasted: The Life and Death of Sarah Kane* for BBC Radio 4. He is also a playwright and recent works include *Beachy Head* (2009), *Theatremorphosis* (2009), *Static* (2008), *Mile End* (2007), *Outright Terror Bold and Brilliant* (2005), *Here's What I Did With My Body One Day* (2004), as well as adaptations of *The Midwich Cuckoos* (2003), *Dead Souls* (2006) and *Girlfriend in a Coma* (2008) for BBC Radio.

Graham Saunders lectures in Theatre Studies at the University of Reading. He is author of *'Love Me or Kill Me': Sarah Kane and the Theatre of Extremes* (Manchester University Press, 2002), *Patrick Marber's Closer* (Continuum, 2008) and co-editor of *Cool Britannia: Political Theatre in the 1990s* (Palgrave, 2008). He is also a series editor for Continuum's Modern Theatre Guides. He has contributed articles on contemporary British and Irish drama to journals including *Modern Drama, Journal of Beckett Studies, Contemporary Theatre Review, Theatre Research International, New Theatre Quarterly* and *Studies in Theatre and Performance*.

Aleks Sierz is Visiting Research Fellow at Rose Bruford College, Sidcup and author of *In-Yer-Face Theatre: British Drama Today* (Faber, 2001), *The Theatre of Martin Crimp* (Methuen, 2006) and *John Osborne's Look Back in Anger* (Continuum, 2008). He is also a series editor of the Continuum Modern Theatre Guides and of the theatreVOICE website. He works as a journalist, broadcaster, lecturer and theatre critic.

Eckart Voigts-Virchow is Professor of English Literature at the University of Siegen, Germany. He also taught English Literature and Cultural Studies at the Universities of Madison and Milwaukee (Wisconsin), Giessen, Frankfurt am Main, Vienna and Chemnitz. His *Introduction to Media Studies* (Klett Uni-Wissen) was published in 2005. He is also editor of *Dramatized Media / Mediated Drama*

(WVT, 2000) and *Janespotting and Beyond. British Heritage Retrovisions since the Mid-1990s* (Narr, 2004) and co-edited a special edition of the journal *ZAA* (56.2) on *The New Documentarism* in 2008. He contributed the essay 'Heritage and literature on screen: Heimat and heritage' to the *Cambridge Companion to Literature on Screen in 2007* and his paper on 'In-yer-face Victorianism', is forthcoming in *LIT: Literature, Interpretation Theory*. He is on the board of the Society for Contemporary Theatre and Drama in English (CDE), on the Advisory Board of the journals *Adaptation* (Oxford University Press) and *Adaptation in Performance and Film* (Intellect). In addition, he co-edits the book series Studien zur anglistischen Literatur- und Sprachwissenschaft (SALS). He is currently working on a collection of essays on adaptation in the theatre.

Julie Waddington lectures in drama at Manchester Metropolitan University and Edge Hill University. Her research is on contemporary British drama, theories of tragedy and critical theory. She is currently completing a monograph, *Sarah Kane: Posthumanist Tragedy*. She also works as a freelance writer and translator.

Clare Wallace is a lecturer in the Department of English and American Studies at Charles University in Prague. She is author of *Suspect Cultures: Narrative, Identity and Citation in 1990s New Drama* (Prague, 2007) and is editor of *Monologues: Theatre, Performance, Subjectivity* (Prague, 2006) and *Stewart Parker Television Plays* (Prague, 2008). Co-edited books include, *Giacomo Joyce: Envoys of the Other* with Louis Armand (Prague, 2002), *Global Ireland: Irish Literatures for the New Millennium* with Ondøej Pilný (Prague, 2006) and *Stewart Parker Dramatis Personae and Other Writings* (Prague, 2008). She has contributed essays to Cathy Leeny and Anna McMullan's *The Theatre of Marina Carr: 'Before Rules was Made'* (Dublin, 2003), *Engaging Modernity* (Dublin, 2003), *Extending the Code: New Forms of Dramatic and Theatrical Expression CDE 11* (Trier, 2003) *Beyond Borders: IASIL Essays on Modern Irish Writing* (Bath Spa University Press, 2004) and *Irish Literature since 1990: Diverse Voices* (Manchester University Press, 2009).

List of figures

Introduction

Laurens De Vos and Graham Saunders

If it is true, as Aleks Sierz claims in his influential book *In-Yer-Face Theatre: British Drama Today*, that the 1990s witnessed the most exciting wave of new drama since the Angry Young Men almost half a century before (Sierz, 2001a: xi), then Sarah Kane stands out as one of the most important playwrights of that decade. Ten years after her death, her plays are still widely performed around the world.

Yet, ambiguities and paradoxes characterise Kane and her work. Are the plays autobiographical or universal? Is Sarah Kane a late modernist, a postmodernist or a post-humanist? Does her work fit into a feminist aesthetics, or does it refuse any of these labels? Some critics regard Kane as a political writer, whilst others see the work as essentially amoral and nihilist.

Moreover, whilst she was heralded as an important representative of 'Cool Britannia' in the mid-1990s, alongside other writers including Jez Butterworth, Martin McDonagh, Mark Ravenhill, Joe Penhall, Rebecca Prichard and Judy Upton, Sarah Kane's inclusion within this grouping is debatable. Is she really prototypical of so-called 'in-yer-face' drama, and its territory of social realism or is she, on the other hand, its superlative figure, through the preoccupation in her first three plays for depicting graphic scenes of sex and violence onstage? Moreover, her work also displays a reluctance, shared by her contemporaries, to guide audiences to any conclusive moral or political certainties.

This volume consists of two parts. The first examines the literary influences and political implications of the work. The second focuses on what probably became Kane's most compelling preoccupation: namely the question of subjectivity and the problem of representation. Not only did she desperately want to understand what the essential human core consists of, her plays are preoccupied with fragmented, displaced subjects that fitted well into the

1

pre-millennial or postmodernist mood of the late 1990s. Realising that Kane herself would have detested such a division, we are all too well aware of the arbitrariness of each section in the volume. Hence, it is obvious that some of the essays mapping the background of Kane's writing in Part I might equally have found themselves in the second part too, or the other way around.

Given Kane's well known antipathy to the critical establishment, it might also appear perverse that the volume opens with an essay drawing upon the early British reviews which so clearly defined the initial reputation of *Blasted* (1995). Elaine Aston's 'Reviewing the fabric of *Blasted*' engages in an analysis of the cultural and political motivations behind these reactions. In a process derived from Beverly Skeggs's term 'affect-stripping', Aston claims that these early reviewers re-attached the disgust-making affects of the performance on to the play itself and the figure of the young female dramatist. In doing so, the critics uncannily succeeded in demonstrating exactly the message *Blasted* wanted to convey: namely journalistic reporting as a means of avoiding emotional involvement. Consequently, what became disturbing to sensibilities could be easily deflected to ensure a safe critical distance. Moreover, exploring Kane's three unpublished dramatic monologues written before *Blasted*, Aston detects the operation of a feminist sensibility that until now has been largely ignored.

The unpublished dramas are also the subject of Dan Rebellato's 'Sarah Kane before *Blasted*: the monologues', which argues that they inform many of the subsequent plays. Moreover, he demonstrates that significant material from the monologues is recycled, both directly and indirectly, into all her subsequent plays. Aleks Sierz's '"Looks like there's a war on": Sarah Kane's *Blasted*, political theatre and the Muslim Other' also explores the early drafts of *Blasted* as a way of uncovering previously ignored aspects of the play. Sierz concludes that the radical form of *Blasted* came about more by coincidence than by design, and was motivated by two different agendas. Kane wanted to retain the first 'personal' part of *Blasted* concerning an abusive relationship culminating in a rape, yet she also grew increasingly concerned about the effects of war as she watched the unfolding disintegration of Yugoslavia during the early 1990s. For Sierz the genesis of *Blasted* also indicates that the play contains a buried political agenda that has only recently become known – namely the liminal presence of the Muslim Other throughout its unfolding events.

Blasted demonstrated that Kane was never really alienated from the social and political context of the 1990s, yet at the same time her writing was deeply informed by an engagement with past literary and theatrical traditions. Several of the contributors in the volume draw attention to a number of these diverse influences. These range from the classics (Giannopoulou) and Shakespeare (Brusberg-Kiermeier) to Artaud (Wallace and De Vos) and Beckett (Saunders and Chute).

Zina Giannopoulou's 'Staging power: the politics of sex and death in Seneca's *Phaedra* and Kane's *Phaedra's Love*' observes that the two major forces both capable of destabilising the political establishment in Seneca's time were sexual desire and death: these same overt presences are also central to Kane's rewriting of Seneca's tragedy in *Phaedra's Love* (1996). Although writing from a different perspective, Giannopoulou's essay finds common ground with Elaine Aston's arguments. As in *Blasted*, it is the female outsiders, Phaedra and Strophe, who disrupt patriarchal order and offer glimmers of hope in a corrupted world. Unlike Seneca's *Phaedra* (but as in *Blasted*), there is no re-establishment of patriarchal order at the end of *Phaedra's Love*. Both Aston and Giannopoulou also distinguish the bombing of the hotel in *Blasted* and the accusation of rape in *Phaedra's Love* as clear examples of a caesura after which the male world is placed under threat.

A key influence – and one that runs throughout all her work – is Samuel Beckett. Graham Saunders's 'The Beckettian world of Sarah Kane' is sceptical of attempts to make Kane representative of a new school of 1990s dramatists, whose plays can be subsumed under 'social realism'. Saunders argues that she differs markedly from her contemporaries by adopting a far less realistic approach and demonstrates that, from *Blasted* onwards, the plays utilise a variety of dramatic techniques that evoke a Beckettian atmosphere: this is manifested through direct or indirect quotation, the use of pseudo-couples, the recycling of familiar Beckettian imagery and dramatic motifs and the integration of linguistic and rhythmic echoes. Apart from these references within the plays themselves, Saunders concludes that Kane's work – like Beckett's – tends to withdraw into its own subjectivity and explores consciousness alienated from the body.

Saunders's identification of Kane's predilection for the metaphysical over the material is taken up in Stefani Brusberg-Kiermeier's 'Cruelty, violence and rituals in Sarah Kane's plays'. Brusberg-Kiermeier identifies religious rituals as prominent, but she also pays attention to eating, medical and love rituals. Even cruelty is, according to Brusberg-Kiermeier, a ritual necessary in order to explore the human state. Yet, Brusberg-Kiermeier also points out that Kane does not just integrate existing rituals into her plays, but subverts them. The use of a new language and new forms for the old rituals, however, subverts these too for her own (often mischievous) ends.

Sarah Kane is on record as describing her own work as 'experiential' in terms of the effect she wanted to produce on an audience. Clare Wallace's 'Sarah Kane, experiential theatre and the revenant avant-garde' examines the term alongside avant-garde ideas including confrontation, rupture and revolution. Exploring the use of cruelty in expressionist theatre, she concludes that Kane follows on from Artaud's Theatre of Cruelty and Barker's Theatre of Catastrophe. Here, the idea of cruelty is not a means in itself but rather a way to achieve an experiential effect on its audiences. Wallace sets out how in *Blasted* the socio-realist conventions are disrupted, and *Phaedra's Love* subverts the conventions of classical tragedy. *Cleansed* (1998) might be said to combine these two aspects in challenging both the principles of realism and tragedy. According to Wallace, Kane's last two plays, *Crave* (1998) and *4.48 Psychosis* (1999), fall under the label of experiential because they testify to a dispersion of the self.

The various external voices that emerge in Kane's work form the subject of the opening essay of Part II. Ehren Fordyce's 'The voice of Kane' engages in the philosophical issue about the notion of voice. Given the traditions in which her plays exist and the inevitably inherited nature of culture and language, is it possible at all to speak of the author's own voice? However, Fordyce points to the prevalence of voices in Kane's work, which becomes increasingly more important throughout her plays. From *Blasted* to *Crave* he discovers so-called 'chiasmatic structures', which can best be captured by the image of a mirror. Between the characters several symmetrical exchanges and reversals take place, so that roles are continuously overturned. Yet, while the extremities at one pole swap places with the other (and vice versa), the middle remains empty – there is no meeting point. Though displaying features of Beckett's negative ontology, Kane holds up an ethical mirror, to both her audience and her characters. Her plays, therefore, are an appeal to the audience to take responsibility. Interestingly, Fordyce interprets Kane's much quoted phrase 'you no longer know where you stop, and the world starts' (Saunders, 2002a: 112) metaphorically and ethically; rather than a psychotic state of mind, according to Fordyce it refers to a 'pre-reflective self-consciousness' that does not find solid ground in the self or the character. Very hard to situate, it is impossible to address. So, when it comes to taking responsibility, how far does this responsibility go? Where do I, along with my responsibility, stop and where does the world start?

Realising that this ethical stance cannot be upheld in the framing concept of a character, Kane started integrating in her plays more and more voices that destabilise boundaries and hierarchies. This way, different roles that were still easily attributable to specific characters in her first three plays intermingle. These hierarchies also include the position of the authorial voice towards the dramatis personae; Fordyce convincingly demonstrates that in the course of her subsequent plays 'the mark of Kane' subsides and blurs into all the other voices. Thus, the playwright's ethical point of view has substantially altered her attitude towards dramatic representation. Fordyce's essay also reveals how subjectivity, responsibility and representation are inextricably linked up in Kane's work. Her desire to mould the play's form and to question theatrical representation goes hand in hand with the content of her plays. This concerns the dissolution of identity and the wish to unite with the Other. This idea, along with its consequences in regard to representation, recurs in subsequent essays throughout Part II.

In *Arguments for a Theatre*, Howard Barker outlines his ideas on how a play should affect its audience. Barker's theatre refuses to choose sides or impose a moral stance upon its audience. Robert Lublin's '"I love you *now*": time and desire in the plays of Sarah Kane' shows how Barker's ideas of a Theatre of Catastrophe influenced Kane's conception of characterisation and moral certainties. Unlike Aston, who marks out the feminist possibilities in Kane, Lublin focuses more on the human, making recourse to Lacanian psychoanalysis and the notion of human desire. Pain and desire are as much bound up as downfall and salvation. Lublin surveys the drives urging on Kane's characters and regards them as victims of their desire caught up in time. Given the separation of mind and body and the split subject that is a leitmotif in Kane's work, Lacan's triangular structure of the Symbolic, the Imaginary and the Real offers a useful terminology and theoretical frame to approach her plays.

Laurens De Vos's 'Sarah Kane and Antonin Artaud: cruelty towards the subjectile' examines the common ground between Artaud, Lacan and Kane. Firstly, both Artaud and Kane attribute a pivotal role to desire as the quintessential core of humanity. In addition, and maybe even more importantly, through cruelty and language, they have explored similar ways to find an adequate means to express these desiring forces. De Vos picks up on Artaud's use of what he calls the 'subjectile': the receptacle to a work of art by which it should unite. This idea ties in with Kane's wish to make form and content one. Hence, De Vos argues that it is not her earlier plays but rather *4.48 Psychosis* that approaches Artaud's Theatre of Cruelty most. He illustrates this with reference to the much-acclaimed 2002 production by Claude Régy which featured the actress Isabelle Huppert.

There is a voice of the mind in Kane's plays that is constantly at odds with the subject's own status. On the one hand, there is a humanist approach to identity, falling back on Cartesian dualism and proclaiming that an *a priori* unalterable essence is always present independent of any cultural interference. The anti-humanist idea, on the other hand, ignores this quintessential split and attributes the core of being to a subject based entirely on one's environment, rather than some divine given. Julie Waddington's 'Post-humanist identities in Sarah Kane' perceives an oscillation between a humanist and anti-humanist position in Kane which – while only fully explored in *4.48 Psychosis* – actually starts in *Blasted*. She points out how the tension between fragmentation and autonomy permeates Ian, Hippolytus, Grace and the figures in *Crave* and *4.48 Psychosis*. Kane's plays, in this respect, are experiments in order to see how far a subject can pursue their own autonomy without paying for it with their death. Waddington invokes the Lacanian paradox of the subject in concluding that a subject's split is necessary to become autonomous. To think autonomy and the freedom of consciousness immediately means to restrain it.

The uncertainty about where 'I' ends, and the world starts, is reflected in the dramatic composition of the plays as well. From a semiotic viewpoint, Annette Pankratz's 'Neither here nor there: theatrical space in Kane's work' analyses the theatrical spaces and the relationship between the fictional and the real world. Frames of reference change all the time and deictic structures are deconstructed. These include the mind-spaces where inside and outside are mirrored in the alternation of theatrical settings. Along with space, time becomes indeterminate too, so that fictional references receive a metadramatic connotation. The stage itself is incorporated into the drama, and these kinds of confusion ultimately all enhance the dissolution of the character. When it is no longer clear to whom certain deictic markers refer, the self is increasingly perceived as other.

The collapse of this distinction between inside and outside does have a strong ethical impact too. The division mentioned between perpetrators and bystanders in *4.48 Psychosis* (231) no longer holds true where spectators turn from witnesses into accomplices. In line with Elaine Aston's indignation at critics' distancing and self-protective strategies, Hillary Chute's '"Victim. Perpetrator. Bystander": critical distance in Sarah Kane's Theatre of Cruelty' claims that her work undermines this comfortable critical distance by its metonymic representational ethic. History and reality, distant past and present come together metonymically in the present moment of performance. Chute claims that it is this imperative, on which Artaud's Theatre of Cruelty is based, which in turn influenced Beckettian drama.

Sarah Kane never stopped wrestling over the question of theatrical representation in order to produce an experiential theatre. Although *Phaedra's Love* in terms of its dramaturgy is generally regarded as Kane's weakest play, Peter Campbell's 'Sarah Kane's *Phaedra's Love*: staging the implacable' argues that it is crucial in the development of her exploration of the limitations of representation. How can sexuality and violence be brought to the stage without coming across as *Grand Guignol*? According to Campbell, Kane was so disappointed with the reactions to *Blasted* that she started looking for new forms of dramatic representation. *Phaedra's Love*, then, is a turning point in the development of a more symbolic, suggestive imagery that takes over from the quasi-realism that occupied the first part of *Blasted*. It seems no coincidence that Kane eventually decided to direct the play herself in order to experiment directly in her own work. Campbell explains how in his own work as a director he invented solutions to effectively render a distinction between the visceral and the symbolic, the real and the suggestive, and compares his own choices with alternatives made by fellow directors. *Phaedra's Love*, he concludes, subverts the expectations of tragedy and is at the same time a metatheatrical investigation.

Mateusz Borowski's 'Under the surface of things: Sarah Kane's *Skin* and the medium of theatre' argues that Kane's only film, *Skin*, was the turning point in her approach to theatrical texts. In most analyses of Kane's work, *Skin* is overlooked, but Borowski believes that this one confrontation with the medium of film obliged Kane to question the possibilities of representation both on the screen and in the theatre. One might even argue that the shift towards the grandiose theatricality of *Cleansed* was influenced by Kane's writing for film. Not only does Borowski provide analysis of thematic convergences between *Skin* and *Cleansed* but he also investigates how her work on the screenplay urged Kane to invent a new theatrical language which was to be more abstract and poetic. The mediated nature of the screen also made her aware of the border between reality and representation in both film and theatre. Borowski explains how from then on Kane set out to find ways to include the spectators in the play itself and turn them into accomplices.

As the opening of this introduction points out, Sarah Kane's work is full of contradictions. Eckart Voigts-Virchow's "'We are anathema" – Sarah Kane's plays as postdramatic theatre versus the "Dreary and repugnant tale of sense'" follows on from his earlier assessment of her as a late modernist (Voigts-Virchow, 2001). Here, he traces the postdramatic elements in her work. Kane was amongst the first of the mid-1990s generation of playwrights whose work was immediately embraced on the Continent. Undoubtedly, this enthusiasm is related to her deconstruction of narrative and character, along with the reinvention of a theatre that claims a *hic et nunc* presence. Hence, Sarah Kane has been heralded as an English representative of what Hans-Thies Lehmann has labelled 'post-dramatic theatre'. Voigts-Virchow argues that her success in Germany, France, Flanders and other regions on the mainland seems to express an affinity between Kane and the European tradition of theatre practice.

Yet, despite Lehmann's own recognition of Kane's theatre as post-dramatic, Kane is also very much an exponent of the writerly drama text. While Voigts-Virchow acknowledges that most written plays are not postdramatic, even *4.48 Psychosis*, in which the dissociation of language and characters has been pursued the most in this form of critical discourse, still shows traces of human agency and formal narrative. However, in his reference to Wanda Golonka's dance performance of *4.48 Psychosis*, Voigts-Virchow points out that her plays easily allow for post-dramatic performances.

In an Epilogue, the playwright Edward Bond delivers a more philosophical piece on the importance of Sarah Kane's work as a commentary on what he calls our posthumous society. Bond controversially states that society forced Kane to seek her own death. Owing to the lack of truthfulness on society's part, she needed to be 'suicided'. The Tragic and the Comic are the two basic elements in life, according to Bond, and, since these have become subverted in our posthumous society, Kane's path inexorably leads to death. Just like Van Gogh, Kane tried to cross the white canvas in search of what Bond terms the Invisible Object hidden behind the 'reality' of posthumous society. This is her self-fulfilled drama.

With this collection we have tried to bring together a wide variety of scholars who approach Kane's work from a more theoretical vantage point. Although the ultimate impact of her plays will depend on their representation through performance, we hope that the book may shed a light on Kane as a voice that has drawn on many theatrical, literary and philosophical predecessors and that has simultaneously made all these influences her own in a most innovative way. Kane was a child of her time: neither burdened by the paralysis of Cold War angst nor possessed by the terrorist fear which characterises the twenty-first century.

Part I
Surrounding voices

1

Reviewing the fabric of *Blasted*

Elaine Aston

Introducing *Sarah Kane: Complete Plays,* the playwright David Greig observes that Kane is best known for two 'shocking' moments: 'the extraordinary public controversy over *Blasted*' and her suicide. We should take care, Greig cautions, that these extraordinary events do not detract and 'distract' from the 'qualities' of the plays (Greig, 2001: ix).

To look back at the critical outrage provoked by Kane's professional theatre debut is to evidence Greig's concern. The reviews of *Blasted* truly belied and belittled the power and purpose of Kane's writing. In retrospect, it is not hard to understand why *Blasted* shocked the London theatre critics in the way that it did. As the theatre critic Carole Woddis explained in a talk addressing an audience of contemporary women artists, writers and theatre scholars, in a profession which remains male-dominated, the essential qualifications for a theatre critic are to be white, middle-class, Oxbridge and literary.[1] The acts of rape, masturbation, buggery and cannibalism in *Blasted* were, therefore, hardly likely to accord with white, middle-class Oxbridge tastes, but rather, to borrow from Bourdieu, were found to be '"sick-making"' (Bourdieu, 1979: 56). Moreover, to a literary mind, a hotel room blasted and transformed into a war-torn landscape had no formal or thematic logic, and Oxbridge man felt empowered to dismiss Kane as a young and inexperienced writer. With a vendetta to keep bums off rather than on seats, a reviewing tactic was not to sell the show but to sell it short: to engineer an anti-Kane campaign that also brought into question the wisdom and taste of the Royal Court and its then artistic director Stephen Daldry for selecting the play for performance. Out of concern for the moral and fiscal welfare of spectators, *Blasted* was in short condemned as an awful play and an awful waste of taxpayers' money.

The consignment of Kane and of *Blasted* to the critical dustbin has been challenged since by playwrights, practitioners, scholars and, not least of all, the theatre critics themselves, particularly after Kane's untimely death. Her suicide prompted many critics to revise their opinion of her work, and, as Graham Saunders notes, '[t]he irony concerning *Blasted* is that despite starting out on a trajectory of mock outrage, time has given it a far more favourable assessment' (Saunders, 2002a: 3). Given the critical reassessment of *Blasted* and Greig's concern that the original controversy risks damaging our understanding of the plays themselves, then one might be tempted to make an open and shut case to set aside the reviewing history of *Blasted*. However, I recently found myself returning to those original 'shocking' reviews as, ironically, a means of understanding *Blasted*; as a way of renewing and revitalising the performance affects of Kane's play.

As mentioned, the inspiration for this critical manoeuvre came from Carol Woddis's talk on theatre reviewing, or rather from a particular reaction to her presentation. Peggy Shaw of the Split Britches theatre company responded by talking about the years of Woddis's reviewing of Split Britches' performances as part of the fabric of a show; of the theatre reviews woven into the performance history of her company. The images of reviews, the words on the page, have a physicality, Shaw observed, that makes them a part of the performance fabric. Working with Shaw's idea, I want to argue that the reviews of Kane's work, awful as many of them were, particularly at the outset, are part of the fabric of her theatre, and that as part of that fabric they can serve to revitalise rather than to diminish our understandings of Kane's work, of *Blasted* in particular. Woven out of this critical cloth, and explored in the second part of this essay, is a reviewing of *Blasted* as a gendered, feminist and hopeful fabric.

Act one: *Blasted* and the fabric of reviewing

To talk about reviews as part of a fabric is to talk about them as something physical, tangible, touchable. I might say of the reviews of *Blasted* as I go through them again in my own photocopied collection, or thumbing the pages in *Theatre Record*, that these, like Kane's journalist, Ian, 'stink' – figuratively anyway. Yet they are part of the fabric of Kane's theatre; a textual image of the violent critical reaction to the play that takes me back to the time of its first production. By reducing the play to a list of staged atrocities, endlessly described and repeated throughout the reviews and divorced from the context and purpose which they served in the play, the critics aimed to strip *Blasted* of its power to provoke disgust at the atrocities and violence of war; of the terror of lives and loves laid waste by unexpected and unexplained violence.

'Affect stripping', explains the feminist sociologist Beverly Skeggs, is 'a process whereby affects are detached from the body of production and re-made as an exchange-value when re-attached to the body that does not produce the same affect but can capitalize upon it' (Skeggs, 2005: 971). Kane's dramaturgy explored and staged the experiences of terror and violence, whether this was in the intimate sex wars of the bedroom or in state-sanctioned military warfare, as disgust-making. Detaching the disgust-making affects from the performance, however, reviewers re-attached these to their evaluation of the play and of the writer as 'sick-making'. In this critical, affect-stripping manoeuvre, the play with its capacity to discomfort, to disturb, was re-valued as the product of a disturbed mind.

In *Blasted*, as a tabloid news reporter, Ian exemplifies the affect-stripping tactics of news reporting when, in the hotel bedroom, he dictates over the telephone the story of a 'murder ritual' by a serial killer in New Zealand:

> A serial killer slaughtered British tourist Samantha Scrace, S–C–R–A–C–E, in a sick murder ritual, comma, police revealed yesterday point new par. The bubbly nineteen year old from Leeds was among seven victims found buried in identical triangular tombs in an isolated New Zealand forest point new par. (12)

The local and national interest whipped up in an international news story is instantly recognisable as a media tactic designed to sensationalise, as are the character (stereo)types in the drama: the young and beautiful female victim; the heartbroken mother; and the foreign, murdering maniac. The horror of a violent, unexpected death is sensationalised, made monstrous, in a way that makes it at once familiar and yet distant; it is likely to elicit expressions of sympathy, outrage, or horror, but not the feeling of being touched by, or moved by, these violent events.

Kane explained the origin of the newspaper stories in *Blasted* as based on 'real' stories from tabloid newspapers (Saunders, 2002a: 52). In *Outrage and Insight* and in the context of French culture and literature, David Walker makes a study of this kind of *fait divers* newspaper reporting. The *fait divers*, Walker argues, satisfies 'psychosocial' needs as it deals with 'scandal, sensation, disruptions of the norm' (Walker, 1995: 1). It serves a dual purpose by, on the one hand, translating extraordinary, 'odd or bizarre items' into the ordinary, the everyday, and, on the other, 'because of its secondary status, it marginalizes such items, keeps them at a safe remove from the centre of society'. 'The *fait-diversier* thus', Walker continues, 'lays claim to the off-beat or grotesque on behalf of bourgeois humanism or conventional society'; 'the reporter holds these items at arm's length, labels them marginal or odd in order to fend off any disturbing implications they may have for conventional wisdom' (Walker, 1995: 2). Kane was moved profoundly by the news media coverage of war in the former Yugoslavia (which had a bearing on the connection she made between the rape in a hotel bedroom in Leeds and the atrocities in Bosnia (Saunders, 2002a: 39), but was also outraged by the news reporting that kept events in Yugoslavia at a distance and in other ways trivialised by turning attention away from post-Cold War politics to 'sex scandals (which sell more papers)' (Stephenson and Langridge, 1997: 131). The various influences that this had on the writing of *Blasted* generally and on the character of Ian as a tabloid hack specifically point to Kane's understanding of how the sensationalist news story is a reflection of what needs to be kept 'at arm's length' in the interests of 'conventional society'; of the 'social sickness' (Stephenson and Langridge, 1997: 131) it makes visible.

By analogy, the switching between news- and scandal-reporting is one which applies to the reviewers' treatment of *Blasted*: a serious play is reported as a scandal. By way of illustration I shall quote the opening to Roger Foss's review of *Blasted* for *What's On*, but, as I do so, mirroring Ian's tactic of inserting and speaking the punctuation (which as Saunders observes (2002a: 52) heightens the distancing effect) in order to reveal the reviewer's scandal-making tactics: '[Caps up] Only one person walked out on the press night of Sarah Kane's [K-a-n-e] shocking new play, [comma] which ought to be retitled [italics] *Nightmare on Sloane Square* [close italics; stop]' (Foss, 1995: 38).

To sensationalise the play in this way is designed to keep it at a safe distance. However, perversely, or subversively even, the extreme outpourings of disgust, hysteria and outrage in the reviews are the very experiences, reactions and responses that *Blasted* stages. Complaints of upset stomachs, 'a sour taste in the mind' (Kingston, 1995: 39) or 'feeling inwardly soiled' (Taylor, 1995: 38) suggest that the play has penetrated, soiled or stained these squeaky-clean reviewing bodies. Like Ian, in and out of the hotel bathroom, trying to get clean, the 'dirt' does not rub off. It sticks. Squirming with mounting hysteria, 'giggly with shock' (Kellaway, 1995: 40) or the trembling, 'shaking hand' (Foss, 1995: 38), these shell-shocked reviewers also resonate with the vulnerability and fragility of Cate, whose body faints and fits under pressure. Though, equally, their vitriolic outpourings are evocative of the violence, the brutal acts blasted by the soldier into the hotel bedroom. Indeed, overall, in parallel with the script, the collected reviews read like a chorus in a classical drama: Ian, Cate and the Soldier on the one hand appear as the main, named protagonists; the chorus of reviewers, on the other, discharge their hysteria, disgust and outrage. And this not least of all because, as classical choruses often do, they keep on asking, 'What is the point of it all?'

Blinded by their inability to 'read' Kane's iconoclastic dramaturgy in which psycho-social realism is destabilised by a nightmare world that is 'here', elsewhere, if not everywhere, and unable to explain the play in any way other than as a decontextualised catalogue of horrible acts, then what largely claims the reviewing space is not the play itself but the reviewers' *experience* of it. Of course, common to most reviewing strategies, whatever the play and whatever the response, is the selling of the experience: 'I've seen this play. I've enjoyed it, laughed at it, cried at it. You must see it too.' The affect-based selling strategy is one that gets us into the theatre, or rather, in Kane's case, aims to keep us out.

To market *Blasted* as disgust-making was intended to keep audiences away from that which disgusts. In her discussion of disgust and affect, Skeggs (via citation of Tomkins and Probyn) explains how 'disgust evolved to protect the human being from coming too close', and that 'when something or someone is designated as excessive, immoral, disgusting, and so on, it provides collective reassurance that we are not alone in our judgement of the disgusting object, generating consensus and authorization of middle-class standards, maintaining the symbolic order' (Skeggs, 2005: 970). However, Skeggs also reminds us that 'it is not just moral and physical repulsion generated by ambivalence and proximity', but that 'for centuries theorists have documented how disgust is simultaneously about *desire and revulsion*' (Skeggs: 971). To be disgusted by something requires an acknowledgement of that which we are disgusted by; of getting closer to it in order to overcome it, to create distance from it. Desire and revulsion are again made manifest in the reviewers' responses. *Blasted* was not just 'filth' but, to quote the infamous headline that became a byword for the play, this was a 'disgusting *feast* of filth' (my emphasis; Tinker, 1995). Here too, this unintentionally captures the feast-filth interplay of *Blasted*'s opening act and the cannibalistic hell into which it descends. The hotel room we are told is '[a] *very expensive hotel room in Leeds – the kind that is so expensive it could be anywhere in the world*' (3). '[A]*mazed at the classiness of the room*' (3), Cate pauses before she walks in; stands at the threshold, gazing in delight that will shortly turn to disgust. Meanwhile Ian, abandoning his pile of newspapers on the bed and heading straight for the mini-bar and the gin, admonishes the room with his opening line: 'I've shat in better places than this' (3). Each looks and each sees, 'tastes', differently in line with their respective personal and social histories, marked by gender, sexuality, class and economics. And so begins the sexual feast of desire and revulsion, on the stage and on the critical reviewing page, where I might also cite the Freudian slips and jokes made at Kane's expense but that also suggest prurient fascination and repulsion. So, for example, there are Jonathan Miller's 'duties' as a columnist 'to expose [him]self to the degradation and report back' (Miller, 1995: 41). Or, there is Sheridan Morley wanting not to 'pay good money at the theatre to see babies being eaten, strong men going to the lavatory and somnolent women being raped' because '[he] can get all that at home' (Morley, 1995: 42). Yet if I strip these kinds of comments of their comic value, their sexual, bestial mimicry designed to debase Kane's play, then what they point to is the disgust, the danger at getting up close to, being exposed to, the 'social sickness' Kane staged not as hived off and marginalised into an extraordinary, news-horror-story event, but as being at the very core of contemporary society and culture.

What Kane does in *Blasted* is to take us *inside* these events in a theatrical manoeuvre which is the very opposite experience to the consumption of tabloid columns with their safe horrors and thrills. Walker, drawing on Baudrillard, expands on the attraction of the *fait divers* in contemporary consumer society as:

> the form, at once anodyne and miraculous, that articulates political, historical and cultural information in terms which accord with our fantasms of involvement in the dramas of reality. Baudrillard's argument helps explain why in a society of affluence and security (at least for some) the *fait divers* should continue to have compulsive attractions. The media offer fantasms of violence and disruption – 'le plus vrai que le vrai [...] le fait d'y être sans y être' – for consumption by a public whose comfort cannot be appreciated unless it seems to be precariously, constantly under threat. (Walker, 1995: 6)

Working with the 'anodyne and miraculous', the shifts between the sexual power play in the bedroom and the blasting into a war zone, Kane pulls the spectator not into an experience of 'being there without being there' but of *being there*. This happens because the very fabric of *Blasted*, woven out of the *fait divers* sex-scandal story (of Ian and Cate), the war reporting (of the Soldier) and the apocalyptic aftermath that the conjunction of these two news stories creates, is highly experiential, rather than spectatorial. In contrast to the at-a-distance, prurient consumption of the tabloid rape story, for example, a spectator *feels* the violent affects of Ian's sexual bullying. Similarly, when the Soldier, who embodies the news of war atrocities that are too horrible to print, fucks Ian, he blasts the unspeakable, the unprintable into the tabloid story-body. In sum, Kane's image-infused writing aims to make us see and to feel the affects of violence not as a world outside of ourselves, othered and neutralised, but as inside our lives, value systems, choices and behaviours.[2] Consuming violence in the theatrical event does not afford the reassurance and the comfort that is craved to make us feel safe and certain, but discomforts and threatens. If the scandal story represents a real-life event by making it monstrous and unreal to readers, *Blasted* outmonsters the monstrous to make it 'real'.

Regrettably, since 9/11 and the London July bombings in 2005, the traumas of those who were there, those who survived and those who did not make it have become a regular news topic in a way which risks, Skeggs argues, 'displacing everyday suffering for high-impact affect' (Skeggs, 2005: 971). 'The media coverage of the 9/11 event', she contends, 'showed the extension of high-impact affect, enabling a spectacular suffering to reshape claims for nationhood' (Skeggs, 2005: 978, n10). Personal suffering and trauma are used to urge, to justify an aggressive defence of the nation, of national *security*. By contrast, the aftermath of the bombing in *Blasted* does not allow for this kind of ideological manoeuvre; for us to know whose war this is, or whose side we are meant to be on. Reviewers repeatedly objected to their inability to decipher the territories at stake; to be clear about 'where reality starts and fantasy begins' (Edwardes, 1995: 38); to know for certain what is real and what is nightmare. Kane wanted no such easy categories, but rather sought the dis-ease of knowing, of feeling that our worst nightmares are for real – figuratively and graphically illustrated as Ian is 'buggered' by the violence of his tabloid reporting; the soldier whose cock and gun both penetrate

Ian's arse bring the violence 'inside' close, closer, too close for any scrap of comfort. Thereafter, like Ian with only the newspaper left to wipe his arse, or, finally, with his 'head poking out of the floor' (60), we are, Kane suggests, all up to our necks in it.

In brief, as much as the critics did their best to bury *Blasted* with their affect-stripping, disgust-making tactics, the irony is that, as my discussion of the reviewing fabric thus far demonstrates, this puts us back in touch with the dis-ease core to the composition and performance affects of the play. To borrow from Walker's title, where there is 'outrage' there is also 'insight'.

Act two: a fabric of feminism and hope

As previously suggested, criticism of *Blasted* was directed not just at the play's graphic or as some argued pornographic content,[3] but at what was perceived to be Kane's inadequate command of dramatic form, structure and logic. Literary Oxford man was frustrated and angered by a play that 'he' considered to '[b]lur boundaries' (Nathan, 1995: 35); to be 'half-realistic, half-symbolic' (Peter, 1995: 41), and that 'los[t] its grip on any kind of reality' (Gross, 1995: 39). Here too, rereading the reviews *en masse*, the graphic quality of the reviewing fabric is intensified, while at the same time the list upon list of 'nasty things' that reviewers offered by way of explaining *Blasted* evinces an acute anxiety on the part of critics to deal with a play that was breaking new ground. This is, I imagine, every critic's nightmare: seeing a show and having immediately to comment on, to make sense of something which appears to make no sense at all. As Carl Miller explained in his post-*Blasted* digest on the 'new post-traumatic stress syndrome affecting middle-aged men [theatre critics]', '[w]atching a new play is never easy. There are no guidelines to fill you in on the writer's intentions or the symbolic implications of what you witness ... critics are thus particularly vulnerable, having to sum up responses to complex pieces of work in a matter of hours' (Miller, 1995).

Kane was convinced that 'if *Blasted* had been a piece of social realism it wouldn't have been so harshly received'. However, what Kane understood from the outset was that '[a]ll good art is subversive, either in form or content. And the best art is subversive in form *and* content.' In respect of *Blasted* she maintained that '[t]he form and content attempt to be one – the form is the meaning' (Stephenson and Langridge, 1997: 130); her politicisation of the *fait divers*, as I have argued it here, is as much, therefore, an issue of form as it is of content. Failing to grasp this point, however, theatre critics instead argued that the 'nasty' shortcomings of *Blasted* were a failure on the part of the playwright, rather than a failure on their (literature-orientated) part. More specifically, they chorused that this was the failure of a young and inexperienced writer, and, almost as often, as reviewers pointed out to their readers that Kane was just 23 years old at the time of *Blasted*, they also pointed out that she was a woman. Age and gender both figured in their hostility and Kane was rapidly 'promoted' to 'bad girl' of British theatre (Aston, 2003: 79).

On the other hand, she was not criticised and dismissed on feminist grounds as some pre-1990s women playwrights had been (Remnant, 1987), not least because her work was not immediately recognisable to critics as an explicitly feminist play, in terms of either form or content. For example, Michelene Wandor offers a snapshot of British plays of the 1990s (which includes a discussion of Kane's *Cleansed*) and concludes that '[e]xplicit feminist dynamics are absent from these plays' (Wandor, 2001: 237). Meanwhile, Saunders, in his discussion of Kane's experimental use of dramatic form in *Blasted*, comments 'that Kane played a cruel trick on the Royal Court's target audience who weren't expecting the wrench into Expressionism during the second half' (Saunders, 2003: 106), but rather what Peter Morris calls 'the predictable pseudo-feminist drama that a girl of Sarah Kane's age was supposed to write in order to get staged at the Royal Court' (Morris, 2000: 144).

Kane also distanced herself from a feminist theatre tradition noted for taking the '"woman's side"' (Aston, 2003: 80), stating her view that she felt 'no responsibility as a woman writer because I don't believe there's such a thing' (Stephenson and Langridge, 1997: 134).

As Saunders observes, '[w]hereas a previous generation of female dramatists were perhaps more willing to see their work as an expression of their gender, Sarah Kane always saw the issue as irrelevant when assessing her role as a writer' (Saunders, 2002a: 30). There is, however, a crucial difference between Kane's desire, one shared by most other 1990s *women* playwrights,[4] not to have her work categorised, labelled in terms of being only about gender, or only about sexual politics, and the idea that gender concerns are not important to her work. Clearly they are, or, as Saunders clarifies, '[t]his is not to say that Kane ignores issues of gender in her work – in fact the so-called "crisis of masculinity" and the interplay of power between men and women dominate all her work' (Saunders, 2002a: 30). To this I would add that they 'dominate' or drive both the form *and* content of *Blasted*, and that, in contradistinction to Wandor's general view of Kane's theatre, feminist dynamics are far from absent, but present in a new, or renewed form. In the detritus of the reviewing fabric, it was not just the critical failure to grasp the form and content of *Blasted* that I saw but also a failure to grasp this as a feminist form and content. While many scholars and critics might agree with Saunders's assessment of Kane's 'most impressive legacy' as her 'willingness to experiment and subvert dramatic form' (Saunders, 2003: 106), far fewer might be willing to commit to the idea that this is an 'impressive [*feminist*] legacy'. I propose, therefore, a more audacious (albeit contentious) argument for *Blasted* as an aesthetic and political renewal of a feminist theatre tradition.

In support of this claim I turn first to Kane's trilogy of unpublished monologues, *Sick*, which she wrote before *Basted*. Each of these three monologues is assigned to a 'woman' who tells her story of oral rape (*Comic Monologue* in 1991), of an eating disorder (*Starved* in 1992) and of first-time lesbian and straight sex encounters (*What She Said* in 1992). What is striking about each of these is that the experiences recounted are written from an individual woman's perspective.

Comic Monologue, as a rape monologue, in particular anticipates the sexual-power play between Ian and Cate in *Blasted*. In this monologue, the rape victim describes how, on the evening of the rape, her boyfriend (with whom she had not previously been sleeping), strips in front of her; how she giggles hysterically, and then stops as she realises what he is going to do. She struggles. She fights back. Ultimately she knows she cannot win. She describes the trauma of tasting the sperm and her own vomit, and the after-event of being bathed 'clean' by her boyfriend/rapist. Except that she says she can never be clean; can never get the taste, the memory, the trauma of the rape, out of her mouth. She feels permanently soiled and damaged. It affects all her future relationships. This could be Cate's monologue.

Staging the experience of rape, along with other acts of male-authored violence against women, had a strong tradition in second-wave feminist theatre and performance. In her mid-1970s solo show *The Rape*, for example, Franca Rame narrated a woman's experience of being gang-raped at night in the back of a van (Rame, 1991). In the mid-1980s Eve Lewis's *Ficky Stingers* dramatised one 'woman's' story of being raped by her boyfriend (Lewis, 1987).

Kane's monologue connects to these earlier feminist treatments of rape through the way in which it is the female victim who gives 'voice' to male violence against women. Its feminist standpoint can be seen not only as Kane's rape victim gives a graphic account of being orally raped and of surviving the ordeal but also by her concluding remarks in which she clearly states that rape is an experience, a trauma, from which there can never be a full recovery. When you hear about the woman recovering in hospital, or a judge denying the trauma of the rape experience, do not believe it, the victim tells the audience. She cannot be 'cleansed'.

Had the theatre critics encountered Kane through these first monologues, there would have been a different howl of outrage, of the kind reserved for an earlier generation of *feminist* playwrights. I am thinking in particular of the critical response to Sarah Daniels's *Masterpieces* whose radical-feminist treatment of pornography and the connections made between pornography and male violence against women created a furious, gender-biased attack on Daniels and her work (see Remnant, 1987), by a majority of male critics (many of whom were still the same reviewers of Kane's theatre in the 1990s). Like *Masterpieces*, *Comic Monologue* is unequivocal in taking the 'woman's' side; in identifying male sexual violence against women as an unforgivable act. This is why I feel certain that it would have been viewed, reviewed, as 'unforgivable' by the male critics, and all the more so if Kane had succeeded in her attempts to have the monologues staged by the Sphinx Theatre Company: in an explicitly feminist production context.

Ironically, it was the rejection of the monologues that created the opportunity for further discussion and contact between Kane and the Sphinx's artistic director, Sue Parrish. Parrish explains that she first refused the monologues, thinking that these were more 'suitable for radio and not dramatic enough for theatre', but her admission to Kane that she had been 'precipitate' in this respect, encouraged further dialogue and gave rise to Kane's direction of a staged reading of *Blasted* for a Glass Ceiling event in 1996 and discussion of a Medea commission (Parrish, 2007).[5] At the same time as this evidences her feminist interests, however, there was also Kane's concern and view not to be categorised as a *woman* playwright. As Parrish surmises and summarises '[s]he did have a feminist commitment I think, but was keen not to be pigeon-holed and therefore compromise her work' (Parrish, 2007). Kane's decision that the monologues should not be published and not be performed after her death may well reflect her view of them as 'juvenilia' (Saunders, 2002a: 150),[6] but equally they risk 'pigeon-holing' her work in a feminist past rather than future, which Kane was at pains to avoid.

Hence, while *Comic Monologue* affords a feminist familiarity given the presentational, reporting style of making the violent act of female rape visible, *Blasted*, on the other hand, defamiliarises that feminist 'story'. Rape is still the *inside* story; an epic *fait divers* that links domestic violence in Britain with war in the former Yugoslavia, but the invitation is to see and to know this differently. Writing *Blasted*, Kane was reviewing and renewing her feminist connections, aesthetically and politically. Concerned, on the one hand, not to write out of rigid gender divisions, and, on the other, to create theatre subversive in both form and content, her gender interests evolve differently from the oppression-exposure tactics of earlier feminist playwrights and practitioners, tactics that she herself had essayed in *Comic Monologue*. The more experiential, visceral mode of image writing in *Blasted* does not invest in the materialist-feminist politics and strategy of a making visible of gender violations so much as it serves to pull the audience into the epic rape trauma. This formal shift, from materialist feminism to experiential feminism, also 'forms' a political shift, from a first-person, victim testimony that refuses the possibility of recovery, to *Blasted*'s political aspirations towards the recovery, the hope, the love, in what in most other ways is a hopeless, loveless, world of terror and violence. Unable to grasp the intent of *Blasted*, reviewers were also mostly unable to see the play as anything other than full of horror and despair, whereas Kane was adamant that the play was about hope. To acknowledge the hope in *Blasted* is also to acknowledge Kane's break with a feminist past that takes the 'woman's side' and her focus on the redemptive possibilities of the male oppressor in the interests of *both* sexes and a less violent future.

Hope in *Blasted* stems from the formal and feminist shifts that, unlike the monologue, keep the abuser, the rapist, at the scene of his crime; that include him in, rather than release him from, the traumatic aftermath of his violent, sexual carnage. To elaborate on this point: Ian is 'bad news' – literally and figuratively. He abuses personally (in his treatment of Cate) and professionally as a tabloid writer of sensationalist, sexist, racist *fait divers*. He is the unlovable love object that so fascinated Kane as a subject in her theatre. His aggressive-defensive paranoia that someone is out to get him ultimately is not enough to keep him 'safe', and when his nemesis, the Soldier, 'comes' through the door and up his arse, Ian is penetrated by his own 'filth'. *Blasted* is, to borrow a short but highly effective line from Kane's monologue *What She Said*, '[a] male mess'. It is 'a male mess' which holds everyone, male and female, back from the shared desires to be loved, to be safe, to be clean. To be held in love and affection requires a giving and a receiving that is mutual, non-hierarchical. Instead, the hierarchical and abusive power plays produce a critical, violent tension between the desire to hold and the being 'held': Ian holds Cate captive in a hotel bedroom; the Soldier holds Ian at gun point; Cate, forced to hold, pleasure Ian's cock, bites back. Where there is 'a male mess', the desire to protect, to make and be made safe, is thwarted: Ian's defence of the nation is outmanoeuvred by the Soldier; the Soldier does not save his girlfriend from war; Cate does not save the baby placed in her care. Born into 'a male mess' of war, the baby cannot survive; the elsewhere space of a comforting maternal that Ian, coming round from the hotel bombing, reaches out for, is unattainable, is out of reach.[7] Where there is 'a male mess' then it pollutes each scrap of love, comfort, or pleasure as Kane variously shows through images: Ian's love and abuse of Cate; Ian's arse fucked by the Soldier; the baby held in Cate's arms, cuddled, cradled to death; Ian's shitting, then wiping his arse clean with the newspaper tissue (of lies), and Ian's death that brings him back to a living hell.

As Ian descends further into the hell of his own making, however, this opens up the possibility of seeing differently. Saunders argues that Kane's 'cruel male tormentors, grasping for fragments of goodness half glimpsed within themselves after experiencing or inflicting terrible punishments, provides an alternative [vision] – even if that alternative is bleak and uncomfortable' (Saunders, 2002a: 34). Part of that discomfort is that the victim (Cate) still (as in the monologue) does not recover, imaged in the close of *Blasted* as Cate returns to Ian having been raped by soldiers. It is a discomfort that is also *felt* because structurally there is no relief or release from Cate's fit, the rape trauma into which the play collapses. The pain of that experience remains, while the hope, the 'alternative', 'bleak and uncomfortable' though it certainly is, resides in the suggested dis-ease of a diseased masculine.

In sum, this two-part, two-act essay represents my attempt to hold together the reviewing fabric of *Blasted* with an idea of the play as a gendered fabric: to 'blast' a hole in the critical reviewing that allows us to see the play and its performance affects as those of political outrage and, ultimately, *feminist* insight. Dan Rebellato's 'appreciation' of Kane, written after her suicide, cues a final feminist image of Kane with which I wish to close. Recollecting Kane's enthusiasm at the idea of acting the part of Skinner, Howard Barker's 'feminist witch' in *The Castle* (1985), Rebellato gives us the idea of Kane coupled with Skinner (Rebellato, 1999: 280) – the witch who survives the betrayal (by women) of her radical-feminist creed, the male (sex) wars and, outraged to the last, her body bound with the rotting corpse of her own male victim, faces an uncertain future and the threat of (nuclear) war. Like Ian, she would rather be dead, would rather have perished, but 'it is the pain of [feminist] witches to see to the very end of things' (Barker, 1985: 19). 'To see to the very end of things' is relentlessly painful, but as *Blasted* illustrates, may also be hopeful.

Acknowledgement

This essay began as a conference paper solicited by Anna Harpin and Dan Rebellato as organisers of 'Sarah Kane: a Reassessment' (Cambridge, February 2008). I am indebted to Anna and to Dan for encouraging me to think about new perspectives on Kane's theatre, and to Graham Saunders who helped me further in these endeavours, generously sharing Kane materials and inviting me to develop a draft of my paper into the essay that appears in this book.

Notes

1 This talk was given by Woddis at the international Symposium hosted by the AHRC-funded 'Women's Writing for Performance Project', Lancaster University, April 2006. Footage of the talk can be viewed on the Project website at http://www.lancs.ac.uk/depts/theatre/ womenwriting/pages/Symposiumpages/splbrit.htm (accessed 2 September 2007).

2 For further and fuller discussion of this point see Aston, 2003: 82–3.

3 See Foss, for example, who stated 'I cannot think of one good reason why anyone, apart from a theatre critic or a dirty mac voyeur, would actually want to watch it [*Blasted*]' (1995: 38).

4 See contributions by Clare McIntyre, Winsome Pinnock and Rebecca Prichard to Edgar, 1999: 56–61.

5 The Glass Ceiling events are national women's theatre symposia organised by the Sphinx Theatre Company. Details of the Sixth Glass Ceiling event to which Kane contributed are posted on-line at:

http://www.sphinxtheatre.co.uk/index.cfm?nid=EB95C1F5–3FCF–
4A7F–9C00–156832242382 (accessed 12 September 2007).

6 In this interview, Kenyon also makes reference to having turned
down the monologues when she was at the Royal Court.

7 Ian, recovering from the blast of the mortar bomb, utters a one-word
question 'Mum?' (39).

2

Sarah Kane before *Blasted*: The Monologues

Dan Rebellato

One Sunday evening, in the late summer of 1992, a small fringe theatre in North London hosted a work-in-progress showing of three new plays, collectively entitled *Sick*. Using the set of the show already running, the performance was the result of a few days' workshop with the actress Jane Montgomery and the director Deb Jones. The performance used minimal props and ran at around an hour. The evening consisted of *Starved*, *Comic Monologue* and *What She Said*, billed as 'three monologues dealing with power, pleasure and pain'.[1]

The monologues are evidently the work of a fledgling writer. *Comic Monologue* and *What She Said* are powerful but unsophisticated. *Starved* is much richer and more fully realised but its short length strains to accommodate the complex emotional landscape that it depicts. They are, in other words, apprentice-works, and would probably not be of great interest, had their author not gone on to write some of the most important plays of the decade. These monologues were by Sarah Kane.

The monologues are not widely known and have not been published. Indeed, in the last year of her life, Kane asked friends to return copies of the manuscripts and made it clear that she did not want them performed or printed. Perhaps she considered them juvenilia; perhaps she felt they were too personal, or too provisional. However, the monologues introduce concerns and theatrical ideas that would animate her throughout her work, and contain specific moments that she would later revisit to much greater effect, principally in *Crave*, as I shall show. Kane was an author who thought hard about how she wanted her works to be seen, the ways they might be grouped together. The sense of the monologues forming a body of work that led Kane – somewhat precociously – to gather the three pieces together in a single typescript, entitled *Sick: Three Monologues by Sarah Kane*, is perhaps the same impulse that would later see them omitted from *The Complete Plays*.[2]

Kane did not retrieve all copies of these pieces. During her final year at Bristol University, she gave copies of the three monologues to the University's Theatre Collection and does not appear to have asked for them back, with the happy result that researchers can still read them.[3] In the controlled theatrical environment of the monologue, they offer a unique insight into the prehistory of Kane's emergence as a major playwright; and, while there is much of interest in the monologues themselves, they also give a clear sense of the trajectory of her creative journey when she burst into public attention with the *succès de scandale* of *Blasted*.

Comic Monologue was written in early 1991. Her friend and near-contemporary at Bristol, the playwright David Greig, had returned to the city after a short time living in London, to concentrate seriously on making theatre; to do so, he hired the newly opened Hen and Chickens pub theatre in Bedminster, in the west of the city, for three nights, as the venue for a monologue he had written, *A Savage Reminiscence*. Kane, then in the second year of her degree, suggested that she had written something which she could perform alongside it to make it a fuller evening. This was *Comic Monologue*, and the opening in 23 April 1991 marks her professional debut as a writer. Prior to this she had mainly concentrated on acting (she played Bradshaw in a production of Howard Barker's *Victory*) and directing (she had just directed a programme of Beckett monologues, whose influence would be felt increasingly in her work; she would go on to direct Caryl Churchill's *Top Girls* in her final university year).

Kane also performed the monologue at the Students' Union in Bristol, before taking it to the Edinburgh Festival, where it formed part of a programme entitled *Dreams, Screams and Silences*. This comprised a semi–improvised new play written each night by Vincent O'Connell, Kane's then partner, based on suggested titles from the audience, alongside two works by Kane: *Comic Monologue* and a new monologue, *What She Said*. Under the banner of Sore Throats Theatre – a grim reference to the content of *Comic Monologue* – Kane directed both her plays, but *Comic Monologue* was now performed by Catherine Eschle and *What She Said* by Marie-Louise Hogan. The programme records that the show was 'funded by overdraft, fuelled by Guinness'.[4]

Kane's decision not to perform is perhaps a sign of her growing focus on writing, which flourished in her final year at University.

Figure 1.   Programme for *Dreams Screams & Silences* (Roman Eagle Lodge, Edinburgh Festival, 1991). Designed by Steven O'Neill.

In that time Kane wrote *Starved*, a monologue of much greater depth and sophistication. This was also taken to the Edinburgh Festival, this time performed by Sarah Ogley, as part of a bill entitled *Dreams Screams 2*. It was also at this Festival that Kane saw Jeremy Weller's show *Mad*, which had a decisive impact on the theatre she wanted to make (Sierz, 2001a: 92–3). In London, she saw the three monologues performed together for the first and last time in a one-off performance by Jane Montgomery. A month later, she had enrolled on the MA in Playwriting at Birmingham University, where she would write the first draft of *Blasted*. These three monologues flow directly into that auspicious professional debut.

In this chapter, I want to discuss the development in craft and originality that the monologues demonstrate. In particular I want to consider the way in which their concerns re-emerge in the later, mature work, and explore, too, what these pieces are increasingly *not* like, in a way that throws new light on the politics of Kane's work.

Comic monologue

This monologue describes an oral rape. The speaker, a woman, has been seeing a man, but the relationship has not become sexual. One evening at his place, he demands oral sex. She refuses but after a violent struggle he forces his penis into her mouth and ejaculates. Afterwards, he bathes her, dresses her and drives her home. At the end of the monologue, the speaker observes that rape is an ordeal from which there is no recovery. The text itself is composed of thirty-seven short paragraphs, the longest only seventy-three words.

The piece resembles Franca Rame's *Lo Stupro* (*The Rape*) (1975), the Italian actress's account of being kidnapped and gang-raped two years earlier by a group of neo-fascists, acting with the encouragement of the Carabinieri. But where Rame's monologue begins in confusion, growing to horror and revulsion, Kane's style is plain, measured and factual. Even when it is describing violent acts and emotions, it does so with unflinching clarity. Only towards the end does the speaker pull focus to address the traumatic aftermath of this assault and offer moral condemnation of the act. The tightly controlled, sparse prose in some senses clashes jarringly with the subject matter, but creates a build-up of subtextual emotion that emerges powerfully in the final paragraphs. The economy of the writing perhaps also serves to suggest the annihilation of the speaker's sense of self in that violation, an effect emphasised by the fact that the man is named as 'Kevin' while the speaker remains only 'WOMAN'.[5]

It is a relatively simple text, though the effect is very powerful. John Osborne once wrote that he tried to write *Look Back in Anger* in 'a language in which it was possible only to tell the truth' (Osborne, 1993: viii). Truth and truthfulness are terms that get bandied about in theatre and seem to accrue mysterious and metaphysical significance, but it might be useful to use the more deflationary definition offered by the philosopher Bernard Williams, who simply defines it as a combination of accuracy and sincerity (Williams, 2002): this is something Kane certainly achieves in this first creative flight: Kane's vividly plainspoken descriptions immediately persuade as accuracy, while her unadorned non-literary style persuades us of her sincerity.

Having insisted on the piece's simplicity, *Comic Monologue* hints at a more inventive dramaturgical style. I will discuss later the more subversive effects of the blankly factual style. Elsewhere we note that between the account of that day and the account of the aftermath are four blank lines. Here it no doubt indicates a longer pause than normal but it also suggests a hinge between being in events and out of them, from the present to the past, and the onset of post-traumatic shock. This sort of manipulation of the page would eventually reach its apotheosis in *4.48 Psychosis*. It may seem crass to reflect purely on dramaturgical form when the content is so pressing, but it is worth noting that Kevin's penis hardening and softening over again, which is described during the stalemate phase of the violence, is an original and inventive way of marking the passage of time, and prefigures scene five of *Blasted*, which gives us snapshots of Ian's degradation through time (59–60).

What she said

Kane's second monologue is twice the length of her first. The speaker is seeing a man called Howard, with whom she has an open relationship. For much of the play, she recounts a series of ideological debates with a feisty lesbian friend called Deb, who is scornful of the speaker's proclaimed bisexuality and urges her to understand men's fundamental hatred of women. Her relationship with Deb continually promises to become sexual though this

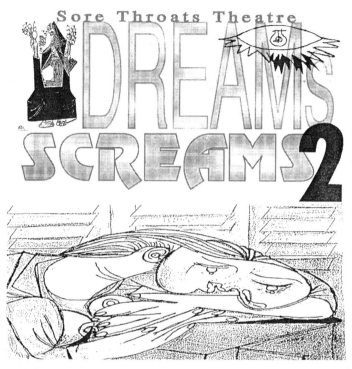

Short Plays by Vincent O'Connell
& a One Woman Play by Sarah Kane

Figure 2.   Poster for *Dreams Screams 2* (Roman Eagle Lodge,
Edinburgh Festival, 1992). Designed by Steven O'Neill.

misfires badly on one occasion: trying to show how much more open lesbians can be about sex, Deb urges the protagonist to express what she really wants sexually but, when her response is to ask to be tied up, Deb is horrified and rejects her. At their next encounter, the speaker asserts her bisexuality more confidently and finally they make love, the speaker describing herself as deeply happy.

What She Said has a much stronger sense of character than *Comic Monologue*. Wisecracking, confident, infuriating Deb, the weak, passive Howard and, between them, the shy but emergent speaker are all vividly realised in places. Unlike the austere, precise *Comic Monologue*, this play brims with puns and allusions, mostly deriving from the cut-and-thrust of the speaker's banter with Deb. (One typical rally has the speaker invite Deb to hers for Christmas; Deb retorts that a radical lesbian-feminist would hardly want to celebrate the birth of a man; how about Easter then? offers the narrator.) The language is also richer in its rhythms and vocabulary, with short sections recalling the incantatory style of Jim Cartwright's work. Lines are halting and incomplete, the layout itself contributing to the effect of the piece.

Because all three characters are voiced by a single narrator, there are moments of ambiguity, where it is unclear who is speaking. This may be evidence of a writer not yet in control of her craft, but it does, inadvertently perhaps, point to the permeable boundaries of gender that we find in Kane's later plays: the genital transplantation of *Cleansed*, the collective cross-gender chorus of *Crave*, the genderless, self-less semiotic flow of *4.48 Psychosis*. This gender-confused impression is confirmed when the (female) protagonist admits her inexperience with lesbian sex and wonders if the right way to ask for oral sex is to ask to be sucked off. The central character is outshadowed for much of the play by Deb, but even so intrigues with her alternation of savage misandry (as when she recalls winning money at a game of pool, joyful that she'd won it from a man) and wide-eyed idealism (as when she wonders why we build houses when we could live in trees).

This is the only one of the three monologues to exist in two different versions. The later version of the play which is included in the typescript for *Sick* has a handful of extra lines. When these additions were made it is hard to tell, though it's interesting that Kane hadn't yet acquired her taste for cutting her texts down to the bone, which would take root in the process of drafting *Blasted*.

Starved

The brutalised protagonist of *Comic Monologue* recalls that, after her violation, she didn't eat properly for a year. As if taking its cue from that, *Starved* follows a teenage girl with a serious eating disorder as her weight drops to four stone and she is hospitalised, force-fed and returned to her family. These events unfold in a bleak social landscape of a warring, uncomprehending home and a school which is little more than a battleground for predatory sexual warfare. The monologue begins with the speaker recounting in minute detail all the food she eats and she vomits it up, like a bulimic Bridget Jones. As her weight diminishes, the piece's dramaturgical syntax disintegrates and the second half is fragmented, impressionistic and sometimes numbed with apparent horror at the brutality of the world.

The monologue is a great step forward in depth and complexity compared to the two earlier works. The language has rhythmic echoes of Beckett, in the narrator's frequent announcements that she feels, in a single word, Better. Formally the piece is rich and evocative, charting, through its own structural collapse, the terrified breakdown of a mind. This technique would be repeated, on a grander scale, in the sudden and decisive departure from narrative, spatial and temporal coherence after scene three of *Blasted*. Even more decisively, the fragmented, subjective style produced by this breakdown would come to define the style of Kane's final two plays. Just as *What She Said* showed a marked development in the handling of character, *Starved* now paints a much more fully realised picture of a world, even if it is a world from which the speaker is deeply alienated. When her father snaps at her to live in the real world, the speaker replies that she thought this *was* the real world, and her private reaction is to be very sick indeed. 'Sick', which was the title Kane gave to the three monologues, is here a floating signifier, whose meaning can be applied to the speaker's eating disorder, but also to the values of the world around her. She feels alive when she's half-dead, and, when she's forcibly fattened up again, she feels dead. Indeed, what is for the first time fully worked out here is the inversion of values that the speaker experiences between her and the world around her that we will see recur through the later plays. In *Crave*, M asks C if she's ever been hospitalised for 'Anorexia. Bulimia'; 'No' replies C (173). We might wish to take this exchange from that personal, almost private, play as an acknowledgement that

FREE ASSOCIATION PRODUCTIONS PRESENT A WORKSHOP PRODUCTION OF

SICK

THREE MONOLOGUES BY SARAH KANE

STARVED

COMIC MONOLOGUE

WHAT SHE SAID

PERFORMED BY JANE MONTGOMERY

DIRECTED BY DEB JONES

PRODUCED BY JO SMITH AND DEB JONES

Three monologues dealing with power, pleasure and pain. The performance is the result of a few days workshop, performed around another show's set and using the minimum of props. Tonight's performance is very much a 'work in progress', so please take the opportunity to discuss the reading with the company later this evening, or for more details contact 071 263 7833. The three pieces run consecutively with no interval for approx. 1hr.

*   *   *

Figure 3. Typed programme for *Sick: Three Monologues by Sarah Kane* (London 1992), the first and only public performance of all three monologues together (document kindly loaned by Harriet Braun).

Starved is a work of imagination rather than documentary, and it is all the more impressive for that.

Starved is the last thing Kane wrote before the plays generally accepted as her canon. It's a token of just how close she was to this work that the blunt irony of *Comic Monologue* and the theft of a song title by The Smiths for *What She Said* sound like nothing else in her work, whereas *Starved, Blasted, Cleansed* are all of a piece. As Kane embarked on writing *Blasted*, she was making the leap from monologue to dialogue. In some ways, the early drafts of *Blasted* with their reputed long Howard Barker-like speeches (Sierz, 2001a: 101), sound like monologue disguised as dialogue. As she pared away, and found her own distinctive voice in dialogue, she was forging a fully mature identity for herself as a playwright. That play has a scale and theatricality that is beyond even the best of the monologues, but we should not underestimate the decisive leap from *What She Said*'s conventional unconventionality to the raw, splintered descent into psychological hell that she discovered in writing *Starved*.

Things to come

I have indicated a number of ways in which these plays prefigure the later, mature work. When the protagonist of *Starved* asserts that after her medical treatment there's no point getting up, we hear an echo of Grace's nihilistic mantra at the end of *Cleansed*:

> Think about getting up it's pointless
> Think about eating it's pointless
> Think about dressing it's pointless
> Think about speaking it's pointless
> Think about dying only it's totally fucking pointless (150)

When Howard in *What She Said* insists that he just wants her to love him, not die for him, we hear a resonance of Rod and Carl's brutal disputing of romantic clichés (109–12). However, such connections perhaps only suggest that these plays are all written by the same writer, addressing the same ongoing concerns.

However, there are some far stronger and closer links between the monologues and the later plays. In *4.48 Psychosis* Kane describes (presumably) herself as the 'Last in a long line of literary kleptomaniacs' (213). Her indebtedness to other authors, like Shakespeare, Beckett and Bond has been thoroughly set out (Saunders, 2002a). Less well recognised is the extent to which Kane stole from herself, reworking motifs and images from the early monologues in the later plays, and at one fascinating moment conducting a wholesale cannibalisation of this early work to rebuild her playwriting identity.

Blasted echoes *Comic Monologue* in a great many ways. In the earlier work, Kevin strips off and stands naked in front of the woman; her initial reaction is to laugh hysterically. The same sequence of events happens in *Blasted* (7–8). Cate remarks that she's going out with 'Shaun' but they haven't slept together (16), which is the same relationship the speaker has with Kevin before the events of the monologue. In scene two, when Ian ejaculates in Cate's mouth, her immediate reaction is to brush her teeth (31), the same reaction described in *Comic Monologue*. Where they part company is Cate's resistance. *Comic Monologue*'s protagonist remarks that she couldn't go to the police, because of the prurient, sneering questions she felt they'd ask, like why she didn't bite his penis to stop him. Cate does have the presence of mind to do that (31), perhaps as a belated act of literary revenge on Kevin. In the closing moments of *Comic Monologue*, the narrator recalls reading about a young boy caught up in a civil war, forced by guerrillas to murder his own parents. She finds that she understands and identifies with his resultant withdrawal into silence. This connection between a singular rape in a domestic setting and acts of global atrocity is exactly the connection elaborated in *Blasted*. As she would later tell me, 'I thought what could possibly be the connection between a common rape in a Leeds hotel room and what's happening in Bosnia? And suddenly the penny dropped and I thought of course it's obvious, one is the seed and the other is the tree' (Saunders, 2002a: 39). The events of *Comic Monologue* and *Blasted* – perhaps as seen by Kevin/Ian – are eerily combined by A in *Crave* when he declares: 'We checked into a hotel pretending we weren't going to have sex [...] We made love, then she threw up' (178–9).

Comic Monologue's account of oral rape is echoed and multiplied in a variety of complex images. In *Starved*, when she determines to keep quiet at school on her eighteenth birthday, the protagonist is both refusing sexual adulthood and keeping her mouth closed, in a context where the boys remark that she always has something in her mouth, and sneeringly ask her to suck their cocks. Images of oral rape are also found in *Blasted*, *Phaedra's Love* and arguably *Crave* (31–2, 81, 175). Tinker's force-feeding of Robin with a box of chocolates in *Cleansed* is a similar image, again symbolised by food (139–41).

Crave and the monologues

Crave remains Sarah Kane's most beautiful and cryptic play. The text is a patchwork of languages and registers, citations and references, stage poetry and private messages, expansive humour and dark despair. One of the generally unrecognised features of it is that, in writing the play, Kane returned to the monologues and raided them, lifting large sections to build her new structure.

There are direct quotations from all of the monologues in *Crave*. *Comic Monologue* gives us 'my bowels gave way' (181), 'Empty / Sickened / White' (184). *What She Said* gives *Crave* 'I am much fucking angrier than you think' (189) and 'Something clicked' (196). *4.48 Psychosis*'s painstaking descriptions of all the pills being ingested in hospital grimly echoes *Starved*'s obsessive itemisation of all the food the protagonist is eating. Otherwise, there is one lone citation in *4.48 Psychosis* from the early works: Kane's first monologue furnishes her last play with the line 'the morning brings defeat' (231).

But it is *Starved* that she draws upon the most. All of the following lines from *Crave* derive, sometimes very slightly altered, from that piece: 'death is an option' (173), 'I have children, the men come, I am fighting but they take them, I realise, the men, they came, they said, in the night, they said',[6] 'she touched my arm and smiled', 'GOT ME' (178), 'not my fucking mother neither', 'Starved' (179), 'He buys me a make-up kit, blushers and lipstick and eyeshadow. And I paint my face in bruises and blood and cuts and swelling, and on the mirror in deep red, UGLY', 'What does that mean, what does that mean, what does that mean what you're saying?', 'Be a woman, be a woman, FUCK YOU' (180), 'it's real, it's real, dead real, dead real' (183), 'out, out into what?' (189),[7] the line 'What have they done to me?' repeated seventeen times (191), 'Weight / Don't know / Date / Don't know / Fate / Don't know', 'Shit on a plate. Look enthusiastic or your own mother will take you apart' (195), 'Get the Night Men in' (196), 'Fat and shiny and dead dead dead serene', 'When even dreams aren't private / Best to forget' (198), 'Cured my body can't cure my soul' and 'Patch and paint and paste a look onto my face' (199).

This decision to recycle and reuse material from an earlier stage of her life echoes Kane's adoption of a pseudonym (Marie Kelvedon) constructed out of her middle name and the town she grew up in. Perhaps burdened by her reputation as an *enfant terrible*, Kane wanted to recover something of herself before *Blasted* made her notorious. Further, as is well known, Kane was taken into Eileen Skellern 3 Ward, at the Maudsley Hospital in South London shortly before writing *Cleansed* and *Crave*. (*Cleansed* is dedicated to 'the patients and staff of ES3' (105).) It is unsurprising to see her turn to her own fictional account of a hospitalisation from five years earlier to re-examine it, turn it inside out, to find the kernels of authenticity there. Of course, the use Kane makes of all of this material is to fundamentally transform it into a quite new experience. *Crave* is, as the critics noted at the time, a great leap forward (Saunders, 2002a: 102), but in one important way it is also an act of careful retrospection across the entirety of her work.

Politics

On the surface, the subject matter of these three monologues looks like standard feminist theatre fare: rape, sexuality, eating disorders. In the first two, the endings take on a tone that is recognisable also in the work of a playwright like Sarah Daniels.

In the grim insistence that rape is a trauma from which there is
no recovery, we hear both a conclusion but also an avoidance of
rhetorical climax, which resembles the closing lines on Daniels's
Masterpieces, 'I don't want anything to do with men who have knives
or whips or men who look at photos of women tied and bound, or
men who say relax and enjoy it. Or men who tell misogynist jokes'
(Daniels, 1991: 230). Earlier, Rowena, a social worker, looks for
the first time in her life at pornographic magazines and is horrified
by what she sees. 'How they must hate us' she declares (204). The
same sentiment, in similar words, is expressed by Deb in *What
She Said* in her attempt to persuade the speaker to give up her
attachment to heterosexuality. As a whole, *What She Said* feels
like a description of feminist consciousness-raising, both for the
speaker to feel confident in her bisexuality and also for her to have
the confidence to sleep with a woman.

However, in both monologues, the endings are not wholly
consistent with their contents. In *Comic Monologue*, the tonal
blankness of the prose means that, for the whole description of
the rape, there is very little clear sense of moral condemnation
of the man's actions. We are plunged so quickly into the action,
and so little context is given, that the piece is disorientating; we
are thrown into this violent experience without explanation. The
actions are horrifying, but this is not something Kane feels the
need to underline editorially. Indeed, in an unsettling moment,
after her assailant has washed and dressed, she describes him as
stunning, and as beautiful. As he lifts her into the bath, washes
her, dresses her, the text daringly takes on a tender, even gentle
tone, which speaks vividly of deep psychic confusion, that places
the onus on the audience to make their own judgements of the
events described. In that sense, we see a clear prefiguring of one of
the dramaturgical strategies that would prove so perplexing to the
first reviewers of *Blasted*. Noting the lack of a clear moral message,
those critics denounced the play's 'numbing amorality', its lack of a
'coherent moral framework', and for having 'no message to convey'
(Kingston, 1995; Hemming, 1995; Tinker, 1995). Kane agreed,
describing the play as deliberately 'amoral' (Saunders, 2002a: 27).

Comic Monologue, however, ends with a *very* explicit moral
message, emphasising the traumatic effects of rape. What we have
seen before is more powerful than the explicit moral denunciation
precisely for its lack of ethical moorings and its requirement of the
audience to respond directly to the material. The explicit message
raises further problems for the politics of the monologue, by its

pessimism: throughout Kane's protagonist describes her rape at the hands of this man as if it were inevitable, and ends by saying there is no getting over such a thing. This complicates the positive assertion of a feminist principle (no means no) in a way that is politically problematic. The piece is in complex dialogue with its ending, and the tone of the two sections is not easily reconciled. *Comic Monologue*, in a sense, is a rehearsal for the much more decisive destruction of the theatrical frame in *Blasted*. In both there is a clash between blankly observed violence and clear editorial commentary. Here it is the blankness that gives way to commentary; in *Blasted*, the rational lucidity of naturalistic form is explosively abandoned in favour of escalating atrocity.

Something analogous happens in *What She Said*. Much of it is taken up with the speaker's insistence on her bisexual identity in the face of Deb's scepticism and disdain. The most emotionally wounding row comes when Deb refuses the speaker's sexual desire to be tied up. Neither of these disputes is resolved; Deb continues to argue her line that bisexuality is just a form of false consciousness and the protagonist's desire for a sadomasochistic relationship is dropped. At one point, neatly, their differences are encapsulated when the protagonist asks Deb why she has to take her politics into bed with her, to which Deb retorts why the speaker leaves hers behind. The precise articulation of sex and politics was one of the key debates for feminists in the 1980s in what is sometimes called the 'Feminist Sex Wars'. But if the audience hope to find some resolution and development in the debate, they are disappointed. Instead, without much explanation, the two women end up making love. Sincere no doubt, and in its own way rather affecting, but it's hard not to feel that, by going to bed with Deb, the speaker has foreclosed rather abruptly on the complicated questions that the piece has raised.

At one point *4.48 Psychosis* identifies three subject-positions: 'Victim. Perpetrator. Bystander' (231). As in the first production of the play at the Royal Court in 2000, these have often been taken to suggest a cast list, a division of the text to create a scene: the witnessing of an atrocity. The key thing to remember is that Kane's plays are populated by all three of these positions, and one is increasingly aware throughout her work that Kane saw herself just as capable of being a perpetrator as a victim. 'I gassed the Jews, I killed the Kurds, I bombed the Arabs, I fucked small children while they begged for mercy, the killing fields are mine, everyone left the party because of me' begins one famous passage (227).

Sadomasochism is an interesting terrain to explore some of the ambivalences of sexual power. In *Crave*, A insists, 'You're never as powerful as when you know you're powerless' (159). The locking together of the sub/dom couple is a motif that we see repeated throughout the plays, extreme dominance and submission that seems to be willed or at least accepted by both parties. Kane's ability to place herself in both positions of the dyad is what gives this a peculiar richness and complexity.

In *Starved*, the explicit political editorialising has entirely vanished. Does this mean that Kane abandoned feminism or politics? Some have imagined Kane to have turned her back on feminism on the basis of remarks like her famous declaration, 'I have no responsibility as a woman writer because I don't believe there's such a thing' (Stephenson and Langridge, 1997: 134). To conclude that this represents a withdrawal from politics, sexual or otherwise (Gottlieb, 1999: 209), is in my view mistaken, because it is to confuse one particular formulation of political theatre with political theatre as such. As I've suggested elsewhere, changes in the political structure of the world in the 1980s and 1990s – in particular the relative decline of the state and the broadening of our ethical commitments in an era of globalisation – meant the obsolescence of certain theatre forms designed for an earlier era (Rebellato, 2007). Sarah Kane was by no means alone in seeking to move beyond the categories of political identity and action that had been developed in the 1970s and 1980s. Her contemporaries and near-contemporaries such as Mark Ravenhill, David Greig, Philip Ridley and Martin Crimp also showed a preference, throughout the 1990s, for avoiding precise social references or straightforward political commentary in their plays. This was not a flight from reality but a suspicion of those totalising ideological forces whose power over reality had never seemed more complete: reproducing reality perhaps just reproduces its ideological forms. The playwrights of the 1990s, and none more strikingly than Kane, eschewed naturalism for utopian, ironic forms, marshalling great impossible oppositions of power and powerlessness, always insisting, even metaphysically insisting, that this world is not all that is possible, and defiantly keeping open a sense of otherness.

Conclusion

Sarah Kane's first three monologues show a remarkably swift evolution in confidence, daring and sophistication. They mark the first appearance of a set of concerns that would continue to animate her work right to the end; at times, she turned directly to her early pieces as a storehouse of fragments and intense feeling that she used to animate the later plays. What they also show, very clearly, is a deliberate reconstruction of political playwriting: away from the models that had dominated the two decades before and towards a revaluation of formal experiment as a locus for a new utopian politics.

Acknowledgements

I'd like to thank, Harriet Braun, Graham Eatough, David Greig and Lucy Macaulay and Graham Saunders for their help in preparing this essay.

Notes

1 This description of the performance of *Sick* draws on a photocopied programme for the event given to me by a friend of Kane's. The programme is undated, but it seems to me likely that it took place in or around September 1992, after her second visit to the Edinburgh Festival (with *Starved*) and before she moved to Birmingham to begin her MA in Playwriting. The individual texts are marked with her third-year Bristol address.

2 Sarah Kane's Estate are currently upholding her wishes in respect of the monologues and for that reason they have not granted permission for them to be directly quoted in this essay. Their concern is that once they start being quoted in print it might eventually become possible to reconstruct the texts and then samizdat productions might start appearing, which they are keen not to see happen. I am, of course, happy to accept their judgement and have described but not quoted directly from the monologues. I have also decided not to give page references to the manuscripts, on the same grounds, though the texts are short and researchers will be able to find the sections referred to in the manuscripts.

3 The holdings of these plays at the University of Bristol Theatre Collection are as follows. There are two identical typescript copies of *Comic Monologue*, both bound, with the shelf numbers WTC/PS/000246/1, and WTC/PS/000246/2. There are three identical copies of *What She Said*, with the numbers WTC/PS/000247/1 (loose-leaf), WTC/PS/000247/2 and WTC/PS/000247/3 (bound copies). There are two identical bound copies of *Sick* (which contains *Starved*), at WTC/PS/000245/1 and WTC/PS/000245/2. The version of *What She Said* has some small changes and additions to the text. All of the

typescripts have unnumbered pages. The Theatre Collection can be contacted at http://www.bristol.ac.uk/theatrecollection.

4 I'm grateful to Graham Eatough for tracking down a copy of the programme.

5 WOMAN would also be the only name given to the speakers of *What She Said* and *Starved*. *Blasted* is the first play to give the speaking characters names, though from there the journey is back to the annihilated self: From Cate (a real name in *Blasted*) to Hippolytus (a literary figure in *Phaedra's Love*) to Tinker (stealing the name of a hostile theatre critic in *Cleansed*), the Woman in *Cleansed* to A (a single letter in *Crave*), to no names at all in *4.48 Psychosis*.

6 In *Starved* this line is a description of a nightmare and refers to these children being kept in from a blast; which suggests that this is also a source for *Blasted*.

7 This line may be a half-reference to the opening of Beckett's *Not I* (1972), '... out ... into this world ... this world ... tiny little thing ... before its time ...' (Beckett 1986: 376). Beckett's protagonist, Mouth, seems to be recalling her premature birth. Kane at this point of *Starved* is describing her infantilisation in the hospital (she has earlier described herself as looking and perhaps feeling like a baby), so the reference is apposite.

3

'Looks like there's a war on': Sarah Kane's *Blasted*, political theatre and the Muslim Other

Aleks Sierz

One of the most persistent myths about British theatre in the 1990s is the idea that the decade experienced the death of political theatre. Young writers, the story goes, abandoned the big political plays of the 1970s and 1980s, and opted instead for small domestic dramas about private issues in which – to reverse the feminist slogan – the political was personal. Clearly, like all myths, this one has a vital kernel of truth: large-cast political plays on main stages did become rare in British theatres, but that does not mean that writers lost either their political passion or their political intelligence. Nothing illustrates this better than Sarah Kane's debut, *Blasted*, which has now been firmly established within the canon of 1990s British drama – here is a play that was political in origin, political in content and political in its effects.

Although Kane's work has been widely admired and discussed, with numerous productions mounted all over the world, it took several years for revivals of her plays to appear on British stages. Following the first production of *Blasted*, in 1995, at the Royal Court Theatre Upstairs, and a revival on the Court's main stage in 2001, other productions of *Blasted* have included the Citizens Theatre in Glasgow in 2002, and Graeae Theatre, in 2006. In 2008, there was a site-specific production directed by Felix Mortimer at the Queen's Hotel in Leeds. Although Kane's work has not been revived very often, it has affected other playwrights. For example, in September 2000, Holly Baxter Baine – whose *Good-bye Roy* was part of the Royal Court's Exposure season of young writers – said that her favourite playwrights were Bertolt Brecht and Sarah Kane. Baine was just fifteen years old (Royal Court Press Office, 2000). In February 2003, the final stage image of debbie tucker green's *dirty butterfly* (2003) – a '*damaged*' young woman with blood running down her legs – was a powerful echo of Cate's last appearance in *Blasted* (tucker green, 2003: 38). More tangentially, the opening scene of Kevin Elyot's *Forty Winks* (2004) featured a hotel room with a closed bathroom that concealed a secret visitor, a subtle homage to Kane (Elyot, 2004: 7; 9).

One example of Kane's political influence is Kaite O'Reilly's *Peeling* (2002), about three women chorus members in a postmodernist production of Euripides' *The Trojan Women*, one of the classic plays about war. At one point, there's a litany of horrors: each character says, in turn, 'Fire'; 'Smoke'; 'Pestilence' – then they all say: 'Men' (O'Reilly, 2002: 22). The characteristics of war are: 'Woman's body as battlefield'; 'Rape as a war tactic'; 'Mutilation as a reminder' (O'Reilly, 2002: 23). Along with Beaty's speech about surviving a massacre in her village (O'Reilly, 2002: 24), such lines are clear examples of *Blasted*'s influence on contemporary playwrights; they also provide an indication of the way that the experience of the Bosnian (Muslim) wars haunts the European imagination, and of how political theatre remains urgently alive.

It is also interesting to consider how *Blasted*'s meaning has mutated. In the text, and in Kane's recorded conversations about the play, there is a gap, a silence, an absence of the explosive word 'Muslim'. Although the play was inspired by massacres in the Bosnian (Muslim) war, and Kane was moved by the image of a Bosnian (Muslim) woman hanging in a forest, the word 'Muslim' is absent from the play.[1] After '9/11', the absence of this Muslim Other is even more noticeable. While the word 'Muslim' is on everyone's lips, oddly it has disappeared from a play inspired by the plight of European Muslims. So it is significant that Thomas Ostermeier's Berlin production of *Blasted* (*Zerbombt*) at the Schaubühne am Lehniner Platz in 2005 tried to redress this by using a constant CNN news commentary about the war in Iraq (widely perceived by Muslims as anti-Muslim). *Blasted*, of course, is set in Leeds, home coincidentally – or presciently? – of three out of the four '7/7' London suicide bombers. However, if Muslims are absent in *Blasted*, what's present is Ian's racism, part of which is explicitly directed against those of Pakistani (Muslim) origin. Ten years before the London bombings, Kane instinctively, if unconsciously, suggested the politics of Muslim disaffection, and of English reactionary racism. However, if the Muslim Other is always absent from *Blasted*, its shadow falls across the play, and recent events have sharpened its contours.

'You're a nightmare'

When *Blasted* opened in January 1995, most theatre reviewers were appalled by the ferocity of Kane's writing, puzzled by her play's structure and dismissive of its vision. For example, Michael Billington thought that its radically innovative structure, in which the first half is perfectly naturalistic and the second half is metaphorically horrific, did not work. 'The reason the play falls apart', he argued, 'is that there is no sense of external reality – who exactly is meant to be fighting whom out on the streets?' (Billington, 1995). In other words, the prevailing naturalistic and social realist aesthetic of British critics blinded them to the meaning of the radical rupture within *Blasted*. Other spectators were less worried about the play's meaning. For example, the Reverend Bob Vernon, in a letter to the *Guardian* newspaper, defended the play, pointing out that 'Some housing estates in our city look like war zones … my local shopping centre looks like Grozny' (Vernon, 1995). Grozny of course is part of another anti-Muslim war: this time in Chechnya.

Not only did most critics not appreciate Kane's daring innovation in form but they also found the play's central idea, that a civil war could happen in Britain, entirely unconvincing. This is a profound misreading of the meaning of *Blasted*'s structure. The whole point of the play is that this violent break in the middle of the story not only mimics the real effect of war as a radical disruption of normality, but also shows that it can be read in two completely distinct ways. Firstly, the play stays in Leeds – what this means is that, when the Soldier knocks on the door, the play, which at first seemed to be happening today, suddenly reveals itself as a projection into the future. In other words, Kane has violently shifted the temporal aspect of the drama. The play warns against complacency and argues that the antagonisms that create civil wars are always present in society, yes, even in today's Britain. To the conservative mantra of 'It couldn't happen here', it answers with a radical: 'It just has'.

Secondly, the play, which started in Leeds, suddenly reveals itself as an account of Bosnia. In other words, Kane has violently shifted the spatial aspect of the drama. The play breaks down the barrier of distance imposed by geography and transports the audience into the experience of civil war. To the insular idea that 'It's none of my business', it replies with an in-yer-face: 'Try avoiding this then'. So *Blasted* is at the same time both a play that stays rooted in Leeds (then jumps into the future) and a play that stays rooted in the 1990s (then jumps across Europe to Bosnia). Clearly, it also has a number of other metaphorical meanings. And, however disconcerting, the play's shift into a war zone in the second half is a perfect link between form and content.

In theatre, space is vital: in the small studio space in 1995, *Blasted* literally blasted its audiences – it was extreme, experiential and in-yer-face. According to critics, the play's central meaning seemed to be a childish desire to shock by an inexperienced playwright. One of the reasons for their reaction was the fact that the first production was staged on a very small budget. For this reason, the '*very expensive hotel room*' (3) required by Kane's stage directions actually looked more like a squalid bedsit. So the play's opening, which crucially sets the tone of the evening, was misread by the audience. Ian's first line – 'I've shat in better places than this' (3) – is funny if the hotel room looks very classy; when it looks impoverished, the line simply suggests that the audiences are in for an evening of squalid dirty realism. Thus, lack of money meant the first production got off to a fatally humourless start.

By contrast, when the Royal Court revived the play on its main stage in April 2001, the set, designed by Hildegard Bechtler, was immensely expensive and Ian's opening line came across as Kane intended: it caused a laugh. In general, this production not only hit the right mix of black humour and grim horror, but its mainstage setting also made the play seem more like a state-of-Europe play, large, expansive and deeply political. The critic Charles Spencer, who admitted that his original review of the play had got things wrong, said: 'The transition from a world that we recognise as our own to one we have only seen on news footage from the former Yugoslavia, raises all kinds of questions. Is Kane suggesting that racism in Britain could turn into full-scale ethnic cleansing? Or merely that the seeds of unthinkable barbarity lie in us all, or at least in all men?' (Spencer, 2001). Michael Billington also apologised and acknowledged that *Blasted* 'seeks to warn us that we enjoy no special historic immunity from violence and that there is a direct link between private and public fascism' (Billington, 2001). Benedict Nightingale thought that Kane's 'moral, social political' vision reminded him of another political play, J.B. Priestley's *An Inspector Calls* (1947): 'if we don't learn responsibility for each other, we'll "be taught that lesson in fire and blood and anguish"' (Nightingale, 2001). In fact, in July 2001, soon after this revival, riots broke out in Oldham and Bradford after Muslim youths were provoked by racists of the British National Party. Once again, the reality of the Muslim experience in Britain shadowed Kane's play.

'Our town now'

Nevertheless, if it is clear that *Blasted* is an account of civil war, and that its theatrical innovation comes from its radical structure, it did not start like that. The play was conceived not as a big political statement but as a personal account of a domestic rape. As Sarah Kane said, 'Originally, I was writing a play about two people in a hotel room, in which there was a complete power imbalance, which resulted in the older man raping the younger woman' (Rebellato, 1998). Then something unexpected happened:

> At some point during the first couple of weeks of writing [March 1993], I switched on the television. Srebrenica was under siege. An old [Muslim] woman was looking into the camera, crying. She said, 'Please, please, somebody help us. Somebody do something'. I knew nobody was going to do a thing. Suddenly, I was completely uninterested in the play I was writing. What I wanted to write about was what I'd just seen on television. So my dilemma was: do I abandon my play (even though I'd written one scene I thought was really good) in order to move on to a subject I thought was more pressing? Slowly, it occurred to me that the play I was writing was about this. It was about violence, about rape, and it was about these things happening between people who know each other and ostensibly love each other. (Rebellato, 1998)

Kane then struggled with the connection between the two parts of the play:

> I asked myself: 'What could possibly be the connection between a common rape in a Leeds hotel room and what's happening in Bosnia?' And then suddenly this penny dropped and I thought: 'Of course, it's obvious. One is the seed and the other is the tree.' And I do think that the seeds of full-scale war can always be found in peacetime civilisation and I think the wall between so-called civili-sation and what happened in central Europe is very, very thin and it can get torn down at any time. (Rebellato, 1998)

Media images of war had politicised Kane. Next, she 'needed an event' to join the two halves of her play. In early drafts, Ian merely hallucinated the soldier. 'And then I thought: "What this needs is what happens in war – suddenly, violently, without any warning, people's lives are completely ripped to pieces."' Therefore, Kane 'picked a moment in the play. I thought: "I'll plant a bomb, just blow the whole fucking thing up." And I loved the idea of that as well. Just blowing up the set' (Rebellato, 1998).

If what really annoyed audiences about the first production of *Blasted* was the way the naturalistic first half suddenly changed into a symbolic second half, Kane's experiment in form was not a coolly premeditated idea. She didn't wake up one morning and think, 'Oh yes, this is a radical idea – I'll write a play like this.' It was forced on her by the need to turn two different plays into one. Although we now see the radical structure of the play as its most daring aesthetic innovation, it is worth remembering that, when she wrote it, Kane was an apprentice playwright. As a first-time writer, she could control the monologue form, but she was struggling to write a proper play. Her radical structure arose from a meeting between chance and necessity. Her later rationalisation that 'war is confused and illogical, therefore it is wrong to use a form that is predictable' is aesthetically right, but it is still a rationalisation after the fact. The irony remains that her much praised 'experiment in form' (Kane, 1999) was actually a result of improvisation.

'I can't piss. It's just blood'

The idea of rape was central to Kane's vision of war, which is why *Peeling* feels like an echo of *Blasted*. For example, she once said, 'I was working on this with some actors and someone said, "There's nothing kind of unusual about the fact that there's rape camps in Bosnia, or people are raped during war. That's what war is"' (Saunders, 2002a: 48). Indeed, it's interesting that a bestselling book in Britain in 2002 was Anthony Beevor's *Berlin – The Downfall 1945*, with its horrific accounts of what the Soviet army did to German women – perhaps a generation that has not known war is more fascinated by its representation than a generation that has lived through the experience. Kane argued against this essentialist view that war necessarily means rape:

> Certainly the Vietcong it seems didn't rape. They just didn't. And when Western women were captured by the Vietcong and they were finally rescued, and people said, 'Oh God, what happened? Were you raped?' – gleefully, for stories, and there just weren't any. And similarly the Chinese army ... Isolated incidents, but it really isn't kind of used as a war weapon. Certainly, it's happening in Yugoslavia. It's being used systematically to degrade Muslim women. And so I tend to think there's got to be something cultural about that. (Saunders, 2002a: 48)

For a brief moment, the Muslim Other makes an appearance – as a victimised female. And Kane is probably right to say that the use of rape as a weapon of war is cultural. It is also significant that, in *Blasted*, she extended its use to cover the male Ian as well as the female Cate, a case of poetic justice in her contemporary reworking of the genre of Jacobean revenge tragedy.

At this point, it is worth looking at the early draft of *Blasted* – the text used in the first production at Birmingham University as part of Kane's MA in Playwriting (Allardyce Nicoll Studio Theatre, 4.15pm, Saturday 3 July 1993) – to see what it tells us about its original meaning. The most revealing thing about this draft is that the Soldier, later unnamed, is here called Vladek, which makes him more explicitly Yugoslav or Serbian than just the nameless, symbolic character in later drafts. The other thing you notice is that Kane, when she revised her work, systematically removed local references and substituted general ones. For example, in the early draft, she specifies Gordon's gin; in the final text, it's just gin. The other characteristic of her working method was to speed up the dialogue in each successive draft – so that Ian's first question to Cate 'Do you want a bath?' becomes 'You want a bath?' (Kane, 1993: 1; Kane, 2001: 3).

Finally, the early drafts also reveal that the play was a direct response to the events in Bosnia:

> VLADEK. English shit. Why did you fuckers recognise Croatia?
>
> (*Ian is confused.*)
>
> Why are you English spineless dogs sniffing Germany's arse?
>
> IAN. That was the government. I'm not the government.
>
> VLADEK. This is a Serbian town now. And you are English shit.
>
> (*He spits in Ian's face.*)   (Saunders, 2002a: 53)

Such specific references were later dropped, pushing the Muslim Other further into the subtext. What remain in the play are Ian's parochial patriotism and his racist hatred. Although he is Welsh by birth, he has lived almost all his life in Leeds, and has reactionary notions of racial purity: 'Come over from God knows where have their kids and call them English they're not English born in England don't make you English' (41). His constant racist, sexist and homophobic comments build up a powerful picture of a cauldron of emotional anguish and aggression. Tabloid prejudices, football-fan attitudes and pub-bore hatreds combine with testosterone to create a convincing picture of bigoted nationalism. Implicitly, Kane is arguing, this is the raw material of today's social antagonism – and such sentiments could one day be the emotional ammunition of civil war. Furthermore, since blindness is a recurrent motif in recent war drama, it is significant that when Ian 'fails to comply with the soldier's request to report the war atrocities he has experienced [he] is therefore blinded as a nemesis for shutting his own (and the public's) eyes' (Soncini, 2004: 90–1). Like much of Kane's symbolism, this is overtly political.

'He ate her eyes'

Of course, after her suicide at the age of 28 in 1999, most discussions of Kane's work run up against the myth of the tragic genius who died young. The cult of Kane, which is popular among academics and students, tends to blind us to what is good and bad in her work. Nevertheless, as the heat of controversy that made partisans of many critics and theatre workers in the immediate aftermath of *Blasted*'s debut has passed, it is worth pointing out that exaggerating Kane's genius actually does her no favours. On the other hand, those academics who sneer at Kane's talent are less defensible. In one publication, Mary Luckhurst states that 'I find her plays politically conservative and her writing stilted' (Luckhurst, 2002: 73), yet confidence in this judgement is undermined by the fact that in another book Luckhurst both gets the year of Kane's death wrong and believes that her plays were directed by Ian Rickson rather than James Macdonald (Lennard and Luckhurst, 2002: 106; 164). On more solid ground, Peter Buse argues that *Blasted* can be read with reference to trauma theory, although his conclusions are rather unremarkable (Buse, 2001: 172–90), while Elaine Aston acutely points out the link between Ian's destructive patriotism and his selfish conception of love (Aston, 2003: 88).

Theatre people have a similarly mixed record. For example, in defiance of the text, Richard Eyre and Nicholas Wright insist on believing that '*Blasted* starts with an abusive sexual relationship between father and daughter' (Eyre and Wright, 2000: 374). With a greater feel for rhetoric than for sense, the playwright Peter Morris argues that 'what makes Sarah Kane thrilling as a writer is her punk resistance to being commodified' (Morris, 2000: 151). More controversially, Dominic Dromgoole (director of the Bush theatre in the 1990s and once Kane's employer when she was a literary associate at the theatre) writes that 'the only problem

with Sarah, in my view, is that I'm not sure she's a natural writer'
(Dromgoole, 2000: 162). He has a point: Kane is not primarily
a writer of easy dialogue – her exchanges always serve a larger
purpose, and it would surely not be ridiculous to suggest that this
purpose is political.

Worthwhile criticism has to look at the writing itself. Therefore,
in *Blasted*, what is interesting is how Kane rewrites theatrical
predecessors such as Bond and Beckett – and the most fascinating
moments are precisely those in which there is a dissonance that can
be felt in the text. For example, Ian's offhand 'You have kids, they
grow up, they hate you and you die' (21) sounds more like Beckett
than Leeds in a text whose main register is the naturalism of 'Sarky
little tart this morning, aren't we?' (26). A bit more successful is
Kane's rewriting of Hamm's line about God in *Endgame* – 'The
bastard! He doesn't exist!' (Beckett, 1986: 119) – which comes
out as: '**Cate**: God– **Ian**: The cunt' (57). And while the psychology
of the relationships always feels right, and the characters have
been fully imagined, there remain some dissonant notes: in the
naturalistic first half, would a character as shy as Cate talk about
masturbating? (22–3). Like many great playwrights, Kane was
also rewriting Shakespeare, especially *King Lear*.[2] However, if at
the core of her rewriting of theatre history is politics, what are
Blasted's politics?

'They buggered her. Cut her throat'

Most commentators on Kane's work, perhaps paralysed by the
full-frontal assault on the emotions that *Blasted* embodies, have
accepted without question the central premise of the play. For
example, the playwright David Greig, in his lucid introduction
to Kane's *Complete Plays*, defends *Blasted* against the newspaper
critics by saying: 'Her simple premise, that there was a connection
between a rape in a Leeds hotel room and the hellish devastation of
civil war, had been critically misunderstood as a childish attempt
to shock' (Greig, 2001: x). However, he never questions that simple
premise. Moreover, doesn't the equation of a domestic rape with
the use of rape as an instrument of war suggest a moral absolutism
that is quite useless for our understanding of either crime? To say
that a domestic rape is potentially a war crime does not seem to be
the most sensitive way of tackling a personal tragedy – to say that a
war crime, the premeditated use of rape as an instrument of war, is
just an extension of a domestic rape is also a questionable approach

to the issues involved. In *Blasted*, Kane was blinded by her own psychology, by her desire to be morally absolute, to impose her point of view rather than arguing it, and paradoxically this is both the central strength of the play and its central weakness. Kane sums up her play's argument by saying that the logical conclusion of the attitude that produces an isolated rape in England is the anti-Muslim rape camps in Bosnia, and the logical conclusion to the way society expects men to behave is war. In Ian's case, you can recognise the truth of Kane's portrait of male psychology without accepting all her conclusions. It is much easier to agree with her conclusions emotionally than to accept their intellectual implications. After all, not all men are rapists. Nor are they all self-destructive. Not everyone acts out their needs and desires in the manipulative way that Ian does.

The more you think about *Blasted*'s ideas, the more unsatis-factory they are. If you consider the connection between maleness and violence, Kane asserts a connection, then implicitly generalises it, but never offers a dramatised proof of the assertion. You could conclude that the play argues not only that all men are animals but also that, while men abuse vulnerable women, they treat other men with even greater violence. If masculinity is in crisis, then the effects of this are shown as an uncontrollable explosion of abuse. When I asked Kane whether *Blasted* was about the crisis of masculinity, she replied: 'Draw your own conclusions and I'll draw mine' (Kane, 1998b), thus rejecting any narrow or exclusive interpretation. Nevertheless, it must be said that her claim to universality, her desire to be open to many meanings, may in the last instance generalise the play's politics to a point where they become diluted.

Therefore, the paradox of *Blasted* is this: it feels experien-tially like a profound political statement, and emotionally makes links between private abuse and public war crimes, but its moral absolutism and ferocity of feeling are also a way of avoiding political discussion. Conclusions are imposed on the audience, feelings jump across the footlights, but the rational explication so characteristic of 1970s state-of-the-nation political drama is confined to a few brief exchanges about the existence of God (55–7).

Conclusion

It is clear that, although *Blasted* was conceived as sexual politics, it soon became a much more ambitious work. Soon after Kane saw those television pictures of anti-Muslim atrocities, it became a play which argues that the seeds of war lie in men's psychology, and that unthinking racial prejudice creates the conditions for civil war. Looking at the changes that Kane made from early drafts of the play, it is obvious that her removal of local references, whether to Gordon's gin or to Vladek the Serb, was motivated by a desire to make a more universal statement. At the same time, she added more layers of Beckettian imagery. The result of this is a powerful and unresolved tension in the play between a specific political response to the Bosnian war and a general statement about the human capacity to survive atrocity and to endure the unendurable. This tension, perhaps, is one reason that *Blasted* has such a powerful stage presence.

When pressed, Kane usually fell back on the most general interpretation:

> For me, the play was about a crisis of living. How do we continue to live when life becomes so painful, so unbearable? *Blasted* really is a hopeful play because the characters do continue to scrape a life out of the ruins. There's a famous photograph of a woman in Bosnia hanging by her neck from a tree. That's lack of hope. That's shocking. My play is only a shadowy representation of a reality that's far harder to stomach. (Kane, 1999)

As this quotation shows, Kane was haunted from the start by images of anti-Muslim atrocities. So if it is true that *Blasted* can now be appreciated as a passionate political statement, this became clear only after the brouhaha of the first production had died down. Despite the play being described in early reviews as 'no more than an artful chamber of horrors designed to shock and nothing more' (Curtis, 1995), Saunders is correct to say that 'in retrospect it has been seen as an important piece of political drama' (Saunders 2002b: 124). Even the late Vera Gottlieb, not noted for her sympathy for young writers, acknowledged that 'Kane is drawing a serious parallel between Britain and Bosnia' (Gottlieb, 1999: 211). The nagging question remains: how far has Kane's rewriting of her original 'Bosnian play' diluted its politics?

Kane's politics are the politics of moral absolutism. Although she rejected the idea of being a moralist, it is clear that she believed in an absolute idea of morality – it is the essence of her sensibility. She believed in right and wrong as black and white facts, and had no time for shades of grey or compromises. In the main, academics have also discerned a moral aspect to her work. Elizabeth Sakellaridou, for example, has suggestively outlined

Kane's 'non-realistic [and] elusive strategies of moral implication' (Sakellaridou, 1999: 47), while Ken Urban has eloquently described her 'ethics of catastrophe' (Urban, 2001: 37) and more recently situated her in a wider 'ethics of nihilism' (Urban, 2004: 369). These are crucial elements in understanding her sensibility.

Although the play was inspired by a specific event, the Bosnian war, Kane systematically took out these references and replaced them with more general ones: she wanted to universalise the play and generalise its politics. In the process, what was gained is balanced by what is lost: the play becomes an example of cultural memory loss, in which an Other that is repressed or silenced in art (although always implicitly present) returns in the real world to break the silence of their forgetting. At first, as Ian says about Bosnia, 'This isn't a story anyone wants to hear' (48); now *Blasted* itself might be an example of all the repressed stories we need to keep retelling.

Finally, David Greig has argued both that political theatre must show the possibility of change, and that theatre should be an act of 'resistance' to 'the management of the imagination by power' (D'Monte and Saunders, 2008: 212; 214). Clearly, *Blasted's* innovative form qualifies it as a work that does just that. Moreover, Cate's transformation from a naive young woman easily incapacitated by stammering into a symbol of survival amid disaster is a small glimpse of the possibility of change, but, as a vision of human fortitude in the middle of a civil war, it is unforgettable. It may not be theatre's job to provide simple political solutions to complex social problems, but it is part of drama's remit to come up with haunting images that have a multitude of meanings. Shadowed as it is by the invisible Muslim Other, this is exactly what *Blasted* does.

This chapter is an expanded version of a paper given at the 'Civil War(s) in Contemporary Performance Arts' conference at Rennes University 2, Rennes, France, 23–24 May 2002.

Notes

1 For Kane's own account of the Bosnian conflict influencing the writing of *Blasted* see Saunders, 2002a: 38–9.
2 For a discussion of the relationship between *King Lear* and *Blasted* see Saunders, 2002a: 58–63; Saunders, 2004: 69–78.

4

Staging power: the politics of sex and death in Seneca's *Phaedra* and Kane's *Phaedra's Love*

Zina Giannopoulou

In the space of four years from January 1995 to February 1999, Sarah Kane managed to write five highly controversial plays before committing suicide at the age of 28. For her second play, *Phaedra's Love*, Kane turned, quite paradoxically, to classical theatre, despite her own earlier hostile admission, 'I've always hated those plays – everything happens offstage' (Sierz, 2001a: 109). Preferring Seneca's *Phaedra* to Euripides' *Hippolytus*, Kane produced (and directed) a 'public' play which was generally viewed by critics as 'viscerally powerful but intellectually pointless', and its author 'in need of a psychiatrist' (Sierz, 2001a: 108). While these, and other similarly dismissive, reviews comment on Kane's fascination with extreme situations, a better understanding of Kane's dark vision is possible, if we come to appreciate the extent of her debt to Seneca's dramatic ideology.

Kane's predilection for the Senecan over the original Euripidean story of the hopeless love of a queen for her royal stepson should not come as a surprise, given that both playwrights share the same fundamental assumptions about human nature. A. J. Boyle, for example, describes the dramatic universe of Seneca, and, I would add, of Kane, as 'one in which to be human is to suffer, to be alive is to be entrapped in evil, to exist to be located in the middle of a universe conspicuous for its apparent perversity' (Seneca, 1987: 37). Deep associations between Seneca's dramatic preoccupations and some of the central concerns of contemporary literary discourse have already been established: rhetoric, theatricality and power; the contingent authority of canons and norms; and the recasting of history in radical, even apocalyptic form.[1] However, the appropriateness of Seneca's tragic motifs, his politically charged use of sexual violence and death as a way of

coming to an understanding of contemporary issues, has often
escaped notice.

Whilst the political situation of Kane's world is by no means
identical to Seneca's, one can find in her play subtle allusions to the
declining moral standards of the British royal family. As Stefani
Brusberg-Kiermeier observes:

> Kane implies that a royal stepmother falling in love with the princely
> stepson is a plot construction that suggests itself when the royal
> family of your own nation can boast of a prospective king with
> a beloved mistress, a prospective queen who enjoys sex with her
> equerry in the royal stables and a princess who has her toes licked
> by a lover in a fashionable seaside resort. (Brusberg-Kiermeier,
> 2001: 168)

Similarly, Graham Saunders establishes useful connections
between the play's depiction of the mob's hostile reaction to the
monarchy immediately after Phaedra's suicide and the elevation of
Princess Diana to iconic status after her death (Saunders, 2002a:
75). These interpretations gain support from Kane's own admission
that the first thing that struck her about Seneca's *Phaedra* was the
fact that 'it's a play about a sexually corrupt Royal Family – which
makes it highly contemporary' (Stephenson and Langridge, 1997:
131–2). However, Kane's bold theatrical depiction of the royal
family's corruption is not the sole ideological link with Seneca's
socio-political context. The ruthlessly honest portrayal of a spoiled
prince, given over to the joyless consumption of material goods and
to an appreciation of the world as depicted on television, echoes
the morally and politically complacent Rome of Seneca's time.

The destabilising forces of sex and death can be the playwright's
most potent means of attacking the political establishment. In
what follows I shall examine the political dimensions of sexual
desire and death, and the specific ways in which Seneca and Kane
deploy them as tools for envisioning a viable political alternative.
On the one hand, I shall argue that sexual desire shatters a
sense of personal imprisonment resulting from allegiance to
prescribed societal roles, and enables the individual to experience
freedom in the context of a new, imaginary and asocial, realm. In
addition, it empowers the powerless 'other' to wreak havoc on an
existing political configuration, only after they have become an
instrument of enlightenment and salvation. On the other hand,
the theatricalised representation of death reasserts equality as the
inalienable condition of human life, one that challenges the hierarchical structure of power advocated by monarchies. Seneca and

Kane, I shall contend, seem to support a 'horizontal' view of social existence, in which human isolation is replaced by interpersonal communication and man's thoughtless criminality is superseded by kindness grounded in a genuine interest in the affairs of others. This kind of social attitude, in turn, underscores the importance of personal accountability for one's own actions.

The irresistible force of unnatural sexual passion is perhaps the focal point of both versions of the story and the catalyst for the unfolding of the dramatic action. While Seneca's *Phaedra* foregrounds the disastrous outcome of the dramatic interplay between such fundamentally irreconcilable polarities as male chastity (Hippolytus) and female sexual lust (Phaedra), Kane makes sexuality the common denominator of the life of all her characters. In the Roman play, love is portrayed as an irrational force, which, while it frees the individual from the conventions of public life, revives them in a new, imaginary context created by the rhetoric of love. Phaedra experiences lust as a debilitating ailment that aches and burns like fire. Perhaps the most eloquent description of its uncontrollable force appears a few lines before she reveals her feelings to Hippolytus, in this impassioned self-exposition: 'Smouldering love scorches / My frantic heart. A savage fire devours / Me deep inside; it courses through my veins, / Lodged within the body, hidden in the blood, / Like vibrant flame darting through vaulted beams' (640–4).[2] Assaulted by the emotional intensity of her passion, Phaedra appears restless, refuses to eat or drink, experiences frequent fainting attacks, and spends many sleepless nights soaked with tears (360–83). She neglects her socially prescribed female duties (103–9) and indulges in imaginative reenactments of wild hunts, in a desperate emulation of the actions of Hippolytus or his mother (110–11; 395–403).[3] Just as Phaedra's passion causes her to behave in conventionally unacceptable ways, so Hippolytus' sexual repression plunges him into a lifestyle similarly incongruent with his political role. Instead of being interested in the affairs of the city, he prefers hunting in the woods, where he enjoys an idyllic life of moral purity and uplifting solitude (483–564). The natural environment inevitably affects his personality: his 'unbending heart' (413), his fierceness and ferociousness (416) resemble either inanimate objects ('some hard and impenetrable rock', 580) or the behaviour of men from a lower social status ('some harsh woodsman ignorant of life', 461). Both Phaedra's sexual passion and Hippolytus' chastity manifest themselves in a contrived, asocial environment in which the physical, intellectual and emotional absence of the desired or feared 'other' sanctions the moral choices of the two solitary agents.

An opportunity to remedy Hippolytus' lack of political or social awareness is dramatically furnished by Phaedra's frequent self-descriptions as his slave (611–12; 617; 622), which create the illusion of a political context in which Hippolytus is the all-powerful 'king' and Phaedra his slave. Although these expressions may legitimately be viewed as yet another example of the well-known literary *topos* of obsessive love *qua* form of enslavement (Segal, 1986: 158), the overt political connotations of Phaedra's references to her situation lend Seneca's play additional complexity. Both as a woman, whom it befits to obey (618), and as a defenceless suppliant, Phaedra acknowledges her helplessness and seeks protection (613–22). Love transforms her into a being bereft of personal autonomy, an object in the hands of Hippolytus, whose control over her life is deemed absolute (712). Phaedra's irrationality deprives her of the temporary political authority granted her by Theseus' absence and reinforces the conventional, hierarchical stratification of power that makes women subservient to men.

In Kane's version of the play, the sexual act is given unprecedented prominence and, consequently, the politics of sex acquires added significance. Unlike his chaste Senecan antecedent, Kane's Hippolytus is a promiscuous young man who engages indiscriminately in masturbatory, heterosexual and homosexual activities. All these actions leave him emotionally unengaged: he participates in them simply to '[to fill] up time' (79). His inner, emotional passivity is matched by his outer, physical immobility: his environment is the claustrophobic, darkened television-room, which he has not left for 'months' (76). He uses his sexual partners in the same manner that he uses the filthy socks scattered around his room, as a convenient tool for the expeditious completion of a mechanical act whose only value lies in its level of proficiency, its 'technique' (84). His indifference to others' individuality is indeed astonishing: he either looks away from them as they perform fellatio on him (Phaedra) or avows ignorance as to the gender of those with whom he has casual intercourse (76) or even admits that his own facial expression upon reaching orgasm is like that of 'every other stupid fucker' (82).[4] All that matters is the performance of sex, which, for Hippolytus, involves solely the expenditure of minimal physical energy. Most often sex is depicted as a gift whose ungrateful and almost hostile recipient, namely Hippolytus, takes it for granted (74). His sexual behavior captures a key component of the political behaviour of royalty, its preoccupation with the satisfaction of their own interests, which may result in indifference to the individual needs of those with whom they come into contact. Emotional aloofness inevitably attends this sort of attitude toward both sex and politics. Kane's play emphasises this by having a brutal and unemotional Theseus rape Strophe in the midst of a jeering crowd of equally unaffected onlookers.

On the female side of the spectrum, sex is viewed as an offering, an act of self-sacrifice, and becomes the instrument of the beloved's salvation. Like Seneca's Phaedra, Kane's is also consumed by desire, in which she neglects her parental and political duties. Unlike her Roman antecedent, however, Kane's Phaedra feels an emotional affinity with Hippolytus, a sort of deeper understanding that both fuels and transcends her sexual desire (71; 79; 80). For her, sex is the best form of self-expression, as it conveys the full force of her emotion, and the most effective means of curing Hippolytus from his paralysing self-loathing. However, in *Phaedra's Love* it is a selfless (and, ultimately, thankless) gift which, just like the gifts Hippolytus receives from his subjects on his birthday, is meant to be a token of appreciation and love. By treating her gift as coldly and disinterestedly as he treats the presents of his citizens, Hippolytus deprives Phaedra's gesture of its emotional and moral importance, and sees her as interchangeable with the anonymous populace of his kingdom.

When viewed from the perspective of Hippolytus' cruel reception of her love offering, Phaedra's accusation of rape becomes less capricious and certainly more intelligible than its depiction in Seneca's play, because it transmutes into sexual language her condemnation of Hippolytus' disregard for the ethical principles underlying her voluntary sexual encounter with him. As Kane has commented, 'what Hippolytus does to Phaedra is not rape – but the English language doesn't contain the words to describe the emotional decimation he inflicts. "Rape" is the best word Phaedra can find for it … so that's the word she uses' (Stephenson and Langridge, 1997: 132). It is not coincidental, I think, that the false accusation functions as the catalyst for the manifestation of the moral bankruptcy already present in the royal family's world, if until now effectively concealed from public view. Phaedra's talk of rape, for example, eliminates the comfortable distance that Hippolytus has created between the reality of rape and the televised sexual scenes he watches (74), thereby shattering the fantasies of his solitary existence and thrusting upon him the ugliness of public life. It also contradicts his view of sex as a convenient pastime, undertaken in the hope of 'something to happen' (79): while his sexual contact with Phaedra is for him as unengaging and dull as any other, its moral implications endow it with the kind of 'excitement' he has always wished for (86). Life, Phaedra suggests, happens as we are waiting for it to happen; its value lies not in passive acceptance but in the wisdom attained through reflection on, and emotional involvement with, personal experience.

Whereas in Phaedra's case rape is used figuratively, Strophe is actually raped by her mother's new husband, Theseus. It is important to note that Kane establishes the same, exclusive biological bond between her female characters as she does between her male ones: Strophe is Phaedra's daughter but not Theseus', and Hippolytus is Theseus' son but not Phaedra's. The dramatic implications of this apparently coincidental pairing become evident when we consider the political ramifications of sexual violence. According to Saunders, 'both mother and daughter are depicted as outsiders to the royal household, and in a cynical move are brought in by the old order in an attempt to refresh and restore its mystique' (Saunders, 2002a: 75). These 'outsiders' are portrayed as the innocent recipients of punishment issued by the patriarchal political establishment. For the unjust suffering of her female characters at the hands of the ruling authorities at once pinpoints the spiritual emptiness of those in power and, as Kane has commented, 'set[s] off the most extraordinary chain of events leading to the collapse of the monarchy' (Stephenson and Langridge, 1997: 134). Thus, the seemingly weak and powerless become the dramatic instrument of political subversion and the beacon of hope in an otherwise corrupt social environment.

Death is the climactic event in both theatrical versions of the story. In Seneca's *Phaedra*, the heroine's suicide precipitates the revelation of the truth about Hippolytus' nature and actions, while in Kane's *Phaedra's Love* death seals the dramatic fate of all the characters, rendering the stage an empty and desolate space. Both playwrights use death as a powerful tool for criticising the slavish conventions of a hierarchically structured royal power that locks individuals into prescribed social roles. Death makes possible the abandonment of these roles and the experience, albeit temporarily, of complete freedom.

One aspect of the political subversiveness of death emerges from the fact that it not only negates a character's particular kind of life but actually inverts it. By the end of the play, all main characters in Seneca's *Phaedra* are either afflicted by, or willfully invite upon themselves, ruinous actions that are antithetical to those taken while they lived. Hippolytus, who in the prologue emerges as the quintessentially aggressive hunter of animals, is now mercilessly pursued and killed by a strange creature appearing from the sea. Phaedra wastes her life hunted down by an irrepressible passion only to permit herself before her suicide the sweet indulgence of acting out in fantasy a truly Amazonian hunt (1179–80). Even Theseus is transformed at the end from a sacrilegious pursuer of Hades' bride and the barbarians of the far North (906–14) to an ardent suppliant of death. Furthermore, in his last macabre act of attempting to reconstruct in vain his son's body from dispersed limbs, Theseus emerges as a mere caricature of the omnipotent individual depicted earlier in the play.[5]

Similarly, in *Phaedra's Love*, the characters' *modus moriendi* constitutes an ironic reversal of the manner in which they lived. Hippolytus, a pursuer of an utterly solitary existence, dies a most public death at the hands of the mob and his father, whereas the royal couple, two figures of prominent publicity, choose the lonely death of suicide: Phaedra's final act is performed offstage, possibly in the privacy of her bedroom, while Theseus' suicide occurs on a deserted stage, in front of Strophe's corpse and the body of a moribund Hippolytus. Death effectively blurs the fixed boundaries between the real and the imaginary, or the private and the public domain, thereby affording the dying characters a glimpse of a mode of existence alien to them.[6]

In a dramatic world of almost solipsistic isolation, death becomes a powerful means of interpersonal connection: the violent eruption of death generates in those who witness it a heightened emotional sensibility toward – and a healthy awareness of – another's existence, and foregrounds the need to assume personal responsibility for one's actions. Prior to Hippolytus' tragic death, Seneca's Phaedra is locked in an emotionally stifling world, defined exclusively by *furor* (madness) and *pudor* (shame): her illicit desire for her stepson causes her constantly to think of, and pity, only herself. She experiences shame, a social mechanism for maintaining moral normalcy, as the appropriate and painful reaction to her *nefas* (evil), and attempts, in vain, to silence it by rationalising its cause. However, the sight of Hippolytus' maimed body shatters her self-centredness, since it causes her to cease thinking of her psychic condition as violence done to *her* and instead to view it as the originator of evil done to *others*. Her own suicide is thus appropriately construed as a debt and atonement.[7] Likewise, Theseus' emotional apathy regarding suffering, his essentially 'spectatorial' attitude toward corporal punishment in the underworld is transformed by Hippolytus' death into a tragic awareness of his own psychological pain (1117), and results in the need to expiate the wrongdoing he has caused (1201; 1220). For the devastated Theseus, death is no longer the irreparable harm brought down on the powerless by an all too powerful force but the ultimate form of redemption, freely chosen and avidly desired.

While Seneca makes Hippolytus' death the pivotal point of the royal couple's self-awareness, Kane offers a richer perspective on the emotional ramifications of a character's violent demise, not only by increasing the number of deaths but also by embedding them in a tightly interwoven nexus of inexorable causality. The dramatic chain of events is set into motion by Phaedra's suicide, which, unlike that of her Roman counterpart, is enacted offstage and is merely announced by Strophe (89–90). The tragic simplicity of Strophe's words – in stark contrast with the highly stylised, rhetorical force of Phaedra's suicide in the Roman play – brings into sharp relief Hippolytus' unexpectedly affective response, itself the first sign of the awakening of his hitherto dormant emotional being: his hold of Strophe's arms 'turns into an embrace', only to be immediately followed by a thrice repeated acceptance of his responsibility: 'Then blame me ... Yes. Blame me ... Me. Blame me' (89–90). A little later, once Hippolytus has contemplated the meaning and the dire consequences of Phaedra's action, he realises that her death is irrefutable proof not only of his own culpability but also of her love for him. Her suicide thus becomes a symbolic gesture, a sacrificial act that obliterates her physicality in order to make possible the emergence of the spiritual truth of love.

Both Phaedra's suicide and its inevitable consequence, Hippolytus' death, affect decisively the remaining members of the royal family. They transform Strophe, a formerly detached, rational observer into an active participant in the gruesome disintegration of her family. During the third act, and before the catastrophic chain of events begins to unfold, Strophe, like Seneca's Nurse, functions as the principle of reality to the delusions of her mother. She elucidates the true nature of her feelings (69), reminds Phaedra of the conventional morality which ought to inform her emotions and actions (71; 73) and offers an objective assessment of Hippolytus' quite unattractive character (70–2). Phaedra's suicide, however, ruins this relatively passive objectivity and launches her into a series of profoundly emotional reactions: she tearfully laments the sudden loss of her mother and declares her indirect responsibility for it (89). As an indisputable indication of her loyalty to the family, she is even willing to share Hippolytus' punishment, should her mother's incriminations prove false (88). And, indeed, Strophe defends her stepbrother publicly, as he is mercilessly tortured, an action which provokes her own rape and subsequent death at the hands of her stepfather.

Finally, Theseus' regret at the senseless killing of his stepdaughter puts an abrupt end to his murderous rampage and causes him to commit suicide. While Seneca's play foregrounds the king's fruitless sense of injustice by having him eternally mourn the loss of an innocent son, Kane deprives Theseus of the knowledge of Hippolytus' guiltlessness; his dead son remains for him as hateful as he was while alive (102). This innovation has interesting ramifications: in the Roman play, although the strong spiritual bond between father and son underwriting the patriarchal order of things is temporarily disrupted by female deception, it is finally reclaimed and emphatically reaffirmed. Theseus' cruel, laconic address to Phaedra's corpse (1199–1200: 'A father's duty to a ravaged son / Let his stepmother teach: tomb yourself in hell' and: 'This one – earth press deep upon her, / And soil lie heavy on her impious head' 1279–80) contrasts sharply with the long and heart-rending invocation of Hippolytus (1247–74).[8] Kane, on the other hand, delineates a hostile father–son relationship, which Phaedra's suicide fails to rectify, because her incriminatory accusation toward her stepson is never retracted. Even as Hippolytus lies semi-conscious, Theseus cruelly proclaims his dislike toward him. His own suicide immediately follows an open admission to having accidentally killed his stepdaughter (102), and this emotional allegiance toward Strophe, an innocent outsider and – as Hippolytus himself acknowledges – 'the one person in this family who has no claim to its history' (88), conveys a subversive political message: regret and an overwhelming sense of personal account-ability can emerge only from the suffering of those uncorrupted by the emotional and moral excesses of royal power.

The notion of human interrelatedness, and its natural concomitant of responsibility toward others, is further enhanced by the fact that for Seneca and Kane death is the ultimate means of reconciliation and unification. Both playwrights foreground the essential commonality of human beings, by associating one character's death with emotional forces deriving from the tortured soul of another. In *Phaedra*, Hippolytus' gruesome demise is brought about by a phantasmagoric creature of extraordinary strength, tossed up by the swelling waves, an animal twice called a 'bull' (1036 and 1067).[9] This maritime bull, I suggest, represents the frustrated murdering force of Phaedra's passion and Theseus' heroic power. In attempting to justify her inexplicable passion for her stepson, Phaedra often imprecates her mother's desire for the Cretan bull, whose unnatural union led to the birth of the Minotaur.[10] As a visual reminder of Pasiphae's monstrous desire, the sea-bull becomes a potent symbol of Phaedra's destructive passion, its force now redoubled by dint of its association with the mother's deadly lust. The maritime *taurus* is also linked with Theseus, both via his divine father's, Poseidon's, ruling of the sea and as a reminder of Theseus' most heroic exploit, the death of the Minotaur. By killing the son of the Minotaur's murderer, the bull exacts punishment for the death of its own son, uniting in the process past and present, the guilty and the innocent.

Death establishes a similarly inextricable nexus of affinities among all characters in Kane's rendition of the story. Phaedra's visceral experience of erotic passion calls for the wish to 'cut open your chest tear it out to stop the pain' (69). This imagined eradication of her painful desire becomes a gruesome actuality when Hippolytus meets commensurate punishment at Theseus' hands (101). Indeed, all characters' punishments are very similar: Phaedra hangs herself, Hippolytus is *inter alia* strangled, Strophe is raped (an echo of her mother's incrimination of Hippolytus) and her throat is cut, and Theseus cuts his own throat. By devising a similar form of death for all her characters, Kane endows them with the kind of unity they staunchly opposed in their life.

Finding themselves in corrupt political environments, Seneca and Kane mounted a powerful critique against the ideological presuppositions that informed and sustained them. The political disruption thus effected is ingenious, precisely because it is predicated on nothing other than a different use of notions, such as violence, sexual perversity and murder, already inherent in the system under attack. Kane borrowed from Seneca the tragic vision of a disintegrated world, and creatively transferred it to contemporary Britain. In *Phaedra's Love*, she attacks with disarming honesty not only the sexual corruption of the royal political establishment but also the broader ideological and moral underpinnings of a social structure that supports it. The end result may hurt, but so did the depravity that gave birth to it. Kane's *Phaedra's Love* is a play as much about ugliness as about beauty: the beauty of hope for a new order of things that leaves the old one safely behind it.

Notes

1 For the rhetorical and theatrical elements of Senecan drama see Boyle, 1997; Braden, 1970; and Michel, 1969. For Seneca's use of canons and norms see Fowler, 1982; Goldberg, 2000; Maguinness, 1956; Mazzoli, 1991; and Tarrant, 1978. For the historical echoes of Senecan drama see Calder, 1976; Most, 1992; and Rudich, 1993.

2 The play's fire-imagery has been extensively studied. See, among others, Pratt, 1963: 220ff; Ruch, 1964: 358ff; and Segal, 1986: 46–50.

3 For the image of Phaedra's longing for the forest see Euripides, *Hippolytus* 221; Ovid, *Heroides* 4.73–7. See also Glenn, 1976: 439ff; Henry and Walker, 1966: 230; Knox, 1979: 199: 207ff; and Segal, 1986: 130.

4 Cf. Saunders, 2002a: 76–7: 'Instead of being the culmination of Phaedra's longing, the sexual act is wantonly deconstructed and trivialised by Hippolytus, and so becomes redundant and passionless, punctuated by the rustle of the bored prince's sweetbag and his cruel comment after ejaculating into his stepmother's mouth – "There. Mystery over".'

5 For an emphasis on the scene's physical violence see Regenbogen, 1930: 208ff. See also Giomini, 1955: 108.

6 The staging of the play, under Kane's direction, at the Gate Theatre in Notting Hill in May 1996 reflects the eventual overlapping of private and the public. See Sierz, 2001a: 108–9.

7 Segal, 1986: 195 discovers another sort of unity when he writes, 'instead of the fantasied union of bodies ... [Phaedra] finally seeks a tragic union of souls and of destinies' (1183f).

8 Theseus' last words to Phaedra have been variously interpreted. See, among others, Herrmann, 1924: 408; Herter, 1971: 77; Leeman, 1976: 209; and Skovgaard-Hansen, 1972: 123.

9 For the nature and symbolism of the bull see Davis, 1983: 114ff; Henry and Walker, 1966: 232; and Segal, 1986: *passim*. For Seneca's elaboration of Euripides' description of it see Garton, 1972: 200; Giomini, 1955: 92–7; and Liebermann, 1974: 39ff.

10 The Minotaur was the offspring of Pasiphaë, Minos' wife, and the bull that Minos injudiciously kept for himself, instead of sacrificing it to Poseidon.

5

The Beckettian world of Sarah Kane

Graham Saunders

In July 2000, to coincide with the production of Sarah Kane's posthumous play *4.48 Psychosis*, the *Guardian* newspaper ran a retrospective feature on the late playwright and her work. Amongst personal reminiscences from friends and colleagues, analysis of the plays and her reputation as a dramatist were a series of photographs. One of these, submitted by her friend Vincent O'Connell, shows a smiling teenage Sarah Kane standing in front of a large poster (which looks to have been made by hand), consisting of just two words, 'Fuck Life' (Hattenstone, 2000). This phrase – the two closing words of Samuel Beckett's *Rockaby* (1980) – on the one hand reveals enagagement at a surprisingly young age to one of Beckett's lesser known late works; yet it also vividly articulates the sense of alienation that would become a dominant and recurring theme throughout Kane's subsequent playwriting career.

Out of the many influences on her work, 'the gaunt shadow' (Billington, 1998) of Samuel Beckett, has been a constant presence. Kane herself had always been frank about the debt: 'I think my influences are quite obvious. Yes, Beckett, of course but not particularly consciously … I was steeped in Beckett so it's not surprising that *Blasted* ends with an image of a man with his head poking out of the floor with the rain pouring through the ceiling onto his head' (Sierz, 1999). This immersion in Beckett's drama is in fact all-pervasive, and extends from direct quotation and manipulation of well known phrases to reworkings of dramatic motifs and a language that echoes the spare compelling rhythms of his work.

Kane's debut *Blasted* is just such an amalgamation of themes, ideas and imagery from Beckett's two most well known plays, *Waiting for Godot* (1952) and *Endgame* (1957). Here, Kane appropriates Beckett's so called 'pseudo-couples'[1] and the mutually interdependent relationships between Vladimir, Estragon, Pozzo, Lucky, and Hamm, and Clov from *Waiting for Godot* and *Endgame*.

Walter Asmus, who assisted Beckett's direction of his celebrated 1975 German production of *Waiting for Godot*, recounts a conversation with the playwright/director on the nature of these paired relationships: 'Gogo and Didi belong one to the stone, the other to the tree. That means they are connected, and at the same time there is always the tendency to go apart. He [Beckett] used this image of a rubber band: they pull together by means of a rubber band and then apart again, and so on' (Kalb, 1989: 175).

As Fletcher and Spurling observe, Vladimir and Estragon 'have been joined in a sadomasochistic relationship for many years' (Fletcher and Spurling, 1972: 66), and a similar co-dependency is established between Ian and Cate in *Blasted*. The pair seem inextricably linked, with Ian's assertion that, 'we're one' (26). While Beckett's characters torment each other verbally, often to pass the time or provoke a response, such as Estragon's pleased exclamation: 'That's the idea, let's abuse each other' (Beckett, 1986: 70), Kane's characters are more reminiscent of the overtly masochistic relationship played out between Pozzo and Lucky, or Hamm and Clov in *Endgame*; where, despite being given the opportunity to leave, a condition of servitude is preferred.

In *Blasted*, despite being raped by Ian and escaping from the hotel room, Cate still returns on two further occasions to him, now blinded and helpless. His occupancy of the infant's grave under the floorboards recalls the buried Winnie in *Happy Days* (1961), and the three imprisoned characters from *Play* (1962–63). The striking image of Ian occupying the makeshift infant's grave also recalls and in a sense dramatises Pozzo's well known speech, 'they give birth astride of a grave' (Beckett, 1986: 82) from *Godot*. *Blasted* also ends in a frozen tableau reminiscent of Beckett's pseudo-couples attempting to leave but being unable to do so, as Cate returns once more to feed her one-time tormentor gin and sausage.

Kane's use of the pseudo-couple is a notable feature of her work up until *Crave*. In *Phaedra's Love*, the eponymous queen talks of how much Hippolytus' presence draws and overwhelms even in his absence: 'Can feel him through the walls. Sense him. Feel his heartbeat from a mile' (70–1). In her penultimate play *Crave*, where the four characters are replaced by the letters A, B, C and M, a still recognisable pairing of trapped and destructive relationships exists between the two pairs. B rejects M but is compelled to return, and C attempts unsuccessfully to escape from the influence of A, who refuses to relinquish their hold: 'don't say no to me you can't say no to me' (178). At the end of the play all four characters embrace an end which involves 'Free-falling / Into the light / Bright white light' (200).

Blasted also reworks other well known Beckettian themes such as the activity of waiting and deferral of death. Here, Ian speeds up the imminent process of his own demise from lung cancer through drinking and smoking in order 'to enjoy myself while I'm here' (13). Whereas in Waiting for Godot and Endgame music hall routines, game playing, bickering and questioning are employed to pass the time, in Blasted and Phaedra's Love sex is the principal activity that attempts to fill the void. This is made explicit through Kane's reworking of the Phaedra myth and the queen's passion for her stepson. Despite Hippolytus admitting, 'I think of having sex with everyone', he gains no pleasure from the activity and indulges in it only because 'Life's too long' (79).

Ian's and Hippolytus' enjoyment of the cruelties they inflict upon the women trapped with them is also reminiscent of the pleasure Hamm in Endgame takes in tormenting Clov. Beckett has described Hamm as 'the remains of a monster' (Fletcher et al., 1978: 22), where his blindness and physical decrepitude render his behaviour more pathetic than morally reprehensible. The same is also true of Ian and Hippolytus. Ian's terminal illness, and eventual sodomy and blinding at the hands of the soldier, and Hippolytus' crippling depression act to make their characters more deserving of pity than condemnation.

Beckett's characters are often defined by their ability to endure, seemingly consigned to never being released from death. Richard Coe comments that, 'for Beckett's people, the boundary between life and afterlife becomes progressively vaguer' (Coe, 1968: 60), where May in Footfalls (1975) or the protagonists from Play exist in liminal, indeterminate states. Again, here Kane is at her most Beckettian in Blasted where Ian after being blinded by the Soldier, is left alone in the bombed-out hotel room, and whole seasons pass. Eventually he crawls into the infant's grave where he 'dies with relief' (60). However, Ian's release into the afterlife is granted only for a short period, and he is brought back from the dead to continue life inside the shattered hotel room. As in Waiting for Godot and Endgame the final scene avoids closure, and seems to suggest an infinite period of time stretching out for the couple. Ian's fear of 'not being' (10), earlier in the play, returns to haunt him, and despite physically dying he is brought back to life to endure indefinitely. As David Greig observes in his introduction to Kane's Complete Plays, the final images of Ian and Cate sheltering inside the wreckage of the hotel 'are not unlike those moments in Beckett where the human impulse to connect is found surviving in the most bleak and crushing places' (Greig, 2001, x).

While this idea of a deferred state is returned to at the end of *Cleansed*, in which the mutilated figure of Grace is finally left to her fantasy world – 'safe on the other side' (150) – Kane differs from Beckett, in that predominantly she wishes to release her characters from suffering through the escape provided by death. Hippolytus in *Phaedra's Love* for instance willingly lets himself be ripped to pieces by the rioting mob outside the palace, ending the play with his dying words, 'if there could have been more moments like this' (103); the four characters in *Crave* collectively embrace their own destruction – while in *4.48 Psychosis* we learn that one of the speakers is 'charging towards my death' (207).

Whereas in Beckett individuals such as Victor Krapp in *Eleutheria* (1947) and the tramps in *Waiting for Godot* muse upon the subject, Kane's plays are notable in that on every occasion individuals either attempt to take, or finally succeed in taking, their own lives. By the time of *Crave* this has become an irresistible impulse for all the characters, as it is in *4.48 Psychosis* with the speaker(s) calling on the audience to 'watch me vanish' (244). This is an important distinction to make between Kane's work and Beckett's, and calls to mind a question raised by the Irish critic Vivian Mercier 'why so few of Beckett's characters carry their distaste for life to its logical conclusion in self-destruction' (Mercier, 1977: 238).

Part of the reason for this distinction might come from the two dramatists' different responses to Cartesian models of selfhood. Whereas Beckett's characters, such as Mouth in *Not I* (1972), seem to exist, albeit in a state of suffering, between indeterminate states, Kane has commented that the only point of unity and reconciliation is the moment when the subject takes their own life:

> With Hippolytus [in *Phaedra's Love*] ... in his moment of death everything suddenly connects. He has one moment of complete sanity and humanity. But in order to get there he has to die. Actually that's a bit like the Soldier in *Blasted*. There, the only way he can ever learn what his girlfriend had to go through is when he's pulling the trigger. But of course the next moment is the moment of his death. (Tabert, 1998: 2)

In her last play, *4.48 Psychosis*, one of the speakers asserts: 'Body and soul can never be married' (212), which for Kane is 'what madness is about' (Tabert, 1998: 2). One of the speakers however finds they gain a nightly moment of clarity when mind and body become one, but again the implication seems to be from some of the last lines of the play – 'watch me vanish' (244) – that the solution to this alienation between mind and body is suicide.

This growing preoccupation with nihilism in Kane's work perhaps also explains the considerable stylistic changes that take place in the five plays written between 1995 and 1999, which rapidly assimilate the far slower dramatic development that Beckett's work took from the 1950s until his death in 1989. Essentially this concerns the increasing tendency for the plays to withdraw into themselves: setting is made nebulous and character itself becomes reduced to 'men and women talking to themselves' (Fletcher and Spurling, 1972: 37).

For Beckett, this move towards a formal reductivity in his work seems to have been part of a long-foreseen project. As far back as 1931 in an essay on Proust Beckett remarked that 'the only fertile research is excavatory, immersive, a contraction of the spirit, a descent' (Beckett, 1965: 65). Because of the shortness of Kane's career, this trajectory seems to progress far more rapidly and intensely, and is marked by the change of style in *Crave* and *4.48 Psychosis*. Speaking in regard to Beckett's drama in 1968, Ronald Hayman took issue with this process of sparse reduction being worthy of praise, or those critics who saw the technique as a new way of presenting 'universal' insights on human nature contemporaneous to Shakespeare (Hayman, 1970: 80). The erosion of formal character that Hayman finds so problematic in Beckett's later work is also shared by the dramatist Phyllis Nagy in regard to Kane's last three plays: 'Beginning with *Cleansed* she became the subject of her work – often in a very liberating and surprising manner, and sometimes in a very dangerous manner' (Saunders, 2002a: 156). This aspect of the writer becoming sole subject and addressee is also seen by Fletcher and Spurling in Beckett's later drama as 'neither humane nor friendly, for the simple reason that it is addressed to himself' (Fletcher and Spurling, 1972: 37).

Beckett's lack of interest in his own plays by the time they came to be performed is well documented, and, while Nagy admires the formal construction and power of Kane's final two plays, she questions their authenticity as works for actual performance and their seeming refusal to formally acknowledge the presence of an audience:

> There is only one character in both of those plays [*Crave* and *4.48 Psychosis*], despite the number of voices present. Narrative hasn't been abandoned. There is a narrative both in *Crave* and in *4.48*

Psychosis, but there is not really what I would call 'character'. When you abandon character you abandon drama, so for me she has effectively abandoned drama … Something else I think we must remember is that Sarah did not call these works of 'performance art'. They are plays, and she wrote them as such … there is a diminishment of dramatically viable image structure in both of the last two plays, which renders them, for me, viable works of experimental literature rather than viable works of drama. (Saunders, 2002a: 159–60)

Peter Morris believes that *Crave* 'is just Sarah Kane doing herself in different voices' (Morris, 2000: 150); while Kane's agent Mel Kenyon believes that 'throughout her career, the effort was not to write monologues' – and that *Blasted*, *Phaedra's Love* and *Cleansed* were in fact constructed from a spirit of writing against dramatic instinct. Kenyon believes that while the plays' 'incredible restraint is part of their beauty', eventually the effort proved too much but: 'as a writer she thought "fuck it! I'm not going to write a play in the way they think I'm going to write a play." However, what I should have noticed is that now she was refusing to deal with the outside world' (Stephens, 2001). Enoch Brater, writing in relation to Beckett's drama, calls this 'genre under stress', whereby 'the theatre event is reduced to a piece of monologue and the play is reduced to something else, something that looks suspiciously like a performance poem' (Brater, 1987: 3). Fletcher and Spurling also identify much the same trait in Beckett's work: 'The truth is that [the plays are] intended in the first place to satisfy himself, as sole audience' (Fletcher and Spurling, 1972: 37).

Kane's first three pieces of dramatic writing before *Blasted* had all been in the form of monologues, and in an interview with Aleks Sierz she explained, 'I needed to find out if I could write a full length play with more than one person in it.' The monologue privileges the individual with its mode of the confessional, and, while it does not necessarily reject the audience out of hand, neither does it overtly choose to include them. Asked in the interview with Sierz if she considered her audience while writing, Kane was unequivocal: 'I suppose what I'm thinking about when I'm writing is how I want a particular moment or idea to effect me, and what the best way of eliciting that response from myself is. And if it can make me respond in that way, then the chances are that there will be at least one other person who will respond in the same way' (Sierz, 1999).

Yet, Kane's work never fully becomes a private discourse with itself in the same way that plays such as *Eh Joe* (1966) and *Rockaby* (1980) do. In the 2001 revival of *Blasted*, Benedict Nightingale took issue with those critics who picked up on the Beckettian echoes in *Blasted*, and pointed out the essential difference between the two writers: 'Beckett's vision was metaphysical, Kane's moral, social, political and very much of our times' (Nightingale, 2001). Even *4.48 Psychosis* has scenes in which there is recognisably more than one speaker; and, while it will always be vulnerable to the obvious interpretation of essentially being a dramatic suicide note, the play also concerns itself with the treatment of the mentally ill individual in British society.[2]

Fellow playwright (and another significant influence on Kane's work) Edward Bond, despite misgivings that the territory of 'existentially spaceless' writers such as Beckett was 'also a place where Sarah Kane began to wander', also argues that *4.48 Psychosis* creates a world for itself, and is not just a retreat into the writers psyche: 'You cannot talk of any play – as "private" – because it always involves a world … For the play to have value we have to know what the play has to do with our world and the way we live in it … She [Kane] forces us in a sense to live with our own annihilation – by having to live with hers. The sacrificed victim always returns to haunt the sacrificers' (Bond, 2002).

However, Beckett's trademark process in language of 'reduction, intensification and simplification' (Lyons, 1982: 3) increasingly became an integral element of Kane's drama from *Phaedra's Love* onwards. This manifested itself in both language and staging. With *Cleansed*, for instance, Kane was looking for a purity of language approaching that of Büchner's *Woyzeck* (1837), which she had directed in a production at The Gate Theatre in October 1997. She describes it as 'an absolute perfect gem of a play to look at for this. Anything remotely extraneous or explanatory is completely cut and all you get is those moments of high drama' (Rebellato, 1998). Taking this as the model for *Cleansed* Kane set out, 'to strip everything down; I wanted it to be small, and when I say small I mean minimal; poetic, and I didn't want to waste any words. I really hate wasted words' (Rebellato, 1998). Kane reworked the practice in a different manner for her next play: '*Crave* is at the other end of the scale, it's got more words than any of my other plays, but it's actually half the length of anything else I've written. Again, there's no waste, I don't like writing things you really don't need, and my favourite exercise is cutting – cut, cut, cut!' (Rebellato, 1998).

This process also slowly manifested itself gradually in the ongoing staging of the plays. Despite setting *Blasted*, *Phaedra's Love* and *Cleansed* in claustrophobic rooms, reminiscent of *Endgame* and *Krapp's Last Tape*, Kane's theatre was extravagant in its conception of look and dramatic incident. While Ronald Hayman observes that, in Beckett, 'scenically, a single tree is the greatest extravagance he has ever allowed himself' (Hayman, 1970: 39); in Kane's theatre, amongst other things, we see the stage set in *Blasted* torn apart from a mortar bomb (39); a vulture circling overhead in *Pheadra's Love* (103) and a host of daffodils bursting through the stage in *Cleansed* (113).

Yet, by the time of *Crave* stage directions had been abandoned entirely. While the designer Georgia Sion and the director Vicky Featherstone in the first British production gave the voices of the actors a context by setting the play within the genre of a televison chat show, one could see this decision to be essentially an arbitrary one: especially in the knowledge that one of Kane's early staging ideas was to set *Crave* completely in the dark, so that the actors' voices would appear to come out of a void (Saunders, 2002a: 137). While *Crave* in some respects imitates Beckett's practice of replacing names with letters in plays such as *Cascando* (1962) and *Play* (1962), Kane's next play, *4.48 Psychosis*, had dispensed with any form of nomenclature entirely; to the extent that from the written text alone it would be difficult to ascertain even the number or gender of speakers. James MacDonald, director of its British premiere, saw the last two plays as part of a dramatic process: 'with *Crave* she made another jump forward into an abstraction of character, and with *4.48 Psychosis* she realised she could go further – beyond Beckett even' (Saunders, 2002a: 121).

Both *Crave* and *4.48 Psychosis* also resemble Beckett's later drama in their attempts to articulate 'the image of a mind, alienated from its body' (Lyons, 1982: 4). This abstraction is accompanied by an intense scrutiny of the physical presence of the actor on stage by both dramatists in their later work. In part, this is shown by their shared practice of mutilating and confining their protagonists on stage. Katherine Worth believes that in the case of Beckett the practice allows both playwright and audience 'to concentrate on the fine shades of their inner life' (Worth, 1986: 245). Like Pozzo in *Waiting for Godot*, Ian in *Blasted* is rendered blind – while in *Cleansed* Carl is ritually mutilated by Tinker to the point where his tongue, hands and feet are removed. And while Beckett in *Not I* (1972) famously reduces the actor to a disembodied mouth, Kane goes even further in reducing and refining physical presence – at least textually – to speaking voices rather than bodies on stage. Of course, the opposite can be argued, in that the voices in the text are ultimately embodied by the physical presence of the actors on stage. This can be seen in the British premiere of *Crave* where director, designer and Kane herself eventually chose to confine the characters almost exclusively to chairs, a decision which forces an audience to scrutinise the actors continuously.

This concentration on the rhythm of language in *Crave* is just one feature of this most overtly Beckettian-influenced play. There is a sense that at times the rhythms of the language dominate over meaning. This is something that Beckett incorporated into his own work, often through his characters mouthing fragments of well known biblical and literary quotations. Beckett himself has commented: 'I am interested in the shape of ideas even if I do not believe in them ... There is a wonderful sentence in Augustine ... "Do not despair; one of the thieves was saved. Do not presume; one of the thieves was damned." That sentence has a wonderful shape. It is the shape that matters' (Hobson, 1956: 156).

Beckett uses this 'shape' as a basis for the discussion Vladimir and Estragon conduct over the differing accounts of the thieves at the crucifixion. Like Beckett, in *Crave* Kane outlines how this process developed further, where the shape and rhythm of the words at times became the signifier of meaning:

> Normally, when I am writing, I know what the intention and the meaning of the line is. With *Crave* I knew what the rhythm was, but I did not know what I was going to say. There were a couple of times I used musical notation, only the rhythm without actual words. (Thielemans, 1999: 12)

Although T. S. Eliot's *The Waste Land* (1922) is of primary importance in shaping *Crave* through direct quotation, as well as borrowings from its themes and structure (see Saunders, 2002a: 102–5), the critic Michael Billington observes that 'you can actually hear the rhythms of [*Waiting for*] *Godot*' (Billington, 1998). At times this comes from direct quotation such as the use of its famous opening line, 'nothing to be done' (182), but is at its most explicit in the following exchanges:

A Life happens

B Like flowers

C Like sunshine

A Like nightfall

C A motion towards

A It is not my fault. (191)

Vladimir They make a noise like wings.

Estragon Like leaves.

Vladimir Like sand.

Estragon Like leaves.

Vladimir They all speak together. (58)

While Beckett's later drama is also predominantly language-driven, it differs from Kane's in that there is always a central visual image to each play: the wide-brimmed hat on the centre of the table in *Ohio Impromptu* (1981); May's measured and obsessive pacing in *Footfalls* (1975), or the unveiling through light of The Protagonist in *Catastrophe* (1982). In *Crave* and *4.48 Psychosis* such distinct images have been abandoned.

However, this is not to say that such explicitly realised imagery is absent. It is perhaps better to say that it is *buried*. In the case of *Crave*, one reason behind this might be the strong adoption it seems to make of the structure and imagery from Beckett's *Play*. Despite introducing a fourth character, Kane retains Beckett's device of replacing nomenclature with letters to designate character, and despite forgoing the memorable image of the imprisoned speakers in urns, there is the same sense of entrapment and limbo. Both plays also examine the damage that the pursuit of love can inflict on the characters who appear compelled to talk about obsessions and betrayals involving their trapped counterparts. Vicky Featherstone, the director of *Crave*'s British premiere, believes that in Kane's play, 'they are four voices in the darkness – and only exist to speak because people will listen to their sorrow' (Saunders, 2002a: 132). Both plays also use repetition to suggest a circular Dantesque vision of hell for the protagonists, although Kane's speakers seem more aware of their counterparts than Beckett's.

Also employed in both is the central motif of light, although as mentioned Beckett realises this in *Catastrophe* as a physical presence on the stage. In *Play* Anna McMullan believes that the use of light functions as a stark interrogatory tool directed at the speakers, and is associated with 'revelation and judgement' (McMullan, 1993: 17). While the final stage direction of *Cleansed*

– 'The sun gets brighter and brighter ... until the light is blinding'
(151) – also exposes Grace and Carl to the same state of exposed
vulnerability, the image also holds revelatory experience in Crave
through the speakers embracing it as a comforting yet ultimately
nihilistic oblivion, 'free-falling / Into the light / Bright white light'
(200). It is also an image of simultaneous solace and destruction
in 4.48 Psychosis, where the speakers often repeat like a mantra,
'Remember the light and believe in the light' (206).

Ultimately, within Crave and 4.48 Psychosis these harrowing
journeys Kane takes into her own psyche are what really unites
her with Beckett. Ronald Hayman writing in 1970 observes that
neither a well known Beckett enthusiast such as Harold Pinter
'nor any other Beckett followers have inherited his purity or his
integrity' (Hayman, 1970: 79). However, I would argue that Sarah
Kane has consciously followed what Hayman also calls Beckett's
'unshakeable fidelity to his own vision' (Hayman, 1970: 79),
and, despite making a case earlier that Kane's work has more
of an engagement with the outside world than Beckett's, that
her concerns predominantly occupy a metaphysical terrain. This
aspect of her writing places her far closer to being a follower of
Beckett – certainly closer than her own contemporaries writing in
the mid-1990s. Whereas many of them chose to look at aspects of
contemporary urban Britain, Kane like Beckett increasingly took a
path of 'the mind turn[ing] in on itself, analysing the conditions of
living, and the nature of the energy that drives [us] on' (Hayman,
1970: 75).

From the repetition of Hamm's curse in Endgame – 'The bastard!
he doesn't exist' – to Ian's ephiphet in Blasted – 'The cunt' (57)
– Kane's drama, like Beckett's before, has unsparingly interrogated
questions concerning the reason for suffering, the existence of
God and the afterlife and the nature of love as both an ecstasy
and a torment. There is also the feeling that Kane is more earnest
concerning matters of religion and the afterlife than Beckett's
often mocking or contemptuous response. In Ken Urban's view, 'for
Kane, hell is not metaphysical; it is hyperreal, reality magnified'
(Urban, 2001: 45); it may have come from her former Christian
faith (Saunders, 2002a: 22–3).

Beckett's and Kane's perhaps most lasting legacy has been their
ability to occupy simultaneously the plateaux of avant-garde and
popular culture. Fletcher, Smith and Bachem argue that Beckett's
formal methodologies in 'setting out the metaphysical doubts that
torment us, have quickly passed from being innovative to seem

natural and inevitable' (Fletcher *et al.*, 1978: 22). Johnathan Kalb, however, believes that it was the relative speed of Beckett's inclusion into the western canon that made it possible for him 'to smuggle certain progressive ideas across the boundary of mainstream culture' (Kalb, 1989: 158). Peter Morris argues that with Kane's death in 1999 she had simultaneously 'been reconfigured as a kind of easily-assimilated icon, like Duchamp's urinal now placidly enshrined in some vast museum' yet also, 'far from being eternally avant-garde, she too has become a commodity, a trademark, at last: Brand Kane' (Morris, 2000: 152). Beckett too has become a brand – his distinctive features emblazoned on T-shirts promoting Ireland or advertising Microsoft computer software. However, ultimately the importance of both dramatists' legacy is dependent on the energy and relevancy that come from revivals of their work.

Notes

1 Beckett used this term in the English translation of his novel *The Unnameable* (1958: 297).
2 For a fuller discussion see Saunders, 2003: 105–6.

6

Cruelty, violence, and rituals in Sarah Kane's plays

Stefani Brusberg-Kiermeier

While a considerate amount of attention has been paid to the cruelty and violence in Kane's plays, the role that rituals play has been neglected so far. Although Kane rarely makes use of the word 'ritual' itself, the concept is of great relevance in coming to an understanding of her plays. In *Blasted*, for instance, Kane shows an awareness of the close connection between violence and ritual: 'A serial killer slaughtered British tourist Samantha Scrace, S–C–R–A–C–E, in a sick murder ritual, comma, police revealed yesterday point new par' (12). This is how the news story starts that journalist Ian reports on the hotel telephone to his boss at the beginning of *Blasted*. With this story, Kane prepares the ground for the important role that violence plays and at the same time introduces a theme that is central to her work. Throughout all her plays Kane uses ritualised cruelty for her discussion of the human state and human relationships, as she is clearly fascinated and at the same time repelled by the omnipresence of violence in human existence.

Kane adapts rituals from different contexts of life – love, eating, religion, and medicine – and portrays, explains and questions their form and function. Since ritualised actions are symbolically and emotionally charged, they prove helpful for her project to explore the limits of theatrical representation. Their use is also an ideal vehicle for Kane to combine the realistic with symbolic representation. Following what Graham Saunders calls her aim 'to redefine the representation of staged violence' (Saunders, 2002a: 89), Kane not only depicts and satirises culturally established rituals but also transforms actions into rituals.

Moreover, as a dramatist Kane understands the performative character of rituals. In my view, the importance of the performative aspect of rituals cannot be overestimated, because everyone involved in the ritual acts not *ad libitum* but in close connection with the cultural background. As in the theatre, ritualistic performance communication takes place when actor and audience know each other's codes. A reasonably experienced audience will be able to understand the performance and to decipher the meanings that the ritual is supposed to establish or carry. Kane's presentation shows that performance and meaning are inseparable, whatever their relationship might be: a ritualistic performance can be an empty representation, it can persuasively express established meaning or it can even invent new meaning.

Kane shows that ritual, like theatre, is a staged representation of reality that negotiates meaning and order. The close relation of ritual to 'belief' and 'cult' underlines the important role that violence plays in rituals. As Victor Turner has argued, violent cultic acts serve as rites of passage, and the mutilation of the body symbolises the individual's change of place, position, state or age group. Thus, ritual is a metaphor for the human existence at large, for a limited process circumscribed by the violent act of birth and the cruelty of death. The ritual not only alludes to or uses violence, it also helps to contain or guide the horrors (Turner, 1982).

Love rituals

Kane especially combines the physical and performative aspects of ritual for her discussion of the state, function, and relation of human bodies. Throughout her plays, she shows that a successful performance of rituals can decide social standing or membership of a certain group: therefore, rituals are often related to gender and status. In *Blasted*, the first entrance of the actors into a hotel room starts off a series of expectations and rituals. Kane also takes up this game with rituals in *Crave*, when A says: 'We checked into a hotel pretending we weren't going to have sex' (178). Rituals are closely linked to the display of power and control in *Blasted*, which also becomes clear in scene three when the soldier stands on the bed and urinates on the pillows like a dog (39).

Kane continuously parodies love rituals through her presentation of Ian and Cate's relationship. Kane shows her knowledge of manipulative communication structures when she depicts the relationship between Ian and Cate as a double-bind relation with a long history. Ian changes back and forth between insults and promises of love in order to make Cate sleep with him. The expression of love becomes an empty ritual, because it is used as emotional blackmail. Ian says 'I love you' to Cate nine times in

Blasted in various contexts in order to manipulate her. As Graham Saunders has pointed out, Ian's present of a bouquet of flowers for Cate is only a 'hollow gesture' (Saunders, 2002b: 128) as well. Kane's parody of love rituals reaches its height with the mock seduction in scene two when Cate kisses Ian, undoes his clothes, performs oral sex on him and finally bites his penis in a possible act of revenge for the sexual assault she undergoes during the night (28–31).

Throughout the play, Cate tries to retain her personal freedom and spiritual independence by either dismissing Ian's manipulative statements with laughter, evasive comments and questions or by disrupting the smooth procedure of love rituals. When Ian tells Cate he loves her for the sixth time, she retaliates: 'I don't love you' (24). In this way Kane uses the relationship between Ian and Cate to discuss conflicting desires and fears as well as gender power relations. She poses questions about which fears and desires are necessary for survival and where neurosis starts.

As Graham Saunders has remarked, Cate's Christian faith seems to sustain her throughout the play (Saunders, 2002a: 22–3; 166). Moreover, it induces her to take action and reverse the traditional gender roles. For instance, Cate removes the bullets from Ian's gun before handing it to him. When he fails to shoot himself because of this she says: 'Fate, see. You're not meant to do it. God –' (57). Cate is saving the blinded Ian's life in a ridiculous and yet touching way.

Eating rituals

Kane's connection of domestic cruelty with wartime violence becomes especially poignant with regard to her depiction of cruel sexual acts and the use of food and eating rituals. She makes clear that in *Blasted* sexual acts and the acquisition and consumption of food are interdependent and fundamental for the creation of the play's specific reality. *Blasted* explores the symbolic meanings that food and rituals play. As Georg Simmel has shown, eating is the one thing 'most common' and 'most mutual' – '*das Gemein-samste*' – among all people (Simmel, 1957: 243). It is a social act, which brings people with various interests and from different contexts together and follows special rules that often have a long tradition. Simmel argues that eating is egoistic and close to the bestial aspects of humans, because it is a reaction to an individual's physical needs. Therefore, eating habits and table manners play a central role in the human process of cultivation: different cultures have established different rituals and taboos that must be followed during meals. In *Blasted*, the specific reality of the play does not require traditional eating rituals any more: in a cultural system that is dysfunctional, the tradition of the meal has become boring and meaningless. Although they cannot keep up taboos or hygienic regulations when these do not make sense to them any more in their situation, the characters still try to define their relation to this specific reality with the help of specific rituals. For instance, Ian drinks alcohol and orders sandwiches or Cate tries to avoid eating meat unless it is inevitable.

The staging of eating in *Blasted* displays a relationship of the characters to their own physicality that is more grotesque than, say that of the characters in Mark Ravenhill's play *Shopping and Fucking* (1996), who exclusively live on fast food and microwave meals. Whereas the unseen hotel worker brings food at the beginning of *Blasted*, it is the woman, Cate, who finally provides the food and feeds Ian like a baby. In the beginning of *Shopping and Fucking* the play's only female character, Lulu, similarly follows the gender stereotype of the feeding mother or wife by providing microwave food. However, at the end of the play, Ravenhill has all the characters take turns in feeding each other, thus evoking the positive function that mutual meals can still have for the community spirit (Ravenhill, 1996: 89).

In *Blasted*, the soldier's threat to shoot Ian in the anus, the raping of Cate and her aggressive fellatio can be interpreted as extreme versions of grotesque bodies swallowing the world and being swallowed by the world themselves. The relation between eating and sexuality is naturally a close one as the mother breast-feeds her baby. In *Blasted*, Kane heightens this into a grotesque excess by Ian eating the baby that Cate has found. This can be seen as an extreme attempt to hold on to life, as a grotesque body swallowing the product of the womb. Kane seems to argue that the process of renewal might never end in spite of death, since Ian joins it before he dies when he eats the baby and again after he has died, when he is fed by Cate and ends the play with his words 'Thank you' (61).

Religious rituals

Kane's representation of eating rituals is closely interlinked with religious rituals, so that the acts depicted often also have a religious connotation. Cate's Christian faith sustains her when Ian is blinded and helpless. She leaves the hotel and brings back the baby, which she buries under the floor after it dies. She goes out again and offstage exchanges sex for food, which she brings back onstage for herself and Ian. Although she is continuously confronted with violence, she finally disrupts the mimetic crisis of reacting with violence to violence. While Cate is away the second time, Ian 'eats the baby' (60). A Christian reading of the swallowing of the bodies allows for an element of hope, since the baby becomes the 'holy child' who is symbolically transformed into the Host just as Jesus' body is transformed into the Host in the Holy Communion. Ian can then die with relief, but he also lives on as a baby and is fed by Cate who takes up the function of the mother. In a production that emphasises the religious connotations of the last scene, Ian can be represented as Christ-like when the blood on his mutilated body is being washed away by the rain, while Cate can be presented as a *mater dolorosa* (Brusberg-Kiermeier, 2004: 362). Ian's last words, 'Thank you' (61), are part of what Graham Saunders has called Ian's 'painful journey towards self-awareness' (Saunders, 2002a: 64).

Edward Bond alludes to the performative nature of religion when he says: 'Drama shares its ultimate with religion. Religion is merely theatre claiming to be real. It does this in order to control reality more effectively' (Saunders, 2002a: 190). In my view, Kane shows that religion has similar performative qualities as theatre by appropriating religious rituals. Moreover, she goes even further by first subverting religious rituals and then reinstating the power of ritual with new form and language.

What Kane imitates is the linguistic density and intensity of religious rituals, by using word emphasis, accumulation, repetition or invocation. For instance, in *Crave* the constant recurrence of 'I feel nothing, nothing' has a strong emotional impact (156; 158; 175; 199). Equally powerful are Kane's variations of sentences in *Crave*, since a different speaker or a different context changes the meaning and the relationship of the characters. A good example is the discussion of family relations when one character remarks: 'You could be my mother', and another replies: 'I'm not your mother' (168; 173). Kane's last two plays are more overtly religious in tone than her earlier work: this is partly due to her use of formalised, dense speeches and variations of famous quotes from the Bible, such as 'My love, my love, why have you forsaken me?' in *4.48 Psychosis* (219).

Medical rituals

Kane parodies medical rituals in *Crave* and *4.48 Psychosis*, especially the questioning of the patient and the handing out of medical advice. In *Crave*, the questioning of the patient also implies the doctor's wish to standardise human relationships: 'Do you have difficulty in relationships with men? ... Have you ever been hospitalised?' (172). In *Crave*, Kane discusses the definition of madness and sanity and evokes states of liminality, for instance with the question 'Do you ever hear voices?' (188). In *4.48 Psychosis*, Kane further pursues this discussion in the speaker's inner dialogue with doctors or therapists, referred to as 'Dr This and Dr That and Dr Whatsit' (209), whose interrogations and treatments are experienced as unhelpful and humiliating.

In *Cleansed*, Tinker's treatment of Graham echoes relaxation techniques, when he tells Graham 'Your legs are heavy' or 'Your head is light' while he prepares the heroin. Graham acknowledges Tinker's authority when he accepts the overdose with 'Thank you, Doctor' (108). When Grace repeats Graham's words 'Thank you, Doctor' at the end of *Cleansed* this indicates that her process of transformation from Grace into Graham is completed. Although Tinker apologises for his imperfect operation on her body to make it a male one – 'I'm sorry. I'm not really a doctor' (146) – she reinstates his authority with her penultimate sentence. In my view, Kane indicates that rituals are so important for her drama because they can offer a theatrical reality in which body and mind might be one, in which the identity might not be fragmented.

Redemption through ritual

Kane's drama is most powerful when she parodies rituals and finds new forms for them. Her most impressive and touching scenes in this respect are probably the mock marriage-ceremony between Rod and Carl and Carl's dance of love in *Cleansed*. Here, Kane's romantic version of love as a commitment that includes the readiness to die for the beloved is both discussed and literally executed. Carl's claims that his love for Rod is 'perfect', that he will always love and never betray Rod, are satirised by Rod's comments in scene two and later portrayed as untrue when Carl betrays Rod in scene four. Still, Carl and Rod do exchange vows and rings in scene two, but Rod fills the traditional Christian formula with a new language that he finds is more appropriate for him in his situation, and therefore more honest. In my view, this new formula loses none of the power of the old ritual, firstly because it still claims to be unique – 'Listen. I'm saying this once.' – and secondly because the linguistic variation of the love vows gives the language a strong rhetorical force:

> I love you *now*.
> I'm with you *now*.
> I'll do my best, moment to moment, not to betray you.
> Now.
> That's it. No more. Don't make me lie to you. (111)

Carl confirms that he accepts Rod's honesty and that he will trust him – 'I do' – while Tinker and the audience are watching and thereby function as the traditional witnesses.

In scene four, Carl is tortured by Tinker and an unseen group of men. With one method of torture, when Carl's trousers are pulled down and a pole is pushed up his anus, Kane alludes supposedly to an old form of torture that was used for the killing of King Edward II (Marlowe, 1986: 526ff). Kane also implies that Carl's and Rod's sufferings confer on them Christ-like qualities, e.g. in scene eight when Rod says 'You'd have watched them crucify me' and also asks Carl for his forgiveness, because of the tortures Carl has had to endure as a consequence of his love for Rod. However, Carl's betrayal of Rod serves to purify and strengthen their love.

After Carl's spoken betrayal, Tinker cuts out Carl's tongue and makes him swallow Rod's ring. When Carl tries to express his love for Rod by writing in the mud, Tinker cuts off his hands. When Carl performs a dance of love for Rod, Tinker cuts off his feet. As with the anal impaling, each punishment is a direct violent representation of the corresponding 'crime'. The body's desire to inscribe itself into the world is answered by the inscription of violence on to the body. Kane puts Carl's mutilations in systematic order starting from the head and ending at the feet, so that the series of mutilations acquires the form of a ritual itself. However, Rod laughs at these mutilations (136) and decides to die for Carl. Rod repeats his love vows, but changes them so that they now echo Carl's earlier extreme, romantic version: 'I will always love you./ I will never lie to you./ I will never betray you./ On my life' (142).

Carl's continuous suffering becomes a proof of his love for Rod, which in turn enables Rod to admit the special quality of their love and to sacrifice his life for Carl. After Carl makes love to him, Rod asks Carl to swallow the other ring as well, so that the rings are united inside Carl. As Graham Saunders has pointed out, the swallowing of the second ring also resembles taking the Sacrament (Saunders, 2002a: 98), and I would therefore argue that the systematic tortures of Carl as well as the love rituals can be read as a metaphor for the strengthening of their love, with the ability to lie and betray now removed. Thus the title *Cleansed* implies not only a cleansing from drugs or ethnic cleansing, but also a purification of love, a reduction of life to its essentials, and a triumph of mind and soul over the body.

Conclusion

The productions of Kane's plays have made obvious that an extremely realistic mode of representation and especially a glamorising of violence can greatly overshadow the other qualities of the texts. I would argue, moreover, that a largely realistic mode of representation might also be the wrong aesthetic decision with regard to the depiction of ritual. Kane's use of ritual often points to the special aesthetic qualities that rituals can have and makes clear that rituals can be experienced as beautiful. The 'linguistic beauty of rituals' which is established by the use of poetic speech patterns, such as accumulation, repetition or invocation, may be easily discernible, but a production can easily spoil the 'visual beauty of rituals', for instance of Cate's comforting of Ian in *Blasted* or of Carl's dance of love in *Cleansed*. The specific aesthetic quality of Kane's rituals is closely interlinked with their moral quality: the emotional spontaneity of the act conveys commitment and responsibility, goodness and love. Kane parodies the traditional form and language of rituals and finds new formulas and new language for old rituals. She thereby not only subverts them but also confirms the power of rituals, because they can execute and contain cruelty at the same time. As such, they are part of the human 'web of reason' (233) mentioned in *4.48 Psychosis*, of a frail social net of constructed meanings.

7

Sarah Kane, experiential theatre and the revenant avant-garde

Clare Wallace

In a 1998 interview, Sarah Kane asserted that her plays 'certainly exist within a theatrical tradition … at the extreme end of the theatrical tradition. But they are not about other plays; they are not about methods of representation' (Saunders, 2002a: 25). Of all the playwrights credited with producing the provocative new writing that inundated British drama at the end of the twentieth century, Kane is the most overtly experimental and formally adventurous. And although much of the work classed by Aleks Sierz as 'in-yer-face' theatre has depreciated in value rather swiftly, the formal fluidity and thematic foci of Kane's drama continue to engage directors, actors and audiences across a broad cultural and linguistic spectrum.

Why is this the case? Kane's work defies sound-bite appraisals; it remains difficult to sum up in any concise fashion as each play takes a markedly different tack, so that as a whole it is at best unified by an exploration of the limits of what can be done with dramatic form.[1] Sierz has argued that a defining feature of the new drama of the 1990s is its 'experiential' nature. The term is loosely defined by Sierz in the opening chapter of his book *In-Yer-Face Theatre: British Drama Today* as work that provokes, usually in a violent manner, its audiences to feel as opposed to think. As he notes, provocation and theatre share a long history. However, while his 'brief history of provocation' (Sierz, 2001a: 10–30) is primarily concerned with drama in the English language and British theatre specifically, Sarah Kane's work solicits reference to another genealogy and conceptual heritage.

The premise of this essay is that Kane has achieved international acclaim not so much because of her conformity with a new wave of British drama but rather because of her affinity with a not so new constellation of Continental avant-garde ideas and techniques. In exploring some of the connections between this tradition and

Kane's work, we might approach a fuller understanding of the nature of her 'experiential' theatre and the issues that attend a revisitation of avant-garde experimentation in an age purportedly characterised by postmodernity.

'Experiential' is the term Kane herself used for the theatre she wanted to make.[2] This should be a theatre that has a 'visceral' impact, putting its audience 'in direct physical contact with thought and feeling' (Kane, 1998a), with 'truth' as opposed to social commentary or diversion. It is a theatre that must be lived through, that is not merely a live art that may be affected by an audience (though this is an important element of it) but one that is alive with the potential to stimulate and even transform those who are exposed to it. Kane's proclamation of her commitment to 'the truth, however unpleasant that truth happens to be' (Stephenson and Langridge, 1997: 134) indicates that the experiential goes beyond mere provocation or, as the opening quotation suggests, experimentation for its own sake. 'If', asserts Kane, 'we can experience something through art then we might be able to change our future ... If theatre can change lives, then by implication it can change society, since we're all part of it' (Stephenson and Langridge, 1997: 133). Certainly, the tone and import of this vision of 'experiential' theatre seems quite distinct from the ironic distance characteristic of art or literature that is perceived as postmodern.

Definitions of the avant-garde, its genesis, movements and politics, failures and successes, oppositions and complicities, have tended to gather in multiple and contradictory formations. However, the co-ordinates that Kane identifies as central to her experiential theatre – art, experience, transformation – have been, in both latent and overt ways, of primary importance to the avant-garde. I want to highlight just two of the many critical perspectives on the avant-garde that are of particular interest with regard to these co-ordinates. Peter Bürger argues that the 'historical avant-garde' emerged in the early decades of the twentieth century in opposition to the bourgeois, ingrown and detached nature of nineteenth-century aestheticism, and then developed into a radical critique of the institutions of art itself *vis-à-vis* social praxis. Commenting on Bürger's theory, Richard Murphy notes how such an 'avant-garde consequently champions a form of art whose main goal becomes the reintegration and "sublation" of art and life ... to create a new art, from within [and] ... become possible to conceive of an entirely new basis for social practice' (Murphy, 1999: 11). This is a blatantly political, visionary and expansive objective, and one that Bürger finds unrealised by the specific avant-garde movements (Dada and surrealism) that he chooses to focus upon. In contrast, in his discussion of experimental theatre stretching from Alfred Jarry to environmental theatre of the 1980s, Christopher Innes maintains that the general, recurrent feature of avant-garde theatre is primitivism, 'an aspiration to transcendence, to the spiritual in its widest sense' (Innes, 1993: 10). Yet in its return to 'primal forms' his avant-garde theatre is not wholly dissimilar to Bürger's historical avant-garde, with its radical aim: 'to replace the dominant modes of drama – and by extension the society of which these are an expression – by rebuilding from first principles' (Innes, 1993: 3).

Avant-garde theatre has repeatedly deployed shock tactics and provocation to effect a collision between art and lived experience in a variety of ways. These have been eclectically adopted by Kane. Confrontation as a core element of avant-garde tendencies in theatre was of course put forward powerfully by Alfred Jarry as early as 1896. Described by André Breton as 'the great prophetic avenging play of modern times' (Pronko, 1964: 6), Jarry's *Ubu Roi* through grotesque exaggeration aimed to produce in its audience a recognition of their own vices. *Ubu* consequently binds provocation to a moral project, however crudely rendered. Dovetailing with the confrontational element are those of rupture and rejection – in particular a break with and refusal of the values and modes of representation belonging to realism. Accordingly the avant-garde:

> oppose[s] realism's characteristic gesture of pretending to offer a comprehensive survey and rational explanation of the world. [And] challenge[s] the narrative structures and conventional rational constructions through which reality is interpreted, in order [to] make the inherited realist models of the world less self-evident or 'natural'. (Murphy, 1999: 44)

Yet the goal of such challenges is often recuperative, to access and recover a more profound level of truth, though inevitably such truth is vaguely defined. So, for instance, expressionist theatre adopts non-organic devices and montage to subvert conventional representations of the self as knowable or stable. Similarly, Antonin Artaud rejects the notion that truth can be rendered by psychological realism, language or dialogue, rather via 'magic, metaphysics and *mise en scène*' saying that it can be rendered (Pronko, 1964: 14). Confrontation, rupture, revolution and return then might be seen as the compass points of avant-garde theatre that equally mark out key directions in Kane's drama.

Initial reactions to *Blasted* and later (to a lesser extent) *Phaedra's Love* and *Cleansed* focused upon, and in general decried, the excessive visceral imagery of the plays. What was apparently most objectionable in *Blasted* was the fact that the violent spectacles in the play were severed from a context that would sufficiently explain or alleviate them. They were not just unpalatable but unrealistic, or in the words of *Guardian* theatre critic Michael Billington, '[t]he reason the play falls apart is that there is no sense of external reality' (Billington, 1995). The effect was notably perceived as a physical assault, as reviewers' opinions testify. Paul Taylor of *The Independent* memorably responded as follows:

> Sitting through *Blasted* is a little like having your face rammed into an overflowing ashtray, just for starters, and then having your whole head held down in a bucket of offal. As a theatrical experience, there is nothing wrong in principle with either of these ordeals. Provided, that is, you can feel something happening to your heart and mind as well as to your nervous system as a result. (Taylor, 1995)

With regard to *Phaedra's Love*, Charles Spencer of the *Telegraph* claimed '[i]t's not a theatre critic that's required here, it's a psychiatrist' (Sierz, 2001a: 108), and by *Cleansed* John Peter of the *Sunday Times* felt genuinely disturbed:

> *Cleansed* is a nightmare of a play, it unreels somewhere between the back of your eyes and the centre of your brain with an unpredictable but remorseless logic. As with a nightmare, you cannot shut it out because nightmares are experienced with the whole of your body. (Peter, 1998)

Such comments indicate that Kane's attempts at an experiential theatre were indeed successful in aggravating at least a few of their first spectators. However, it is questionable whether the violent content alone was the most confrontational aspect of the work. In a society conditioned by what Herbert Blau terms 'a warp of specularity' (Blau, 1990: 281), in which spectators are habitually exposed and largely desensitised to violent or sexual spectacles in other media, such a response is somewhat surprising, if not a little disingenuous. Rather, in the case of *Blasted*, initial reactions were triggered by the form of the play, described by Kane herself as 'apparently broken-backed and schizophrenic' (Stephenson and Langridge, 1997: 131).

Kane's first step towards an experiential theatre was a controversial rupturing of socio-realist formal boundaries – as noted above, one of the avant-garde's most traditional manoeuvres.

Blasted threw down a gauntlet to critics and audiences with its cocktail of violent content coupled with an equally violent formal transmogrification mid-play. The blasting apart in the third scene of what has up to that point been a realist drama is a direct attack on any conventional sense of organic unity. By the concluding scene in which Ian is shown in various states (which include masturbating, attempting suicide, defecating, laughing, dreaming and hunger), Kane has adopted an expressionist contraction of time and a rudimentary montage effect that will be developed further in her later work.

Blasted's shift from 'socio-realism to surrealism, to expressionism' (Saunders, 2002a: 40) allows the play to explore the nature of power in a quotidian, domestic shape which is then suddenly displaced and magnified to grotesque proportions. The formal rupture functions metaphorically in Kane's view: '[t]he form is a direct parallel to the truth of the war it portrays – a traditional form is suddenly and violently disrupted by the entrance of an unexpected element that drags the characters … into a chaotic pit without logical explanation' (Stephenson and Langridge, 1997: 78). As a result, while thematically the play deals with manipulation, violation and war, the focus is interior; the topology of subjectivity is a key aspect of the play's exploration of extremes. Like the expressionism to which it tends, *Blasted* has little interest in surface reality or social enquiry. Instead, it is structured by the enigmatic qualities of dreams and nightmares where particular orders of logic are suspended and an alternative set of images comes into play. So, for instance, the character Ian, in the hallucinatory order of scenes two to five, is shown by the Soldier the extremities of his own desires and, whereas in the opening scenes he is metaphorically blind, this later becomes literal. Ian's identity is also shaped by an aggressive relation to others, an overstated masculinity and a desire for control exacerbated by his failing health and imminent physical demise. All these values are cast into question by the Soldier's appearance on stage. Throughout the play acts of seeing signify at different levels of reality and association. The pervasive ocular symbolism foregrounds these questions of self-perception and, by implication, of responsibility.

While *Blasted* explores the territory of power and violation by capsizing realist causality, *Phaedra's Love* and *Cleansed* are thematically linked in their dramatisation of the extremes of desire and love. In both plays, points of crisis are reached when the relationship between the subject and object of desire is carried to absolute extremes and where this extremism is expressed in the plays' formal qualities. *Phaedra's Love*, which Kane wryly referred to as 'my comedy' (Saunders, 2002a: 78), is a provocative version of Seneca's *Phaedra*. Kane's intention was that 'the play could be at one moment intimate and personal, at the next epic and public' (Sierz, 2001a: 108). However, it is debatable whether stagings of the play achieve this effect. Unlike versions by Seneca, Euripides or Racine, the focus is Hippolytus rather than the lovesick Phaedra. His downfall is a result not of purity, as is stressed in the other well-known dramatisations of the Phaedra myth, but his rejection of hypocrisy in the pursuit of absolute honesty. Though the key elements of Greek theatre – 'love, hate, death, revenge, suicide' (Sierz, 2001a: 109) – are preserved, the acts traditionally occurring on stage and those reported are reversed. Phaedra's suicide takes place offstage while a host of other brutal actions including the mutilation and disembowelment of Hippolytus, the rape and murder of Strophe, and Theseus' suicide take place in full view. Both these modifications to the formal and thematic elements of the Phaedra myth seem to undo any Aristotelian description of tragedy as the performance of deeds of seriousness and magnitude with the intention of 'arousing fear and pity' in order 'to accomplish … catharsis of such emotions' (Aristotle, 1954: 230).

The emotions stirred up by the play are primarily the result of the concluding spectacle. However, *Phaedra's Love* deliberately pursues visual excess to terrible and absurd lengths, with a view to trauma rather than a safe cathecting of unhealthy or intense emotion. The outcome of this strategy is an avant-garde dismembering of the conventions of classical tragedy that comments on the violence these conventions traditionally mask.

Cleansed, it might be argued, continues from where *Blasted* leaves off and is most clearly governed by aesthetics of anti-realism, fragmentation and montage. Its title seems to suggest the conventional notion of tragedy's role as a form of socially affirming catharsis. Composed of twenty short scenes set in what the stage directions call a university but is in effect an asylum or prison-like clinic, *Cleansed* is structured around various couples and couplings of characters. The play elliptically cites Georg Büchner's *Woyzeck* (1837), George Orwell's *Nineteen Eighty-Four* (1949) and, to a lesser extent, August Strindberg's *The Ghost Sonata* (1907). Kane was interested in the way Büchner's self-contained scenes might be organised in various ways. *Cleansed* follows an episodic logic, its scenes are, to a considerable degree, independent units arranged according to a loose sequential pattern. In addition, echoes of *The Ghost Sonata* might be discovered in the colour coding of interior spaces each with a specific meaning. As Graham Saunders notes, Strindberg's 'use of rooms as places of discovery and revelation for characters constitutes a form of ongoing journey or pilgrimage and is … an important motif in later expressionist theatre' (Saunders, 2002a: 94–5).

This journey explores love as madness by translating the figurative into the literal and making the body the site of trauma. The theme of self-loss is played out from different perspectives. The imbalance between the first couple, Rod and Carl, is clear from the outset. While Carl's desire is for possession, to fix the relationship through the symbolic exchange of rings and vows, Rod will only make promises for the present: 'I love you *now*. I'm with you *now*. I'll do my best, moment to moment, not to betray you. Now. That's it. No more. Don't make me lie to you' (111). In the surreal space of the 'institution', Carl's absolute vow of loyalty is tested through grotesque physical torture and effectively leads to his mutilation and Rod's self-sacrifice. Following his betrayal of Rod, Carl is forced to 'eat his words' by swallowing the rings and each time he attempts to express love physically he loses the corresponding part of the body used: first his tongue, then hands, feet and, finally, genitals.

Similarly with the Grace/Graham couple, loss of self is mapped out on the body. In a vivid play of negation, Graham, the absent object of Grace's desire, is rendered present through imitation and self-annihilation. Grace wishes her body 'look[ed] like it feels. Graham outside like Graham inside' (126). Grace 'becomes one' with her brother/lover only by the erasure of her own identity; first by wearing his clothes, then by undergoing a lobotomy and rudimentary sex change. Ironically, Tinker's 'saving' of Grace in fact destroys her – both her memory and her sex. Emotional pain is rendered physical. This inevitably presents directors with the dilemma of how to stage such a play without the whole structure toppling over into a series of gory *Grand Guignol* effects. Should real rats attempt to carry off pieces of the protagonists? Even though the acts of physical torture in the play have often been heavily stylised by directors, as was the case in the original production, the effect of the imagery is undoubtedly still extreme.

Evidently, the play's title does not refer to the purgative function of tragic drama, rather like *Phaedra's Love* it concerns a radical stripping away of hypocrisy. The exploitation of discontinuous scenes, the stripping back of conventional characterisation, anti-mimetic strategies which tend towards the 'artificial, exaggerated and rhetorical' (Innes, 1993: 43) and above all the harshness of the play's associative imagery have led to comparisons with Antonin Artaud's notion of a Theatre of Cruelty. Indeed some of the 'unstageable' aspects of *Cleansed* might be compared with Artaud's *The Spurt of Blood* (1925),[3] and James Macdonald, director of the first production of *Cleansed*, observed there is little evidence of 'the psychological signposts and social geography that you get in the Great British Play' (Christopher, 1998).

Artaud's concept of total theatre, which closely echoes the preoccupations of many expressionist dramatists in its appeal to an intense all-encompassing experience of theatre, to some extent foreshadows the renewed focus upon the experiential in dramatists like Kane: 'Everything that acts is cruelty. Theatre must rebuild itself on a concept of this drastic action pushed to the limit' and '[i]f theatre wants to find itself needed once more, it must present everything in love, crime, war and madness' (Artaud, 1964: 65) are among Artaud's most frequently quoted statements on the necessity of cruelty expressed in *Theatre and Its Double*. The emphasis on extremity, cruelty and madness seems particularly in keeping with tendencies in these plays.

Yet as Innes cautions, there is considerable disparity between Artaud's assertions on cruelty and its role in his work:

> In Artaud's actual stage work the 'cruelty,' which appears as a definition of existence in his metaphysical writings, is no more than an agent to heighten response by magnification ... It is in fact the dynamics that are primary, not any intrinsic violence: 'the spectator [...] will be shaken and set on edge by the *internal dynamism* of the spectacle.' (Innes, 1993: 65)

Cruelty then is primarily a tool, utilised to affect the audience to achieve an 'experiential' goal. Similarly, while staging visceral and violent action, Kane denies any interest in glamorising violence.

Beyond their interest in expressing extreme states of being, it is more difficult to find commonalities between Artaud and Kane. Artaud's interests in ritual, in rigid archetypal movement, in breaking down the barrier between stage and audience, do not find powerful counterpoints in Kane's work. This is chiefly because of their divergent attitudes towards the sacred, although one might also point to their differing attitudes to language as a means of expressing 'truth'. What is shared, however, is a vocabulary of disruption, extremity, excess, truth and alternative worlds of interiority, which might be traced from expressionist theatre through to Artaud via Howard Barker's Theatre of Catastrophe to Kane. If one is to accept Murphy's assertion that expressionism emerges in response to radical historical change and crisis (modernity, war, industrialisation), then the echoes of expressionism to be found in Kane's work can be said to emerge from a comparable, but contemporary, crisis. Both expressionism and Artaud have a pronounced interest in the status of the self and the unconscious; what is purged from this concern in Kane's drama is any pretence to the recovery of the sacred. The world of Kane's drama is one in which transcendental values are short-circuited from the outset.

In each of these plays it is clear that Kane's 'experiential' theatre owes a great deal to the avant-garde's rejection of the false reconciliations offered by the organic aesthetic of realism and a dedication to a type of theatrical shock therapy. However, do her last two plays also belong to this tradition or do they mark a return to an aesthetic of formal innovation for its own sake? Given the unrelenting intensity of Kane's first plays, it is not surprising that the formal shift in her later work was greeted with some relief among many critics. At this stage, Kane's work distances itself from the primitive or primal dimensions that Innes uses to define avant-garde theatre. *Crave* marks a move away from the physicality of the earlier plays towards explicitly interior, psychological spaces. The linguistic aesthetic of *Crave* especially and, to a lesser extent, *4.48 Psychosis* was welcomed for its poetic quality. Moreover, although both *Crave* and *4.48 Psychosis* foreground subjective indeterminacy and harrowing psychic states treated in non-naturalistic ways, they also share recognisable aspects of modernist literature, as well as some familiar elements of contemporary confessional monologue.

Eckart Voigts-Virchow sees *Crave* as a modernist retreat from the employment of violence, to an involvement with a poetic methodology of semi-Beckettian 'verbal despair' (Voigts-Virchow, 2001: 209).[4] Yet in this withdrawal from violent spectacle, the plays continue to question and dismantle realist conventions of character. Is this also a retreat from the aspects of the avant-garde in evidence in the earlier work? Not necessarily. As Elinor Fuchs writes in *The Death of Character*, alternative theatre in the latter half of the twentieth century has aggressively questioned the viability of the pretence of unified character in an age typified by 'a dispersed idea of self' (Fuchs, 1996: 9). If in this respect Kane's work again bears the influences of earlier experimental dramatists – notably Samuel Beckett, to name but the most obvious – she certainly does not share Beckett's measured existentialism or distance. While *Crave* and *4.48 Psychosis* find their principal target in the illusion of unified character, the attack again serves an 'experiential' end. Consequently, as character is eroded in the plays they advance a painfully obsessive focus upon subjects in crisis, making and unmaking multiple and contradictory selves through language.

So for example, a sense of inarticulate, impossible desire is the central feature of *4.48 Psychosis*, which dispenses with fixed speakers entirely. Saunders notes the structural similarity the play bears to Martin Crimp's *Attempts on Her Life* (1997), 'bringing together a myriad of unidentified and unnumbered voices' (Saunders, 2002a: 111). However, Crimp's play is overtly a postmodernist game, whereas *4.48 Psychosis* is not. As Kane has described, she wished the play to approximate

> what happens to a person's mind when the barriers which distinguish between reality and different forms of imagination completely disappear, so that you no longer know the difference between your waking life and your dream life. And also you no longer know where you stop, and the world starts. (Saunders, 2002a: 111–12)

The text, like *Crave*, is an assemblage of fragments: possible doctor – patient dialogues, diary monologues, strings of numbers, lists of medications and their effects, lists of verbs and questions. The convolutions of a desire to be loved and self-hatred conclude in projection: 'I think that you think of me the way I'd have you think of me' (243). Ironically '4.48 the happy hour when clarity visits' is the moment of self-annihilation, the vanishing point of the self, which the voice invites one to watch (242; 244). In marked contrast to Crimp's *Attempts on Her Life* in which the 'self', Anne, is absent, always constructed by others, the speaking self in Kane's work, however traumatised and fragmented, remains on stage at the centre of attention.

Voigts-Virchow is correct in describing *Crave* as 'a forceful statement on behalf of an "adversary culture" against stale cynicist posturing as well as against insularity, ephemerality, and anti-intellectualism' (Voigts-Virchow, 2001: 216). However, it is a statement that is a product of these conditions as much as it is a rejection of them. Taking Kane's work as a whole (with its techniques of montage, fragmentation and, latterly, citation), like its expressionist forebears, 'takes up [the] experiential complex of alienation and decentring not as an abstraction, a literary topos or describable "content" – such as the way that the "theme" of "dehumanization" is frequently treated in modernism – but as an unavoidable *effect* of the … text which the reader is made to experience at first hand' (Murphy, 1999: 17–18). Given the heritage of these aspects of Kane's work it should not be surprising that her plays have been greeted with less enthusiasm in Britain than in Continental Europe where, especially in countries like Germany, socio-realism or naturalistic narrative have little purchase in a theatre led by auteur directors.

Identifying the traces of Kane's experimental predecessors reveals a critical point of debate about the possible existence and role of avant-garde practice in a postmodern context where critical resistance is allegedly impossible. In his consideration of the relations between the avant-garde and postmodernism Louis Armand remarks how:

> at the beginning of the twenty-first century, this account of the 'end of the avant-garde' is once again under contention, as the viability of a continuation, renewal or reinvention of avant-gardism – in tandem with the end, exhaustion, death of postmodernism – is raised by artists, critics, thinkers generally, unsatisfied with the pre-millennial wisdom that everything is permitted, hence nothing is any longer possible. (Armand, 2006: 1–2)

Although ghosted by the avant-garde, Kane's experiential theatre is not a mere fetishistic recycling of an earlier experimental theatre severed from radical intent. Rather it is an uncompromising but irreverent mix of anti-naturalistic experiment, absolutist in timbre, truth-seeking in aspiration, provocative in its viscerality, fragmenting of character and excessiveness. It extends the traditions upon which she draws. Her apparently unlikely assertion that the plays are 'about love and about survival and about hope' (Saunders, 2002a: 25) should perhaps therefore be seen as a refutation of 'pre-millennial wisdom' that negates the critical capacity of culture generally and, by implication, of theatre specifically.

Notes

1 An acknowledgement of this is evident even in the title of Graham Saunders's book *'Love Me or Kill Me': Sarah Kane and the Theatre of Extremes* (2002).

2 See Sierz, 2001a: 92 and Saunders, 2002a: 18 for the profound effects

of Kane attending *Mad* by Jeremy Weller: '*Mad* took me to hell ... and the night I saw it I made a decision about the kind of theatre I wanted to make – experiential' (Sierz, 2001a: 92).

3 For example, Artaud's stage directions indicate that the Wet Nurse raises her skirts and 'A multitude of scorpions crawl out from beneath [her] dress and swarm between her legs. Her vagina swells up, splits, and becomes transparent and glistening, like a sun' (Cardullo and Knopf, 2001: 381).

4 Voigts-Virchow here cites Jeanette Malkin (1992: 5), with regard to Beckett.

Part II

Subjectivity, responsibility and representation

8

The voice of Kane

Ehren Fordyce

From *Blasted* to *4.48 Psychosis*, Sarah Kane's oeuvre of five works for the theatre offers a concise summary of late twentieth-century struggles to break open and recast the possibilities of dramatic form. Still, Kane remained wary of talking about her plays in formalist terms: 'My plays certainly exist within a theatrical tradition … But they are not about other plays; they are not about methods of representation' (Saunders, 2002a: 26).

Each of her plays explores, consistently and fiercely, similar content: the difficulty of responding to immeasurable experiences, like love, violence, suffering; and the challenge of making a claim about one's needs and desires that does not do violence to others. Yet each play is different formally: exploded psychological realism in *Blasted* and *Phaedra's Love*; character drama and image theatre in *Cleansed*; choral voices and anti-image theatre in *Crave*; and finally the lack of plot, character, setting and disembodied voice(s) of *4.48 Psychosis*. In this last work one line reads, 'How can I return to form / now my formal thought has gone?' (213). This crisis suggests an impulse that was probably always at work in Kane's restless refashioning of form. How can one represent a world where violence often abolishes social structures only to reimpose them by force; and, simultaneously, how can one break open aesthetic form so as not simply to reiterate the violence present in many social forms?

To trace how Kane's plays deal with these questions, *voice* – interpreted variously – serves as a useful guiding metaphor. In philosophical discussion (Husserl, Derrida), voice poses a paradox: on the one hand, a person's voice is identity. It makes one separate, personalised, individual and solitary.[1] One strives (authors notably) to 'find one's voice'. On the other hand, a person never quite possesses his or her own voice. Culture is inherited (or stolen), and, even when people speak in their own name, they are never sure of all implications of what they say. One unconsciously, possibly with inadvertent violence, makes claims that surpass conscious intentions; while others interpret one's claims – rightly, wrongly, indifferently – in a way other than one intends. Voice, then, exists at a potentially conflict-ridden ethical and aesthetic boundary-line. Additionally, *ethos*, or personal character, is important: it matters to have a standing in the world, to take a stand, to have a voice. At the same time, to be ethical one must navigate the unsettled territory of the interpersonal: to respect how voice is not only one's own, nor the only voice in the world.

Kane's plays investigate these ethical dilemmas, and they explore aesthetic dimensions of how to represent voice. That is, Kane struggles to adapt her voice across the trajectory of her plays (Voice as signature of the Author). Meanwhile, this struggle resembles that of the characters in the plays, who variously try to assert themselves as selves, even as the boundaries of their *ethos* as individuals deteriorate owing to violence, madness, love or other interpersonal conflicts.

In aesthetic terms, the dramatic technique of character falls apart in Kane's plays. Kane begins writing plays with characters who display recognisable psychology. Eventually her characters crumble into the empty spaces of interpersonal speech and lose boundaries between selves, to resemble nebulous residue of language as system. Finally, she resorts to a dramaturgy of disembodied voices, where dialogue occurs between juxtaposed fragments of what the Austrian playwright Elfriede Jelinek has called '*Sprachfläche*', or 'language surfaces' (Lehmann, 2006: 18).

In what follows, I will try to show how Kane's effort to write about 'love and about survival and about hope' (Saunders, 2002a: 26) leads her, for ethical and aesthetic reasons, to dismantle the dramatic technique of character (voice as *ethos*) even as she also breaks down her Voice as Author. I believe that, in writing *4.48 Psychosis*, Kane acquired scepticism about the authorial voice hiding behind character and story, as though Voice can no longer maintain a hierarchical position above the voices of characters. Her Voice can no longer contain voices in a form that would make the world appear overly fixed, yet never could 'fix' the world.

Middles

From *Blasted* on, middles fall apart in Kane's work – eruptions occur that emulate the chaos of violence. In *Blasted*, having written half an Ibsen/Pinter drama, Kane wearies of the convention. While writing the play, she is supposed to have turned on the television to find the war in Yugoslavia suddenly erupt into her own home. A possible recognition: violence is immanent, and violence shatters the difference between 'us and them'. To keep to a consistent, realistic setting, situated temporarily in the Balkans or Britain, maintains an illusion that foreground and background are local and stable; that we remain apart from others' violence. So, half-way through *Blasted*, a Soldier enters Ian and Cate's British hotel room and brings the war abroad home to the 'home-based' journalist Ian. Alternatively, is it equally the case that the hotel room crashes into the Soldier's Srebrenica-like terror? Neither perspective can be said to be authoritative; or can it?

The play's mortar bomb blast, which closes the second scene and opens a hole in the hotel room for the war's intrusion in scene three, makes material what Kane is doing dramaturgically. She puts a hole in the middle of things. She cracks open day-to-day causality to show that ethics at the extreme must go beyond the local and spatially contiguous. Now more than ever the global and local, 'us and them' are one ethical pattern. Boundaries are porous and one may, however remotely, bear responsibility, or at least could take on responsibility, for violence elsewhere. But how? As Kane noted, ethical solutions to such a situation are not clear: 'I don't think *Blasted* is a moral play – I think it's amoral' (Saunders, 2002a: 27). Rather than an answer, Kane poses a broken form to the audience to experience something like Cate's blackouts. In the hole of the bomb blast or blackout (outside consciousness) an assault is taking place; one cannot fully put the images together from before and after; but the fractured, traumatic whole hangs together.

To render how violence tears apart, yet oddly binds people, Kane devises a dramatic form for *Blasted* that reappears in her later plays. As the works pass through a broken middle, a pattern resembling the rhetorical figure of chiasmus occurs in the dramatic structure. With brutal rigour symmetrical exchanges and reversals take place.[2] Initially Ian rapes the unconscious Cate; then the Soldier, in Cate's place, but also in place of his own raped beloved – rapes the now conscious Ian. The abuser becomes the abused, and vice versa. The obligatory symmetry demands that one extreme pass to a different extreme, where two extremes pass and change places. But the two extremes never quite touch as they cross. The middle is empty.

In *Cleansed*, this pattern of a broken, crossed middle becomes even more pronounced and formalised. Here a series of transferences and twinnings occur between characters. As Viola passes for Sebastian in *Twelfth Night*, so Grace tries to pass for Graham. Yet Grace wants, beyond passing, to attain Being; beyond the physical, to attain the meta-physic. She wears Graham's clothes; Tinker puts Graham's genitals on her; but even that will not suffice. As Kane joked, the characters in *Cleansed* are quaintly 'sixties and hippy' (Saunders, 2002a: 91) in their utopian attachment to a radical form of love. Grace wants to lose her Self entirely and become the Other. She wants to experience 'Graham outside like Graham inside' (126).

The Grace/Graham pair is mirrored by Carl/Rod. Carl imagines that he knows what love is – endless and enduring. Rod is sceptical. In the meantime, Tinker operates as the play's surrogate author/director, putting the other characters through experiments in suffering. Through torture, Carl acquires Rod's understanding and recognises the limits of his own love. Carl can bear only so much pain before he is willing to transfer it to his paired Other, Rod. Meanwhile Rod speaks of love as ephemeral, but, when Tinker tortures him, he approaches Carl's ideal of unbounded love by not displacing his suffering on to Carl.

Grace crosses into Graham as Graham enters her body; Carl recognises the burden of claiming a love without end when he experiences his own physical limits; Rod, who says that 'There's only now' (142), proffers an image of love transcending death and life's suffering. As these pairs cross, another pairing emerges between Grace and Carl when Tinker sews the latter's phallus on to Grace. At the play's end Grace wears men's clothes, Carl women's. One smiles; one cries. They hold each other. But still an empty middle remains between them.

Through chiasmatic structures Kane gives violence form, releasing a force that reveals characters at their limits, while she simultaneously contains it, showing how life goes on, and leaving an emptiness to feel violence's after-effects. This merciless logic can also appear mechanical.

In *Cleansed* particularly – and this is both its power and formulaicness – characters occupy a world where a violent *Gleichschaltung*, a tense formal balancing of opposites and pairs, pervades every relationship. Tinker, the play's surrogate, internal author, manages these relationships even while caught up in them. Yet when the play's final brutal stage directions come – '*The sun gets brighter and brighter, the squeaking of the rats louder and louder, until the light is blinding and the sound deafening. Blackout'* (151) – it is difficult not to see Kane's own hand as author and wonder whether the writer abuses her creations as much as the world she depicts.

Kane's fourth play, *Crave*, moves back to the 'ordinary,' an everyday world of love and its difficulty. It also offers the most formal example of a logic of crossed, broken middles; yet, because the logic remains understated, the play appears less obviously violent in its structure. The world as institution recedes; stage directions disappear; a transcending structure of violence diminishes. Instead, we are left with a flatter, less hierarchical world than that of the earlier plays, a world that emerges only immanently in the bare voices of the play's four figures.

In place of character psychology and story, Kane begins to experiment with a technique resembling leitmotivic, musical development. In several instances throughout the play the four characters sing a litany in which B = No, M = Yes, C = No, A = Yes. B is a male who says no, A is a male who says yes. M is a woman who says yes, C is a woman who says no.[3] B and M are in a tenuous relationship, as are A and C. Three examples of this litany demonstrate the chiasmatic structure of the play (166; 186; 190). In the first, when B says no, he is saying no to the relationship with M – 'I don't want to stay.' When M says yes, she is saying yes to the relationship, hoping that 'love would [still] come' (160). Conversely, C says no to A, 'I want you to leave' while A clings to yes, saying, 'Let it [love] happen' (166). By the third iteration, the chiasmus has happened. Now B's no is a no to being denied by M: 'The things I want, I want with you' (190). M says yes, but not to B; she says yes to blindness and to the inevitability of love being not for a person, but for something imaginary that does not exist. Meanwhile, A's yes has turned into a denial of C's love, a repudiation of the relationship by affirming its 'totally predictable and sickening futility' (190) and by declaring A's love to be for 'someone that doesn't exist' (190). C says no, 'I love you' (190). The craved are now craving; the craving craved. The sides cross, but cannot meet.

From *Cleansed* through to *Crave* and *4.48 Psychosis*, the dramatic technique of a bare voice progressively replaces that of character. Already in *Cleansed* one finds voices appearing in ways that draw into question the conventional boundaries of character. For instance, toward the end, Graham's voice starts to speak simultaneously with other characters, as though a figure of death were showing how fragile the autonomy of identity is that we associate with 'character'. 'Voices' are also listed as a character in the *dramatis personae* (134–5). They are unseen and disembodied, unlike Graham's ghost, and yet, when these voices rape Grace in scene ten, we are confronted with their profoundly embodied presence.

In Kane's middle play, the spines of characters begin to collapse. Their middles deteriorate. More and more Kane explores a dramaturgy after the 'death of character', to use Elinor Fuchs's phrase. The ability to situate self, to establish a secure ground for the *ethos* of character, disintegrates as voices crowd in; as they speak simultaneously with other characters; as they whisper instructions in the ear to harm oneself. Voice has this odd, de-situating power: to be embodied and disembodied at the same time; to trouble the boundary between inner and outer, local and remote, phantasmatic and real. Voice reveals how porous the *ethos* of character is, showing the difficulty of ethical identification with others and how hard it is to be connected. Voice creates a world that is radically immanent, where no form guides one to know how to be stable and secure.

Responsibility

Kane's plays seem obsessed with responding to a world where ethical response appears haphazard, non-existent, unfulfilled. While an admirer of Beckett, Kane deals with the world's aporia differently. She adopts an ironic model, a divided subject, a self-deprecating wit, but abandons detachment. Her sorrow smoulders with anger. In *4.48 Psychosis* she says, 'Depression is anger. It's what you did, who was there and who you're blaming' (212).

While Kane consciously forsook a transcendent God, her plays remain haunted by a terrible sense of the transcendence of human responsibility. One way to think of Kane's dramaturgy is this: she adopts Beckett's negative ontology but, in abandoning detachment, she does not assume the antithesis by embracing engagement. She moves from ontology to ethics. Kane's question, phrased differently from Beckett's, may well be 'Not "Why being rather than nothing?", but how being justifies itself' (Levinas, 1989: 86).

One of my favourite descriptions of Kane comes from Annabelle Singer. She writes, 'Kane was a moral hardass who, through her plays, aimed to force others to think through the ethical paradoxes of their lives' (Singer, 2004: 141). Kane's plays are littered with characters who try, ineffectually, to refuse ethical responsibility and who are then forced to confront their paradoxes. The soldier in *Blasted* wants Ian to 'prov[e] it [the war] happened' (47); 'Tell them … you saw me' (48). Ian, however, does not want to be a witness: 'I can't do anything' (47), 'I'm not responsible' (48). If, as the Soldier puts it, Ian is always 'covering [his] own arse' (50) by not taking responsibility, then it makes a certain Dantean sense that the Soldier transfers the rape of his girlfriend on to Ian by raping him and then '*push[ing] the revolver up* **Ian***'s anus*' (49). In *Phaedra's Love*, Hippolytus says, 'I'm not responsible' (94). Paradoxically, his refusal is stubbornly admirable. Hippolytus refuses the Priest's sophistry and bland moral admonitions, sticks to his own ethical principles and prefers to die as he lived, 'in conscious sin' (94). Hippolytus exclaims, 'death for those who try to cover their arse' and 'I have no intention of covering my arse' (96).

The list of ineffectual attempts to refuse – and take – responsibility goes on. In *Cleansed*, Tinker says: 'I'm not responsible, Grace' (114); and to the Woman: 'I'm not responsible' (137). In *4.48 Psychosis*, we hear what seems like the voice of a patient to a doctor: 'You were covering your arse too. Like every other stupid moral cunt' (210).

4.48 Psychosis offers a desperate example of voices trying to be responsible, to be able to respond to the world, and yet without a secure standing from which to issue such a response. At this end-point of extreme, chafed sensitivity, the dilemma of ethical response comes to resemble psychosis, a psychology where, as Kane said, 'you no longer know where you stop, and the world starts' (Saunders, 2002a: 112). Given the play's blurring of self and world, it is possible to view the text as a kind of late self-expressive Romanticism or expressionism in which the form of the play displays an interior truth: 'How can I return to form / now my formal thought has gone?' (213). Such a reading of the play would see form disintegrating to demonstrate the shattered voices of a shattered interiority. This view is not wrong: the play is obviously autobiographical. Yet such a perspective de-emphasises the radical way in which Kane's forms not only express a particular self (usually presumed to be hers) but also enact the challenge of ethical identification *per se*. Once 'I' take responsibility, where does responsibility end? Where does the self stop and the world start? If 'I' must be more responsible than all others, does my responsibility ever end? The desire to justify one's being becomes stupefying and intractable. Taken to an implacable extreme, it becomes impossible to think and choose, and, as Edward Bond has pointed out, one of Kane's maddening virtues is that 'The confrontation with the implacable created her plays' (Saunders, 2002a: 191).

Graham's ghosted voicings of other characters; *Crave*'s open and multiple address, where a character's line may or may not respond to or anticipate lines before or after: these are steps to making addresser and addressee mobile and shifting, so as to eradicate the protective moral mask of a character contemplating a calculable world. In *4.48 Psychosis* a voice sometimes retreats from the responsibility of addressing the world in a singular, self-identical 'I', even as it does so in the 'I': 'It is myself I have never met, whose face is pasted on the underside of my mind' (245). Sometimes a voice stakes its claim to the 'I' even as it declines to speak its own name as the subject of a verb: 'we're all going to disappear / trying to leave a mark more permanent than myself' (241). Kane shows the necessary, yet maddening play of hubris and humility that an ethical relationship between self and world demands. You must pay the rent; I can't pay the rent. You and I are in debt to language and others; You must speak in the I; I can't speak in the I; and yet no Hero is going to come, so I myself have to speak up, even as I wonder at the consequences of taking up my obligation.

While the dramatic technique of character erodes in this mobile state where addresser and addressee intermingle, image also erodes. This occurs because vision and space tend to create the illusion of a sensible world – and a morally calculable one – composed of clear and distinct objects (Ihde, 1976: 26). The placeless voices of *4.48 Psychosis* are, then, not so much subjective and expressionistic as de-objectifying and objectless. They wriggle inside the ear the way responsibility wriggles inside the 'I' and breaks down the borders between the 'I' and the world. One can shut one's eyes, but one cannot blink to shut one's ears.

Performance

With the death and decline of character one also witnesses, in various strains of modernist and postmodernist theatre, a desire to do away with distanced illusions of representation and to achieve a sense of direct experience between performance and audience. From Artaud onwards, how can performance have an impact where one cannot blink to shut it out? And yet, what are the ethics of a performance that so forcefully imposes itself?

In a move towards performance, Kane's plays gradually eradicate dramatic subtext. *Phaedra's Love* offers Kane's last example where characters proceed more by recognisable Stanislavskian subtext than straightforward declaration. The character Phaedra, notably, is a mess of subtext, and the first scenes in the play are among Kane's clunkier in terms of technique. The Doctor and Strophe dole out exposition, telling the audience (in the guise of obviously leading questions to Phaedra) about the queen's subtextual passion for Hippolytus. Dramaturgically, playing the game of subtextual hide and seek requires authorial subterfuge. In order to reveal character, Kane must play at concealing it (and throughout her work, it is hard to ignore an urge to say, 'Enough of covering your arse!'). Therefore, from *Cleansed* onwards, Kane abandons subtextual characterisation.

Even in *Crave*, for instance, where one can piece together a limited overall image of the figures' histories, the impact of the piece derives less from the revelation of characters' pasts as from the effect of fugued voices, resembling and repeating each other even as they seem incapable of imagining their isolated notes as part of larger chords. As the playwright Phyllis Nagy comments, 'Those [later] plays are quite blunt emotive appeals which describe various states of being' (Saunders, 2002a: 155). I agree, but, while Nagy prefers the earlier plays' image structure and social vision, I prefer the latter plays, in part because their blunt emotional appeals actually seem less manipulative than the blunt appeals of the earlier works.

Kane's drive to write a text for performance may stem from a desire to immerse the audience in the being of an experience. However, another motivation may exist, one driven by her need to question the ethical relationships between author and dramatic personae and between performance and audience: dissatisfaction with how conventional dramatic form hides its ethical relationship of control over character and audience.

In *Blasted*, Kane creates equivalence between Cate's sexual assault and the rape camps of Yugoslavia by exploding the hotel room and the battlefield into each other. But ultimately the exchange is not symmetrical. In an odd twist, the narrative voice of the play comes to focus on Ian's story. We witness a dramatic version of third-person limited narration concentrated on the abuser Ian's Christophilic redemption. The play ends powerfully, the rain blindly raining on Ian. Yet a play that shows how Ian's exclusionary attitudes cannot ultimately keep his world at bay ends by excluding most of that world to focus on Ian. A similar twist occurs in

Phaedra's Love in that the play might reasonably be called, in its focus on Hippolytus, *Hippolytus' Truth*. In *Cleansed*, Tinker is the play's surrogate author, the one who puts the characters through their paces. His Artaudian cruelty leads to moments of exquisite honesty, but, in the penultimate scene, Tinker's declaration of love comes across as an almost rote effort to humanise the sadist. Narrative voice must intrude to offer a glimpse of redemption. The stage directions – which function as a quasi-narrator – take over to deliver the final blow to the other characters. One feels the blunt stick. Narrative voice keeps invading to make a point – witness the world's pain; do not be in denial, even the abuser cannot be excluded.

In *Crave*, however, Kane makes a wry joke about the author's complicity with abuse. Kane has suggested that A, the male paedophile, may also stand for 'author' and 'abuser' (Saunders, 2002a: 104), and, in the play, A puns, 'God has blessed me with the mark of Cain' (195). Meanwhile the text itself, in its abandonment of stage directions and punitive image theatre, diminishes the role of narrative voice. Compared to the first three plays, one has less of an overall sense of the author's hand intruding to inform for or against the individual voices in the play. Third-person limited stance disappears.

This evolution of the relationship between narrative voice and figure's voice, between framer and framed, comes together forcefully in *4.48 Psychosis*. The play may arguably be unstageable, a text for reading rather than performance, but it does what a drama can do – it stages dialogue, although now the dialogue occurs as much between registers of speech or language surfaces (medical, conversational, self-reflective, and lyrical) as between voices representing individuals. Narrative Voice and the voices in the play intermingle, but without the hierarchical relationship that would allow narrative to abuse the thing it frames. Is the play in the I? In the third-person omniscient? Is the play the world itself speaking? Or is it the 'oralic institution' of theatre that speaks? Whether one or each of these possibilities, *4.48 Psychosis* constitutes a 'death-of-the-author' play in that it does away with setting, authorial voice, narrative voice, and character voice in concentrically hierarchical rings. A chiasmatic dramatic structure, as well as the tenuous formal balance it provides, has disappeared. Instead, frames collapse as narration crosses with action and action with narration. Implacably honest, the play allows for no standing above or outside of the condition that it represents.

Curtain

The final line of *4.48 Psychosis* constitutes one of the great curtain-lines in modern drama: 'please open the curtains' (245). In its reverberating tension, as a curtain-line that nevertheless craves to be an opening, the line rivals Nora's verbal silence when she slams the door at the end of Ibsen's *A Doll's House* (1889), or the closing lines and action in Beckett's *Waiting for Godot* (1952): 'Well? Shall we go? Yes, let's go. *They do not move*' (Beckett, 1986: 88). Like these other moments, the end of *4.48 Psychosis* moves from language towards gesture and performance; moreover, it offers an ending simultaneously authoritative and inconclusive.

Huge lumps of silence (blank spaces on the page) precede the line. We (the audience or readers) watch a 'me' vanish; we are on a death watch for the voice. And the 'I' does vanish in the final line, even if its vestigial sense remains. We may presume that the same voice has been speaking the last few pages of lines, but we cannot be certain. Indeed, the willingness to hold on to one 'I' across the silences of the last few lines may require an odd form of interpretative control, force, and even violence. 'In death you hold me / never free' (244). Perhaps the voice is talking to its own pain or to other voices in the play. Perhaps the voice is also speaking to the reader, the reader who pins the voice down and holds it out of time in the eternal present of the page or stage, the reader who must exert force to take up the responsibility of reading.

Like the play as a whole, the last line poses a question of address that cannot be conclusively answered because it is unclear who is speaking and who is being spoken to. There is no subject to the verb and no vocative of address. Moreover, it is not clear whether the line is in the optative or imperative, a plea or a command. What can follow? In a nod towards performance, the text does itself out of having the last word.

I find Kane's most convincing endings those of *Blasted* and *4.48 Psychosis* because they are most balanced on a hair. The least convincing is, for me, that of *Crave*. The play is elegant, sad and consistent, but the conclusion – 'Happy / so happy / Happy and free' (200) – seems either mawkishly ironic or mawkishly redemptive. Or perhaps it is quietly ironic. However, I cannot help feeling that the Voice of the Author has intruded again to provide a forced narrative closure for the voices of the characters.

The ending of *4.48 Psychosis*, however, echoes in the bones. It resonates back and forth between voice and Voice, in a determined indeterminacy. The line seems utterly private, yet is issued to a public; it appears ordinarily human, yet almost inhumanly metaphysical: 'Please open the curtains' (245). Perhaps a small voice is making an intense plea: please part this shroud. Perhaps Voice is delivering a calm order that assumes it will be obeyed, knowing that the result is as likely to produce blind terror as hope: let there be a beginning, with whatever consequences follow. Or perhaps it is just an ordinary voice, looking for an opening.

Notes

1 See Stanley Cavell's essay 'Counter-philosophy and the pawn of voice' where he discusses Husserl and Derrida on voice (Cavell, 1994: 126–7).
2 In chiasmus, the beginning and end of a phrase change positions when repeated. See Quinn (1982: 95).
3 The characters were cast this way in the premiere production, but Kane allowed for other gendered possibilities. I retain the genders here to highlight the contrasting pairs.

9

'I love you *now*': time and desire in the plays of Sarah Kane

Robert I. Lublin

Openly depicting acts of extreme physical and sexual brutality, Sarah Kane's *Blasted* challenged its initial audience in ways that few other plays had done. Certainly other works depicted violence and sex onstage, but *Blasted* lacked the moral signposts whereby audience members could readily comprehend the action taking place. The result was a play that assaulted the senses without making easy sense of what was occurring.

Registering the complexity of *Blasted*'s moral world, Ken Urban has convincingly argued that Kane manifests in her works an 'ethics of Catastrophe', invoking Howard Barker's theatrical lexicon to begin to map out the difficult moral topography of Kane's plays (Urban, 2001: 37). Crucial to Barker's notion of a Theatre of Catastrophe is the avoidance of simple notions of good and evil that remove from audiences the responsibility of engaging human beings as multifaceted, often contradictory individuals. Barker calls for 'the abolition of routine distinctions between good and bad actions, the sense that good and evil co-exist within the same psyche, that freedom and kindness may not be compatible' (Barker, 1993: 52). Overlapping seemingly discrete moral categories, the Theatre of Catastrophe offers no simple solutions; nor does it provide a sense of redemption that might assuage feelings of disjunction or anxiety.

Kane allied her work with Barker's theories when she stated that *Blasted* does not provide a moral argument (Saunders, 2002a: 27). To each of these difficult experiences she brings stark fidelity, but not reductive solutions. Kane peoples her plays with morally complex characters who live in a judgement-free universe. We cannot, therefore, seek for the source of their motivations through established morality, in an individual's attempts to do what is 'right' or 'wrong'. Rather, the stimulus for Kane's characters can be found in the overwhelming and amoral 'desire' that compels their actions.

In Lacanian psychoanalysis, desire is the consequence of the fracturing of identity that occurs upon entering into language as a child, when one first realises that there is a separation between the individual perceiving and that which is perceived. Desire is one's wish to fill the gap or 'lack' between the wholeness that precedes language and the uncertainty that defines individuals who have entered into social construction. In an attempt to satisfy this lack and replace what has been lost, subjects go from one experience to another, trying to recover the sensation of fullness (Slethaug, 1993: 531). However, as Judith Butler explains, desire 'is never fulfilled, for its fulfilment would entail a full return to that primary pleasure, and that return would dissolve the very subject which is the condition of desire itself' (Butler, 1995: 381). Because desire cannot be fully satisfied, it continually motivates the choices that people make.

Although desire is endemic to the human condition, the characters in Sarah Kane's plays suffer from overpowering, irresistible desire; one that can scarcely be deferred for a moment before it once again exerts its demands on the subject. For Cate in *Blasted*, desire manifests itself most potently in her need to return to the man who abused and raped her. Although she has begun a relationship with someone else, Ian says 'You're more mine than his' (16). Cate responds 'I'm not', but her actions bear out the truth of Ian's assertion. Cate despises Ian but cannot bear to be away from him. Consequently, even after she has been physically, emotionally and sexually abused in the night and effected her escape the next morning, Cate chooses to come back to the hotel room and to Ian. Only by returning to her abuser can she answer the demands of desire, though she would be loath to ever use the word 'love'. When Ian would kill himself, Cate empties the bullets from the gun to deny him the opportunity. And later, after leaving to find food, Cate returns yet again. Graham Saunders has noted that Cate's determination to go back repeatedly to Ian derives in part from her wish to revenge herself on him (Saunders, 2002a: 68–9), but her initial decision to return is motivated by her literally overwhelming desire to be with him. At that moment, Cate is unaware that the Soldier has rendered Ian helpless; she chooses to be with him even though doing so puts her at risk of being sexually assaulted again.

If the moral universe of *Blasted* was defined by feminist values, one might argue that Cate is in a vicious cycle from which she cannot extricate herself. The play would then forward the simple argument that men are animals and that women must not allow themselves to enter such situations. However, when Cate returns, Ian is in no condition to continue abusing her. He is blind and in pain, and the abusive relationship is rendered obsolete – he cannot take care of himself, let alone continue to offer Cate a physical or sexual threat. Alternatively, the play could be seen as a call to empower women by allowing Cate the opportunity to revenge herself on her abuser. Ian realises that Cate deserves the opportunity: blind and powerless, he says 'You come for me, Catie? Punish me or rescue me makes no difference' (51). In this instant, the play has the opportunity to bend to an easily explainable and widely laudable plot: audiences would likely approve of any violence Cate inflicted upon Ian. Instead, Cate simply ignores Ian's comment and the feminist possibilities of the moment are lost. However, Kane has noted that she does not feel responsible for creating 'woman's writing' (Stephenson and Langridge, 1997: 134). The 'truth' in this instance is that Cate feels compelled to be with Ian. Michael Billington has observed that, in Kane's works, love is a source of 'obsession, corruption, ownership and breakdown' (Saunders, 2002a: 107). Yet, even as Kane acknowledges the most destructive aspects of this relationship, she does not judge it. Rather, she devotes her efforts to faithfully depicting a pair of individuals in a troubled world as they struggle to survive and answer the compulsion of their personal needs.

It is for this reason that Ian commands more pity than disdain. He needs Cate to the extent where 'at times Ian's tactics to keep Cate to him become desperate, even farcical' (Saunders, 2002a: 55). And yet they are driven by love, reaching the point of absurdity only because they have to compensate for the abuse he has inflicted on Cate. What is worth noting, however, is that this abuse results from desire as well. Beyond adhering to Lacan's notion of desire, Kane's plays also demonstrate the understanding of desire prescribed by Gilles Deleuze and Félix Guattari. In *Anti-Oedipus*, they argue that the human, as a complete entity, does not exist: 'We live today in the age of partial objects, bricks that have been shattered to bits, and leftovers' (Deleuze and Guattari, 1977: 42). Consequently, people exist as collections of loosely connected 'machines'. Machines are here understood to be the innumerable sources of desire that can result from one's physical, social or psychological construction.

According to this definition, Ian's penis could be seen as a desiring machine that works to produce the means of its sexual satisfaction. This notion of 'desiring production' is at the heart of

Anti-Oedipus, and suggests that desire is more than an indication of lack: it is a source of action. As Deleuze and Guattari explain, desiring production 'is at work everywhere, functioning smoothly at times, at other times in fits and starts. It breathes, it heats, it eats. It shits and fucks' (Deleuze and Guattari, 1977: 1). Ian's psychological desire obliges him to do everything in his power to convince Cate not to leave. Concurrently, his sexual desire demands instant gratification. The compulsive nature of Ian's libidinal needs can be noted in the fact that mere moments after he holds Cate's hand over his penis and masturbates to orgasm (15), he asks Cate to 'Make love to me' (22). She does not want to, and Ian sexually assaults her during the night. The next morning, Ian has two more orgasms in rapid succession, one when he pleasures himself on her unresponsive body (27) and again when Cate performs oral sex and bites him as he comes (31). Ian literally cannot help but pursue the sexual aggression that will drive away the one he loves. Heiner Zimmerman suggests that, when Ian says 'I love you', it is 'merely the prelude to or excuse for sexual violence' (Zimmerman, 2001: 176). However, it is equally likely that Ian both loves her and sexually exploits her. Insight into the nature of Ian's destructive love for Cate can be found in *Crave* when A says 'And I am shaking, sobbing with the memory of her, when she loved me, before I was her torturer, before there was no room in me for her …' (177).

Like his excessive sexual desire, Ian's smoking and drinking habits are also self-destructively out of control. Shortly after he answers the needs of his addictions, they reassert their control over him and demand satisfaction. One drink is completed and he immediately pours another. The spreading cancer in his chest doubles him over in agony, but after it passes he quickly lights another cigarette. In this manner, time is something to be feared, for it brings with it the renewed compulsion of one's desires mere moments after they have been fulfilled. Ian cannot stop even though he knows the cigarettes and alcohol are rapidly killing him. Kane has created in Ian a man we can truly pity, for he is driven to pursue actions that guarantee both his physical and his emotional destruction.

The Soldier similarly deserves our pity, for he also engages in horrible actions to answer the demands of his desire. When he eats both of the breakfasts and drinks the last of the gin, Ian says 'worse than me' (40), drawing a parallel between the two who differ mainly in degree. But the Soldier may deserve even more sympathy than Ian, for all of the atrocities he enumerates and performs onstage were first committed against the woman he loved. Holding Ian at gunpoint, the Soldier details a series of horrors: 'Col, they buggered her. Cut her throat. Hacked her ears and nose off, nailed them to the front door ... He ate her eyes. Poor bastard. Poor love. Poor fucking bastard' (47; 50). The Soldier's decision to rape Ian and then suck out his eyes results directly from his wish to experience what was done to Col.

More than expressions of violence, the Soldier's actions are part of a sadistic fantasy based on the notion that by enacting this cruelty, he will be able to feel it himself. As Lacan explains, 'For a sadistic fantasy to endure, the subject's interest in the person who suffers humiliation must obviously be due to the possibility of the subject's being submitted to the same humiliation himself ... It's a wonder indeed that people would ever think of avoiding this dimension and could treat the sadistic tendency as an instance of primal aggression pure and simple' (Lacan, 1977: 16). Accordingly, while he rapes Ian, '*The* **Soldier** *is crying his heart out*' (49). After he has opened himself up to what Col experienced, the Soldier feels the pain of irresoluble desire – the loss of one he loves entirely – and takes his own life.

Beyond dictating the actions of the individuals who inhabit *Blasted*, desire also serves to determine the form of the drama itself. As Kane has noted, 'the form and content attempt to be one – the form is the meaning. The tension of the first half of the play, this appalling social, psychological and sexual tension, is almost a premonition of the disaster to come' (Stephenson and Langridge, 1997: 130).

The structure alters to reflect the overpowering desires of the characters. By the end, the play's content and structure are truly one as the *mise-en-scène* conforms entirely to Ian's moment-by-moment needs. Blind and alone in the room, Ian answers the compulsion of his mind and body, with the stage going into darkness between each action he performs. Thus, the lights come up on Ian masturbating, answering the impulse of his penis as a desiring machine that demands sex. Then the stage goes to darkness. When the lights come up again, they show Ian attempting to strangle himself and answer the demands of all of his desires at once. Darkness. The lights next come up on Ian defecating, answering the demands of his anus. Darkness. This continues until Ian 'dies with relief' (60), as he is finally released from the compulsion of desire. Of course, Kane does not make it that easy for him, and he is resurrected again. Rather than continue to suffer alone, Cate returns and gives him the food and companionship he needs to go on. For this reason, Kane considers *Blasted* an optimistic play (Sierz, 2001a: 106). At the end of the play, the irresistible desires that created hell on earth become the very ones that allow Ian and Cate to give each other the gift of survival (Urban, 2001: 46). Detached from morality, desire serves simultaneously as the cause of suffering and the source of its relief.

With each play that Kane wrote after *Blasted*, she further engaged and distilled the exploration of desire. At the heart of her next work, *Phaedra's Love*, is the eponymous heroine's incestuous, uncontrollable need for her stepson Hippolytus and his inability to feel anything. Based on Phaedra's drive to submit herself to the impossibility of her desire, to lose herself within it, Greig has suggested that she is the opposite of Hippolytus (Greig, 2001: xi). Phaedra's passion spills on to the stage in dialogue motivated by desperate need: 'Can't switch this off. Can't crush it. Can't. Wake up with it, burning me' (71). Conversely, Hippolytus demonstrates a stoic unwillingness to feel anything at all. He states that he is not even living his life, but rather 'Filling up time. Waiting' (79). On further examination, however, the two characters are more alike than not.

Imitating a convention of classical drama, *Phaedra's Love* begins *in medias res*, the story already well under way. Where Kane begins her play, Phaedra is already in the thrall of desire and Hippolytus seems impervious to its demands. However, Hippolytus is not entirely indifferent to desire. Rather, he is suffering from unrequited desire. Hippolytus would argue that he cares about nothing, but he becomes furious when Phaedra mentions an unseen character called Lena (83). Hippolytus seems to have experienced the very same desire for Lena that compels Phaedra to seduce her stepson. For both characters, the consequence of unrequited love is shattering.

Hippolytus' love for Lena perverts into his attempt to suppress all desire and avoid further pain. But desire constitutes human subjectivity. Attempts to quash it are akin to killing oneself while still breathing. He eats, he has sex, but he cannot feel anything at all. Phaedra, on the other hand, takes the more direct route of suicide when her desire is rebuffed and its satisfaction refused. Before she does, however, she leaves a letter accusing Hippolytus of raping her. Kane has said that 'what Hippolytus does to Phaedra is not rape – but the English language doesn't contain the words to describe the emotional decimation he inflicts' (Stephenson and

Langridge, 1997: 132). Yet, as Stefani Brusberg-Kiermeier has noted, 'Phaedra's slander is not a betrayal, it is a sign of love' (Brusberg-Kiermeier, 2001: 171). Moreover, it is strong enough to motivate Hippolytus to feel again. Phaedra's accusation, backed by her suicide, thrusts Hippolytus back into the process of desiring production by acknowledging his ability to have a meaningful influence on those he touches. Consequently, Hippolytus openly embraces his own destruction, for it is only by accepting his tragic fate that he can truly live. Accordingly, it is without irony that Hippolytus, broken and dying, states 'If there could have been more moments like this' (103). As painful as this moment of feeling is, Hippolytus finds it preferable to his previous abnegation of desire.

Kane considered the relationship between desire and pain further in her next work, *Cleansed*, which almost completely discards traditional notions of a realistic plot to explore the nature of love in what appears to be a series of experiments. Throughout the play, couples are tortured by the doctor/drug dealer/guard Tinker to determine the extent of their love for one another. Here, Kane tests the theory 'love conquers all' to establish what people can ask of their lovers. She writes, '*Cleansed* was written by someone who believed utterly in the power of love' (Sierz, 2001a: 117). However, the optimism of *Cleansed* is a considered optimism; one that acknowledges the complexity of human desire. Accordingly, the first relationship presented includes an idealist and a realist, with the play giving preference to the latter.

Convinced of love's ability to transcend all boundaries, Carl puts his ring on Rod's finger and says 'I'll always love you … I'll never betray you … I'll never lie to you' (110). To each of Carl's assertions, Rod responds with laughter. The older of the two, Rod realises that love is not outside of time. Thus he asks if, after only three months together, Carl would die for him. Carl does not hesitate before saying yes, but he fails to convince Rod, who will not swear the same. Rather, all that Rod will promise is that he loves Carl now (111). Carl wants more, but Rod knows better than to promise more than he is capable of delivering. And he is right to do so, for, when Carl is tortured by Tinker, he betrays Rod in order to save his own life. At the moment of his suffering, the former idealist's desire for life outweighs his desire for love.

The fact that it is the realist who chooses to die for his lover suggests a more profound form of optimism than a blind embracing of love as all-powerful. By having Rod choose to die for Carl, Kane shows how one can love genuinely in a flawed world. Moreover, it is only by rejecting idealism that Rod can stay with Carl after being lied to and betrayed by him. Rod cannot forgive Carl, but he also will not stop loving him. The image of Carl crying at the end suggests that he truly has learned to love Rod and will continue to do so even though he is gone.

The notion that love does not end with death is treated in the relationship between Grace and her brother Graham. Although Graham dies in the first scene of the play from a heroin overdose, Grace's actions continue to be motivated by her love for him. In this way, Graham continues to exist as a source of Grace's desire, the object of her love. Kane has Graham appear, interact and even make love to Grace, showing the presence that people can have in others' lives even after they are gone. The relationship between Graham and Grace is an incestuous one, but Kane chooses to emphasise the power of their love that defies moral proscription and reaches the heights of sexual fulfilment (120).

Truly in love, Grace and Graham are the object of and resolution to each other's desire. Consequently, each serves in large part to constitute the other's subjectivity, and it becomes difficult to determine where one ends and the other begins. Kane manifests the symbiotic nature of their relationship onstage by having Grace subsume the identity of the dead Graham. She dons his clothes, assumes his mannerisms, and later has her breasts removed and appears wearing strapping around her groin suggesting that she has a prosthetic penis.

With this relationship specifically and the play generally, Kane suggests that love offers the possibility of answering the demands of desire in a full and complete way (Saunders, 2002a: 91). Even Tinker, who spends most of the play systematically destroying love in others, ironically wants to find love himself (Saunders, 2002a: 98) and, in Cleansed, Kane challenges the notion that desire cannot be fulfilled by suggesting that love offers the possibility of complete satisfaction.

With Crave,[1] however, Kane offers a darker notion of love that is epitomised in A's comment, 'Only love can save me and love has destroyed me' (174). In this work, Kane maintains her belief that love has the power to answer fully the demands of one's desire, yet also stresses its consonant, opposite ability to destroy the person who embraces its possibilities. As Sierz has noted, 'the play is about aching need and suggests that what we most crave may be the same thing that cripples us emotionally' (Sierz, 2001a: 118). Kane's complex play lends itself to a multiplicity of meanings with the characters simultaneously constituting discrete personalities and diverse aspects of a single subjectivity. Yet, the play's depiction of desire is clearest in its presentation of two couples: A and C, B and M.

A and C seem reminiscent of Ian and Cate from *Blasted*: A could be seen as the male, older, dominant half of an abusive relationship; C perhaps female, younger and the recipient of A's abuse. When *Crave* begins, the relationship between A and C appears to have already ended. Different from the optimistic 'Thank you' that concludes *Blasted*, the lines delivered by A and C are prompted by a failed relationship that has left both broken. C responds to the relationship in a manner similar to the way Hippolytus reacts to being burned by Lena: they remove themselves from the process of desiring production and begin a kind of living death. C says: 'I feel nothing, nothing. I feel nothing' (175).

The pain that A feels after losing C finds articulation in the longest monologue of the play. A's unremitting desire compels an outpouring of the love which has now gone. The words seek to fill the vacant space and are doomed to continue unabated since A has destroyed the object of desire. The longest monologue A delivers reads like an aria to love (170). However, the monologue is interrupted by C, who starts saying, over and over, 'this has to stop this has to stop' (170). The love A felt was the one that destroyed C. Now their absence leaves A empty, with no apparent likelihood of finding respite or relief.

Death similarly seems to offer the only possibility for release in the relationship between B and M. Throughout *Crave*, their relationship goes back and forth as each hurts the other in an attempt to get what he or she needs. Both seek loving relationships and M wants a baby, but neither is able to answer the other's desires. Rather, they repeatedly hold out to each other the hope of satisfaction, only to withdraw it at the moment when the possibility of happiness appears. As B says, 'I keep coming back' (175). Their cycle of abuse continues, as they keep needing what they refuse to give one another.

Structurally, *Crave* conforms to the dictates of the various characters' desires that compel their dialogue and constitute the play. Time thus exists entirely as a subjective experience, understood by the audience in the way it is expressed in the anguished discourse of the characters. Kane employs this dramaturgical approach and its concomitant subjective representation of time again in *4.48 Psychosis*.

In her last play, Kane pushed her exploration of desire to the threshold of insanity, examining in detail the subjective manner in which a single consciousness experiences the irresistible and overlapping desires that find representation in all of her plays. Near the beginning of *4.48 Psychosis*, the speaking subject makes a list of the poignant 'lacks' that define themselves in the moment: 'I am sad / I feel that the future is hopeless and that things cannot improve .../ I can't eat / I can't sleep / I can't think' (206–7). Continuing for three pages, this inventory records the multiple points of desire that currently overwhelm the subject. Each line reveals a shortcoming that the speaker acknowledges in the self, but more importantly the list in total highlights the multifarious desiring machines that are working concurrently to achieve satisfaction. All at once, the speaker wants to attain happiness, experience a hopeful future, eat fully, sleep soundly, think clearly, love deeply, touch sensually and share completely. As Kane has noted, 'Many people feel depression is about emptiness, but actually it's about being so full that everything cancels itself out' (Sierz, 2001a: 110). The various, competing desires are crushing, driving the subject to find some way to relieve the tension of living.

Three possible solutions present themselves in the course of *4.48 Psychosis*. The first is to find a love that will answer all of their needs at once, but the play suggests that such a love does not exist: 'fuck you God for making me love a person who does not exist' (215). The speaker's unmitigated desire drives them to find a second solution, and seeks respite in prescribed medicine: 'let's do the chemical lobotomy, let's shut down the higher functions of my brain and perhaps I'll be a bit more fucking capable of living' (221). This line from the play reflects what Kane has said in an interview: 'I think to a certain degree you have to deaden your ability to feel and perceive. In order to function you have to cut out at least one part of your mind' (Saunders, 2002a: 114), but the drugs have side effects, essentially producing their own needs as additional drugs are required to handle the pernicious consequences of their side-effects.

The third and last solution *4.48 Psychosis* offers for desire's overpowering compulsion is suicide. The fact that this is the choice Sarah Kane made herself has, naturally, coloured responses to her final play. Yet, since this work builds so carefully on the psychological territory that Kane explored in each of her earlier works, we would do best to consider it primarily as a work of art, and not as a suicide note. Through its complex composition *4.48 Psychosis* offers the reader and audience member the unique opportunity to grapple with the forces of desire that compose (even as they threaten) our very subjectivity.

Notes

1 Special thanks to Matthew Flynn, Wendy Nystrom, Geordarna Poulten and Lynneric Powell, students at UMass Boston, for taking part in a reader's theatre performance of *Crave* to help me as I worked on this play.

10

Sarah Kane and Antonin Artaud: cruelty towards the subjectile

Laurens De Vos

When Paule Thévenin, a close friend of Antonin Artaud, and Jacques Derrida collaborated in 1986 on the publication of *Antonin Artaud: dessins et portraits*, in which both their essays comment on the artist's drawings, they touched upon a notion that had remained far too unnoticed. Only three times in his extensive oeuvre does Artaud use the term 'subjectile', but, despite the low frequency, his whole work is permeated with the idea of it. Apparently, every time he was speaking of his drawings, it was perceived as a hostile element. The first time Artaud came up with the word was in a letter of 23 September 1932 to André Rolland de Renéville, which he concluded by expressing his disappointment of being betrayed by the subjectile: 'Enclosed a bad drawing where what is called the subjectile has betrayed me' (Artaud, 1970: 171). This part of the letter was torn off, as Paule Thévenin comments, 'doubtless to make the trace of this treason disappear' (Thévenin, 1998: 16). Describing another drawing in 1946, Artaud is somewhat more forthcoming in his explanation about the subjectile.

> This drawing is a grave attempt to give life and existence to what until today had never been accepted in art, the botching of the subjectile, the piteous awkwardness of forms crumbling around an idea after having for so many eternities laboured to join it. The page is soiled and spoiled, the paper crumpled, the people drawn with the consciousness of a child. (Thévenin, 1998: 26)

To Artaud, the subjectile is an impediment to his artistic creativity, as he longs to mix genres whereby form and content coalesce. Although he never explicitly dwells on what he exactly means by this word, and in what way it could possibly betray him, from the numerous fragments with complaints and illustrations we may get a fair picture of the subjectile. In a third extract from a text written in February 1947, Artaud once again expresses the sabotage by the subjectile that he tries to bypass, or rather, that he fights back against most vehemently.

> The figures on the inert page said nothing under my hand. They offered themselves to me like millstones which would not inspire the drawing, and which I could probe, cut, scrape, file, sew, unsew, shred, slash, and stitch without the subjectile ever complaining through father or through mother. (Derrida, 1998: 136–7)

With regard to his drawings, Artaud faces difficulties in the treatment of the paper, which most often behaves like a passive receptacle, an inert support of the representation above. One of the notes added to Artaud's texts in his *Oeuvres complètes* comments on the subjectile as follows:

> Translation of the Latin *subjectilis*: what lies beneath, the subjectile designates in painting the external surface of a material which must be coated with tar, paint, varnish or a similar coating. Synonym: support. It is in this sense of support that Antonin Artaud uses it, the support being like here the sheet of paper on which he draws. (Artaud, 1984b: 356)

The paper itself, then, just like the painter's canvas, appears as an adversary, and to draw or to paint comes close to a battle or a conquest. It should suffer under the pen or paintbrush as a living being that is being cut, stitched in, carved up and scraped in order to take hold of the pure expression of life. As Derrida remarks in his philosophical treatise on these drawings, Artaud seeks to find a means to incorporate the material used for a painting or drawing into the piece of art itself. The canvas or paper should not merely be the support of a representation but rather become an integral part of the body proper. According to Artaud, there must not be any distinction between the subjectile and the representation. On the contrary, both should merge in a presentation, as he makes clear in his astonishing, prize-winning essay on Van Gogh. Artaud describes the canvas almost like a hymen; Van Gogh's paintings bear 'the suffering of the prenatal' (Artaud, 1988: 499). With his wild, vivid strokes, the painter almost literally tears apart the canvas. Here, the subjectile belongs undifferentiated to the body itself without being degraded to prosthesis, as has so often been the case in western art. Artaud's drawings too bear witness to the closure of representation in favour of an uncontained, unframed and autonomous work, as he burned holes in them with cigarettes, carved them up and scribbled notes in every possible corner.

The traces of burning and perforation belong to a work in which it is impossible to distinguish between the subject of the representation and the support of this subject, in the *layers* of the material, between the upper and the lower, thus between the subject and its outside, the representation and its other. It is really a question of destruction. (Derrida, 1998: 88–9)

Completely against western tradition, the subjectile must be botched and moulded until it conforms to what it evokes. Artaud does not so much believe in the form of a piece of art, which should on the contrary be deformed in order to launch its impact on the senses and to give free rein to its forces. Artaud's attitude towards his drawings is similar to what he had argued in his correspondence with Jacques Rivière, who had shown faith in his poems, if only they would attest to more craftsmanship. While Artaud defends the apparent awkwardness of his drawings as being not of 'a man who does not know how to draw, but of a man who has abandoned the principle of drawing' (Artaud, 1984a: 340), in the same way he had done so at the start of his career to claim vigorously for his poems the right to exist:

For I cannot hope that time or effort will remedy these obscurities or these failings; this is why I lay claim with so much insistence and anxiety to this existence, aborted though it be. And the question I would like to have answered is this: Do you think that one can allow less literary authenticity and effectiveness to a poem which is imperfect but filled with powerful and beautiful things than to a poem which is perfect but without much internal reverberation? ... It is the whole problem of my thinking that is at stake. The question for me is nothing less than knowing whether I have the right to continue to think, in verse or in prose. (Artaud, 1988: 32)

In order to actually botch the subjectile, to make it suffer instead of just using it as a passive support, one must be cruel. If Artaud wants to succeed in replacing the dead material of the subjectile, which is foreign to the work itself, with its reappropriation, he must find a letter beyond the letter, in order to express the inexpressible. The subjectile bars the way to the real thing, the truth, the infinite. Artaud goes to war repeatedly combating the order of the linguistic which he feels imprison and chain him. To go back, one needs to traverse the subjectile, the hymen, back to the prenatal. It goes without saying that this is a most painful and cruel process, and Artaud knows that, in the pursuit of the botching, the perforation, the scratching and the laceration of the subjectile, he is staking his life. To draw, to write or to paint are, therefore, cruel acts. Ink has become a metaphor for blood, which is being shed while writing. As long as the subjectile remains dead matter, no more than an inert and exterior receptacle to the subject, it had better be immediately abandoned: 'The screen must be traversed by an expression that attacks the subjectile, hurls its projectiles against it, bombarding it until it bleeds, sets it on fire, and perforates it. Cruelty is always unleashed *upon a subjectile*' (Derrida, 1998: 103).

It is the notion of the subjectile that can provide an explanation for Sarah Kane's use of cruelty, as well as for her 'linguistic turn', whereby cruelty apparently has disappeared. Cruelty has a similar function in Kane's plays to Artaud's Theatre of Cruelty. Although Kane had only started reading Artaud relatively late in her career as a writer, all of her plays bear the mark of ideas from the Theatre of Cruelty, which aims to unite 'the spiritual and the physical' (Knapp, 1980: 23). Form ought to comply with force.

According to Jacques Lacan, the human subject is burdened with a rupture, a lack that emerges from the introduction in the Symbolic Order. This entry takes place when the infant is forced to leave the pre-oedipal world of the Real, after which this castrated subject now needs to compose their identity by means of the external, linguistic source of the Other. The idea that the self cannot be found within oneself but emerges from a 'borrowed' identity, gives rise to the subject's sense of rupture which Kane's characters cannot bear. Consequently, the denial of the symbolic castration and man's self-alienation results in the artistic endeavour to abolish representation in favour of presentation; in other words, to pierce through the subjectile.

What Kane and Artaud share is not just a predilection for violence onstage but the presentation of a motherly, pre-oedipal world that has not been corrupted by the Symbolic Order. Cruelty reaches beyond language and cannot be controlled or contained by words. Contrary to one's thirst or hunger for something, one's hatred for or fear of something, pain is entirely internally directed: 'physical pain – unlike any other state of consciousness – has no referential content. It is not *of* or *for* anything. It is precisely because it takes no object that it, more than any other phenomenon, resists objectification in language' (Scarry, 1985: 5). It destroys its relations to the external world. 'Physical pain does not simply resist language but actively destroys it, bringing about an immediate reversion to a state anterior to language, to the sounds and cries a human being makes before language is learned' (Scarry, 1985: 4). In other words, pain contributes in attacking the subjectile of language, and offers a way to terminate its impediments. A reversion to the pre-symbolic world that is marked only by groans and cries as the result of the infliction of pain involves the disintegration of language.

In Kane, this is an ongoing process beginning in *Blasted* with Cate's hysterical fits and the snapshots exposing a speechless Ian. Phaedra's inability to speak in front of Hippolytus' rudeness is repeated in Carl's silent scream as he looks at Grace in *Cleansed*. *4.48 Psychosis* is written in a language that is reduced to a bare minimalist script. After the bodily amputations, language as a means of communication is being amputated here. The 'consolations of form' (Murdoch, 1961: 20) are being severely attacked; neither does language still suffice to give shape to the hidden truth. Instead, silences, single words or phrases take over.

In fact, Artaud's development is not entirely dissimilar to Kane's. After all, at the end of his career, Artaud seems to have had greater confidence in the spoken word to express the ideas behind the Theatre of Cruelty. With his radio play, *Pour en finir avec le jugement de Dieu* Artaud 'believed that, through a theatre of voices, he had come closer to the *Théâtre de la cruauté*' (Finter, 1997: 18). Moreover, some months before, Artaud had stunned his audience with a performance given at the Vieux-Colombier in which he manipulated his language until it met his requirements. Hence, language and text are by no means erased from the Theatre of Cruelty; on the contrary, in the end, voice is the only remaining element. It would be a mistake to devalue these performances as off-course experiments that had drifted away from the idea of a Theatre of Cruelty. In fact, Artaud expected that his radio play would 'provide a reduced model of what I want to do in the *Theatre of cruelty*' (Artaud, 1974: 127).

Thus, paradoxically, although it was her visual theatricality and cruelty that had acclaimed Kane as an inheritor of Artaud's theatre, it is my belief that *4.48 Psychosis*, more than *Blasted*, *Phaedra's Love* or *Cleansed*, is the most faithful to the spirit of the Theatre of Cruelty. Cruelty has not been abandoned, only now it is no longer caught in theatrical imagery but is internalised in language itself. The corporeality of cruelty has been transferred to the verbal nature of language, and thus contributes to the process of words becoming spatial. Artaud's language crisis poses the same questions, yet comes up with slightly modified answers. Helga Finter too recognises the cruelty in Artaud's later work in which the voice is given additional prominence.

The retreat to the theatricality of radiophonic work makes sense in that the voices appeal directly to the individual subject's imaginary relationship to the body and thereby displace cruelty with a physical attack that puts to the test the relationship of the individual to language. (Finter, 1997: 18)

Kane's plays completely replace the visual impact that her cruelty had provoked with language. They not only depict the body on the verge of disintegration, as in Ian's snapshot series, Hippolytus' lynching, Carl's amputations and Grace's transformation, but the body of the text is under attack as well. In fact, as Howard Barker explains with regard to his Theatre of Catastrophe, 'the attempt to abolish the word becomes an attack on the body itself – a veiled attempt to remove the body from dramatic space' (Barker, 1993: 30). Thus, however big the gap might seem between the atrocious scenes in her first period and the reduction of language to almost complete silence, the latter is no more than the logical outcome of this cruelty. The breakout from the Symbolic Order that cruelty attests to, shifts from the text's contents to the body of the text itself. Whereas, intra-textually, cruelty is bodily inflicted on the characters within the drama, Kane's wish to move out of the Symbolic is extrapolated to the medium of drama itself. The plays' content – which comes down to the restoration of the Real, prelinguistic state of self-fulfilment as in Hippolytus' final state of bliss: 'If there could have been more moments like this' (103), a brightening sun in *Cleansed* or C's comfort in *Crave*: 'Happy and free' (200) – becomes increasingly more reflected in their mode of representation. This affects the drama and its audience much more, for the representing frame can no longer fulfil its sustaining function.

If Kane seeks to accomplish a reunification of the split subject, she understands that her enterprise can succeed only if she takes language itself as her target, if she burns holes in the subjectile she uses. Given the symbolic nature of words, Kane realises that such a merger necessitates a stripping down of language to its own nakedness. Language, in that case, would not merely serve as a support, a material used to build up meaning, but becomes involved in the cruelty of the Real. Once the Real has overflowed the Symbolic, the signifier has become 'an unmediated physical presence' (Sontag, 1988: xxv).

In other words, as Derrida has outlined, the subjectile ought to free itself from its material passivity and start to be colourful and rhythmic. Kane actually wants to get rid of the signifying function of language, which must, therefore, be traversed and annihilated. Hence, cruelty is an attempt to purify life of what is regarded redundant. Cruelty entails a process towards absence.

If one has the ambition to turn the subjectile from an adversary into an accomplice, one should treat language in the same cruel way as the body. Whereas previously limbs were chopped off, the next step leads to the amputation of words in the process of desubjectivity. The drive to the Real should cut down to the bone its symbolic opponent. Immediately after the persona has considered the tortures, reminiscent of Tinker's bestialities to Carl ('Cut out my tongue / tear out my hair / cut off my limbs ...' (230)), the persona has recourse to an enumeration of verbs with a destructive connotation that point at the wish to penetrate the canvas of the subjectile. Words acquire a capacity to intrude into one's physical integrity. Like the voices thrashing Grace in *Cleansed*, signifiers cease to be a mere medium, but become the thing itself. They exchange the value of receptor for the value of actor.

> flash flicker slash burn wring press dab slash
> flash flicker punch burn float flicker dab flicker
> punch flicker flash burn dab press wring press
> punch flicker float burn flash flicker burn (231)

As words have assumed this new role, they no longer pose a threat; they are a threat in themselves. Six such speech fragments succeed each other, interrupted only by small fragments of sentences. One of these, after the third series, runs: 'Victim. Perpetrator. Bystander' (231). Although most characters in Kane switch roles throughout the plays, this actually holds true for language itself too. The inertia of words as a bystander which only, like the journalist Ian in *Blasted*, render and represent things, switches to the active part of perpetrator. Harold Pinter's comment on *Phaedra's Love* perhaps applies even more to *4.48 Psychosis*, as 'the violence ... jumped right out of the page. The page itself was violent. The act of turning the page was violent. She was so naked, and her work was evidently so naked. She had no protective skins at all' (Hattenstone, 2000). In similar terms to Kane's, Artaud has challenged the substance of the subjectile against which he has struggled all his life: 'The figures on the inert page ... which I could probe, cut, scrape, file, sew, unsew, shred, slash, and stitch' (Derrida, 1998: 136–7).

As life and work merged in the work of Artaud, Kane too was determined to erase this distinction, as Pinter acknowledges:

'she was her work. It was one thing' (Hattenstone, 2000). Unity
has always been the main goal of a real Theatre of Cruelty.
Also, *4.48 Psychosis* reflects a strong inclination to make form
and content one, although this was a major preoccupation from
Blasted onwards, about which she said: 'The form and content
attempt to be one – the form is the meaning' (Stephenson and
Langridge, 1997: 130). A psychotic state demands a free form, in
which all kinds of texts come together that are no longer divided
in monologues and dialogues: medical prescriptions, biblical
passages, diagnoses, psychiatric tests merge in her last play. Even
the most basic distinction in dramatic literature, between play text
and stage directions, has become blurred. If 'Hatch opens / Stark
light' was written in italics or put between brackets, the purpose
would be clear enough. Differing in nothing from the other bits
of text among which it regularly reappears, more doubt moves in,
and some theatre companies indeed opt to have the actress say the
lines.[1] Moreover, the number of characters remains unclear; that is,
if we can still speak of characters, for the undifferentiated nature
of the psychotic has replaced personal identities with fragments of
sentences uttered by voices. Since these do not have names either,
it becomes difficult to distinguish between actor and character.

Language vanishes into thin air and along with it all certainties
of the symbolic world. The whole play is contaminated with
undifferentiated discourse and shrouded in doubt. Whereas many
productions opt for a pure monologue, Daniel Goldman in his
UK production for the Tangram Theatre Company (2006) even
staged seven women. Claude Régy's French production consisted of
Isabelle Huppert assisted only by Gérard Watkins, who remained
in the background, behind a semi-transparent veil.[2] Although
Watkins spoke the lines of what may be the doctor, his voice
inflection revealed that he was primarily the inner voice of the
psychotic body on the stage. Watkins used the same croaked,
dehumanised voice as Huppert. She sounded staccato, deprived
of every kind of emotion. Each syllable was minutely articulated,
but emerged from a mouth that seemed no longer supported by a
heart: body and soul are separated from each other.

With the internalisation of violence, language does not merely
serve as a support, a bearer of a representation or meaning, but
it becomes the message itself. As with Artaud's drawings, Kane
turns the linguistic subjectile into an active player that presents
the message by its material physicality. Signs should not refer any
more; they should speak by themselves by means of their tonality,

sound, intonation and musicality. For instance, the rhythm in *Crave* prevails over its meaning, or rather, *becomes* its meaning. Violence is incarnated in the body of language, the subjectile of the playwright. Kane carries this Artaudian, almost dadaistic materialism further towards its limits by also paying attention to typeface and type page. Thus, with *4.48 Psychosis* Sarah Kane has written a play that not typically represents, but primarily presents a psychotic condition. Especially towards the end, singular words are spread all over the page, with a lot of blank space in between them to render the silences physically.

At the end the persona is stepping out speaking her very last words: 'please open the curtains' (245). This metadramatic allusion is highly ambiguous, and, depending on the interpretation given, leaves room for two almost contradictory endings. In a first reading, the opening of the curtains symbolises a last acceptance, an eleventh-hour admittance of the world. After the unrequited love, the self-mutilation and the lobotomy, the persona eventually feels prepared to reconcile themselves to the world's imperfection. The play's last sentence, then, is a plea at liberation from their psychosis and opens up the gates to the symbolic world, which would enable them to function properly in it again. This optimistic outcome is at least supported by director James Macdonald: in the play's first production at the Royal Court's Theatre Upstairs the shutters of the studio theatre were opened, letting in the urban noise from the streets outside. This seemed to dissipate the claustrophobic atmosphere, and, as Graham Saunders commented, 'Through the choice of ending, Macdonald ensured that the intense emotions that have built up during the performance have somewhere to go' (Saunders, 2003: 102).

In my opinion, though, a return to the (in)sanity of the world in no way fits into the play's mood. *4.48 Psychosis* is a play that is utterly bleak: its atmosphere approaches *Mad* by Jeremy Weller, a play which was much admired by Kane and which equally involves 'constant exposure, without resolution' (Saunders, 2003: 102). Nowhere does the individual give the impression of attempting to shake off their depression. Rather, therefore, they open up the curtain to the Real, out of the world of language and drama into the world of silence where body and mind meet again and the subject's inherent split is undone. This is not the curtain onstage opening another fictitious world before the audience, but the curtain behind the scene, beyond the expressible, beyond the twilight zone of madness and psychosis. Speaking of Artaud's Gnostic project in which he set out to end all dualisms, Susan Sontag argues that such an attempt is a lost cause, and must end in one of three irrationalities: 'their practitioners collapse into what society calls madness or into silence or suicide' (Sontag, 1988: liii). It is no wonder that the last page is almost completely blank, for only silence can adequately render what lies beyond the Symbolic. Kane's appeal refers not to a presentation being shown as it is the case in the theatre but to the transgression of the Symbolic Order.

Once they have almost completed their trajectory towards the Real, Kane's characters experience what Lacan calls *jouissance* (ecstatic enjoyment), which brings them in a state of limitlessness and senselessness. Their pain gives way to the ecstasy of the sense of re-unification with the self, most powerfully expressed in Hippolytus' final line. In normal circumstances, the infliction of pain should prevent them from achieving this self-unification in the Real by urging them to return to the safety of the symbolic world. Yet in some cases, and Lacan abundantly refers to the excesses by the Marquis de Sade, pain is perverted into something enjoyable, depriving the pain stimulus from its protective function. In *4.48 Psychosis*, the persona overindulges in this perverse enjoyment. They cut their own arms, and on being asked why the persona responds: 'Because it feels fucking great. Because it feels fucking amazing' (217). Clearly, the subject moves on a very dangerous fault line. Through physical violence they endeavour to infiltrate the Real that remains inexpressible, the Thing that rules the realm of the *hors-signifié*.

Cruelty, thus, plays an ambiguous role, as it occurs on the brink between the Symbolic and the Real. If it provides an escape route from the chain of signifiers, it will simultaneously produce signifiers that cut short this escape and come to the rescue of the subject that is in danger of meeting the Real. Cruelty withholds the subject from erasing their essential human lack and, with it, themselves. Even the auto-mutilation that they have recourse to in *4.48 Psychosis* should be seen as an extreme attempt to comply with the Symbolic. The body is, as it were, called back in extremis to the law. Signifiers are literally carved or slashed into the skin (Verhaeghe, 1999: 172).

In addition, the cruelty that permeates Kane's first three plays fulfils this double function. On the one hand, the wish to break through the wall of language necessitates violence yet, on the other hand, the same violence also prevents this transgression by alarming the body. As much as cruelty tears down the walls of the

Symbolic in an attempt to attain the Real, it remains – however rudimentary – a kind of language too. In other words, as long as cruelty is at play, the attraction towards the Real is eventually undone by a repulsion and a retreat within the order of the Symbolic. The cruelty we meet in Artaud and the early Kane, then, is a *fort/da* game in which the subject dallies with a transgression into the abyss of the Unspeakable, but never really merges with it. This is why hope is not altogether absent in *Blasted, Phaedra's Love* and *Cleansed*; no matter how despondent Kane's worlds may be, they always return to the understandable world of the Symbolic.

In *4.48 Psychosis*, self-torture initially enables the persona to secure their existence as a subject: 'beautiful pain that says I exist' (232). Extreme measures like mutilation have to stop the subject from going beyond, for a normal, verbal use of language hardly succeeds in curbing the *jouissance*. Unconvinced by its beneficial effect, the subject asks themselves: 'How do I stop?' (226); the provisional answer to which the psyche expresses by self-inscription. Besides these instances of self-mutilation, some other signs prevent the subject from not entirely disconnecting. A set of numbers appears twice in the play, first scattered at random over half a page, later in a series beginning from 100 in which each time 7 is subtracted from the previous number.[3] These are remainders of the Symbolic Order by which the patient still keeps a grip on their mental stability. At this point, the subject does not glorify suicide, and is prepared to try to get back to the sanity of the linguistic world. The abbreviations 'RSVP ASAP' (214) are a cry for communication; the engagement to enter into a dialogue is genuine, but we comprehend that these abilities to communicate evaporate, resulting in a series of aborted words.

The persona shares the preoccupation for unification with Kane herself. The intra-textual content is extra-textually reflected in the form. Both find themselves on the brink of collapsing into the Real; during the play, however, the persona can still fall back on symbolic elements to sustain the existence, and likewise, despite the attempt to represent a psychotic mind through dramatic means, Kane does not succeed in abolishing the representing nature of her medium and turning it into pure presence. Although her plays tend to move inwards, Kane affirms that, as long as she is writing, she is framing the unrepresentable, thus making it representable after all and neutralising the dangerous affects underlying it. Graham Saunders believes 'the expression of that despair is part of the struggle against it, the attempt to negate it' (Saunders, 2003: 105): in other words, as long as the Real is downgraded to mere representation – the subject still finds themselves on sure ground. The persona in *4.48 Psychosis* knows very well that the Real cannot be rendered into words: 'I had a night in which everything was revealed to me. How can I speak again?' (205). At the end of the play, we realise that Sarah Kane, despite everything, has actually spoken again and thus presented us with a representation of the Real. We have been guided beyond the normal reality, to a point that we will never be able to face as such. *4.48 Psychosis* draws an image that has an alliance with the Real, yet it will always be a deformation of the Real. No matter how severely words are manipulated and moulded to express this dimension, as it defines itself as the Thing that can never be expressed within the symbolic dimension, this attempt is doomed to fail. There will always be a discrepancy between representations and the intentions behind that representation. At the end of the play, the persona still feels alienated from themselves, as the penultimate line reads: 'It is myself I have never met, whose face is pasted on the underside of my mind' (245). Although constantly connected with their essential self, it is a double, a shadow that always follows them closely, yet with which it is impossible to unite, until the moment the curtain is opened; but no play will ever be able to fully represent this moment satisfactorily. Here, at this point, where we leave the stage, there is no hope or respite.

Only in silence can content and form merge. Artaud too admitted that despite his adage that 'an expression twice used is of no value since it does not have two lives' and that 'once a form is used it has no more use' (Artaud, 1999: 57), every gesture, every word, was one too many. All over in the play, language is reduced to a skeleton, almost literally fading away along with the subject. In Régy's production, the series of numbers, along with the six series of destructive verbs were illuminated on the semi-transparent screen behind Huppert. Gradually, however, these three-dimensional projections appeared optically closer or deeper, so that the space behind the screen seemed to become a three-dimensional emptiness in which words and numbers were suspended. This Nothingness subtly represented the abyss before the persona. The words that the subject in Régy's production still utters and the wounds that she inflicts upon herself, are the remainders of the Symbolic Order from which she is taking her leave. The projections are the last differential reference points that are somehow a last attempt to structure the chaos of the emptiness. After a while, though, they faded away, until they were completely gone. This perfectly resembles the persona's trajectory; they too will end up in silence in order to unite body and soul and erase the human lack in favour of the completion of the self that, paradoxically, must lead to death. At the very end of the play, the subject utters: 'watch me vanish / watch me / vanish / watch me / watch me / watch' (244). To bring about the perfect and harmonious unity that escapes the Symbolic, the only possible means is through the silence that follows the dissipation of the subject. If language is an extension of the body, as Elaine Scarry contends, 'only in silence do the edges of the self become coterminous with the edges of the body it will die with' (Scarry, 1985: 33). Moreover, indeed, the persona is prepared to lay down their life in order to enjoy this 'instant of clarity before eternal night' (206), an instant that Hippolytus also embraces and wishes to experience repeatedly.

Notes

1 This was done, for instance, by Nanette Edens in a Dutch performance of the play by ZT Hollandia directed by Olivier Provily. It premiered 24 March 2005 in Den Bosch, and travelled in the Netherlands and Flanders. It was selected for the annual theatre festival 2005, which comprises the best productions of both Holland and Flanders. For details of the production see De Vos, 2005.
2 *4.48 Psychose* directed by Claude Régy with Isabelle Huppert and Gérard Watkins in a co-production by CICT/Théâtre des Bouffes du Nord and Les Ateliers Contemporains, 2002.
3 These enigmatic series of numbers are part of the 'mini mental test', which is used in psychiatry to measure the patient's lucidity.

11

Posthumanist identities in Sarah Kane

Julie Waddington

> I write about human beings, and since I am one, the ways in which all human beings operate is feasibly within my understanding. (Stephenson and Langridge, 1997: 133)
>
> Do you think it's possible for a person to be born in the wrong body? (*silence*)
>
> Do you think it's possible for a person to be born in the wrong era? (*4.48 Psychosis*, 215)

Sarah Kane's approach to questions of identity is complex. A tension can be discerned between the writer's claims and developments in her plays. On the one hand, and as illustrated by the tone of the opening citation, her comments often display strong humanist tendencies. Her claim to be able to understand other human beings by virtue of the fact that she herself is human does not appear to take into account the extent to which her understanding is mediated by her own social context. By claiming that the source of her understanding is within herself, Kane is falling back on one of the main assumptions of Cartesian humanism, which maintains that an ideal human essence is located in the capacity to reason and that it is this capacity which links all human beings. This positive appeal to a universal humanity, which assumes that 'deep down' all human beings are the same in that they are endowed with reason and conscience, is, to some extent, a precondition of social transformation. This point can be elucidated further by reference to the Universal Declaration of Human Rights, which has as its aim the advancement of improved rights and conditions for all human beings. Article 1 of the Declaration states that: 'All human beings are born free and equal in dignity and rights. They are endowed with reason and conscience and should act towards one another in a spirit of brotherhood' (United Nations, website). Neil Badmington argues that the Declaration – a document which

139

underpins western approaches to humanitarian issues – 'reveals a fundamental Cartesian humanism at work' (Badmington, 2000: 4). This is most clearly visible in the assertion made that all human beings are 'endowed with reason and conscience'. Whilst, on the one hand, the elevation of reason as the very essence or source of humanness helps to justify the establishment of a code intended to ensure the rights of all human beings, this elevation is problematic in that it assumes that human reason is given prior to, or outside, history, politics and social relations and thereby negates the significance of the social environment in the formation of reason.

Kane appears, then – at least in comments made outside her work – to subscribe to the humanist 'idea that "man" possesses some given, unalterable essence which is what makes "him" human, which is the source and essential determinant of "his" culture and its priority over conditions of existence' (Dollimore, 2004: 250). Critical challenges to this fundamental hypothesis of humanism have come from such divergent fields as feminism, Marxism and psychoanalysis. Although differing in other aspects, these 'antihumanist' approaches converge on one crucial issue: they insist on challenging the humanist assumption that the subject is given *a priori*. At first sight, the questions posited in *4.48 Psychosis*, given in the second opening citation of this essay, appear to be founded on the humanist assumption that an essential subject precedes cultural and historical conditions. These questions could be interpreted as a straightforward attempt to express the speaker's dissatisfaction with their own body or gender and the feeling of being out of sync with the dominant attitudes and beliefs of the time they live in. But given other developments in the play, particularly in terms of the formal innovations, the questions posed here could also be interpreted as an attempt to explore problems related to subjectivity in general. The idea of being born in the 'wrong body' or the 'wrong era' thus implies an incompatibility between the (essential) person or body and era in which s/he finds her/himself. However, whilst the formulation of the question instigates a split between person/body and person/era, the very possibility of such a split is what is being considered in the question. 'Do you think it's possible?', asks the voice. The question is met with a silence.

Although a theoretical departure from humanism may be espoused by anti-humanists, a complete break away from the former remains impossible, as Badmington argues: 'While the anti-humanists were declaring a departure from the legacy of humanism, Derrida was patiently pointing out the difficulties of making such a break. Precisely because Western philosophy is steeped in humanist assumptions, he observed, the end of Man is bound to be written in the language of Man' (Badmington, 2000: 9). Drawing on the work of Derrida, Badmington thus establishes a link between post-structuralism and the emergence of post-humanism. In the same way that post-structuralism does not signal a simple break away from structuralism but, rather, seeks to challenge or deconstruct its structures from the inside, post-humanism provides an opportunity to interrogate the assumptions of humanist thought without assuming that it can just step beyond these and leave them behind. Kane's work, I will argue throughout this essay, articulates the tension between a humanist and anti-humanist approach to identity and, as such, can be linked with a theoretical movement toward post-humanism. In the same way that the 'post' in postmodern does not necessarily designate an 'after' or a complete break with the modern, post-humanism announces something more like a crisis in humanism rather than a complete break with it. This crisis is not conceived as something which comes, as it were, after humanism or at the end of humanism, but as a critical flaw at the very heart of humanism. Kane's writing contains an acute awareness of this critical flaw and of the crises generated by humanist thinking.

Edward Bond claims that 'Blasted changed reality because it changed the means we have of understanding ourselves' (Saunders, 2002a: 190). In literary terms, at least, this understanding was framed by the emphasis on the identity categories that preoccupied criticism during the 1990s. Different critical approaches, including 'feminist criticism', 'postcolonial criticism', 'lesbian/gay criticism' and 'Marxist criticism', which had emerged during the 1970s and 1980s, were increasingly assumed to offer more politically progressive reading strategies than previous approaches to literary studies which, as Barry indicates, are negatively referred to during this period as examples of 'liberal humanism': 'The term "liberal humanism" became current in the 1970s, as a shorthand (and mainly hostile) way of referring to the kind of criticism which held sway before theory. The word "liberal" in this formulation roughly means not politically radical, and hence generally evasive and non-committal on political issues. "Humanism" implies something similar' (Barry, 1995: 3). Kane's approach to writing – which takes the human as its central focus and is generally evasive and noncommittal on political issues – could be regarded as a throwback to the liberal humanist tendencies that were seen as outdated and politically retrogressive by the 1990s. Yet, possibly because of the innovative and challenging nature of her work, this criticism was not levelled in the playwright's direction even though her work was criticised for lacking a clear political focus. What I want to suggest is that Kane's ambivalence and refusal to convey a clear message signals an attempt to disrupt dominant reading strategies, thereby challenging the reader and audience to think beyond received paradigms and to look beyond categories such as gender, race, class and sexuality which, by the time Kane was writing, had become a yardstick by which literary works were measured and critiqued. But this is not to say that she was dismissive of advances made in critical theory in terms of exposing and interrogating assumptions and prejudices concerning questions of human subjectivity. The playwright was concerned, however, that an overemphasis on identity politics might exclude from its enquiry critical questions facing all human beings (Stephenson and Langridge, 1997: 134). Kane's attempt to write about critical questions facing *all* human beings represents a shift in focus from the culturally and histor- ically specific concerns of the time to questions relating to human existence in a wider sense.

One difficult aspect that is explored throughout Kane's work is made manifest by the playwright's comments in the early stages of writing *4.48 Psychosis* which indicate that she is returning to a familiar theme: 'yet another play, which is about the split between one's consciousness and one's physical being' (Saunders, 2002a: 113). Although this split appears to be more pronounced in *4.48 Psychosis*, it is not, as Kane's comment indicates, the first time that she engages with this problem. In fact, it is a theme that recurs throughout Kane's writing and can be discerned from *Blasted* onward.

The question of a split between consciousness and being is a critical point upon which a line of demarcation is often established between humanism and anti-humanism. In the case of the former, Descartes's inauguration of modern subjectivity – which is often taken to represent the inauguration of humanism – institutes the split between mind and being. Descartes's deduction 'I think, therefore I am' (*cogito ergo sum*) effects this split by separating the act of an 'I' thinking (*cogito*) from its being (*sum*). This split, or 'Cartesian dualism', is introduced in Descartes's Sixth Meditation:

> Although ... I possess a body with which I am very intimately conjoined, yet because, on the one side, I have a clear and distinct idea of myself inasmuch as I am only a thinking and unextended

thing, and as, on the other, I possess a distinct idea of body, inasmuch as it is only an extended and unthinking thing, it is certain that this I ..., is entirely and absolutely distinct from my body, and can exist without it. (Descartes, 1997: 181)

Despite, as he discusses throughout this Meditation, the 'apparent intermingling of mind and body' (183), Descartes reaches the conclusion that the essence, or soul, of Man is located outside the body and, as such, could even exist independently of the body. Opponents to this idea of the Cartesian subject have objected to (amongst other things) the way in which this principle sets up a hierarchy in which the body is subordinated to the mind. The mind is, according to critics of Descartes, estranged not only from the body but also from other subjects and the world it inhabits. The inauguration of the modern subject thus signals a simultaneous splitting of that subject. As such, a society founded on the principle of the individual subject is, at the same time, one which is based on the violent splitting of that subject.

This hierarchical split between mind and body is exposed and dramatically overturned in Kane's first two plays, *Blasted* and *Phaedra's Love*. The literal blasting apart of the stage set at the end of scene two in *Blasted* announces more than a departure from naturalistic theatrical conventions. It also signals a challenge to 'the most basic and apparently reassuring category of the humanist aesthetic' (Dollimore, 2004: xxix): the category of the individual character who represents and reinforces the idea of the Cartesian, or humanist subject. Ian is presented at the outset of the play as the main protagonist who, as evidenced by his manipulation of both dialogue and action, is master of the situation he finds himself in and of those he finds himself with. His gradual loss of control represents a challenge to the idea of the 'I'-centred subject as the locus of meaning. The increasing fragmentation from scene three onwards emphasises the split between consciousness and physical being by foregrounding the human body and bodily practices to such an extent that the hierarchical ordering of consciousness and being is theatrically overturned. Instead of the action being motivated by Ian's consciousness, it is Ian's body that begins to direct proceedings. The stage directions towards the end of the final scene gradually take precedence over dialogue and centre increasingly on bodily functions: 'masturbating'; 'strangling himself with his bare hands'; 'shitting'; 'laughing hysterically'; 'having a nightmare' (59). A similar development occurs in *Phaedra's Love* in which Hippolytus' initial status as an isolated, self-contained individual is presented in order to be theatrically overcome. Unlike Ian however, Hippolytus actively embraces his own fragmentation and loss of control at the end of the play as evinced in his last words: 'if there could have been more moments like this' (103).

The violent division of self is made explicit in *Cleansed*, which conducts an experiment in overcoming the split: on reuniting consciousness with physical being. When asked to consider what she would change about herself, Grace responds 'My body. So it looked like it feels./ Graham outside like Graham inside' (126). Grace objectifies her own, external body and finds it to be incompatible with the way she feels inside. Descartes's assertion that an essential 'I' exists independently of the material, external body appears to be borne out here. Grace's essential self is constructed as being oppositional to her external, material self. Grace's comment is overheard by the character Tinker who takes it upon himself to grant her this wish. The mutilation of Grace is thus shown to be not an act of random violence but one provoked by Grace's previous objectification of her own body. This character's fate in the play illuminates Descartes's insight that to think the human is simultaneously to fragment and divide the human. When reflecting on what she would change, Grace separates herself into thinking self on the one hand and non-thinking body on the other. The latter is then projected out of herself and constituted as an object of and for consciousness. Once transformed into an 'extra-human' or inhuman object, the body becomes the site of violence.

Having enacted the violent separation of Grace into essential self and inessential, bodily self, the play then proceeds to explore the possibility of resolving this split. The final scene of the play shows Grace's transformation to be complete: '*Grace now looks and sounds exactly like* **Graham**. *She is wearing his clothes*' (149). The first line spoken by the double, or fused, character of Grace/ Graham is 'Body perfect' (149). The line recalls Grace's earlier wish to change her body to make it look like it feels: to resolve the conflict between inside and outside. The 'body perfect' thus signals the reconciliation of consciousness with physical being. However, the context in which Grace/Graham speaks this line produces an effect of grotesque irony as the 'body perfect' referred to is being gradually eaten away by rats throughout the scene. Rather than resolving Grace's identity conflict, the play enacts the barbaric deterioration which results from her own separation of self into an inside and outside. *Cleansed* explores the mind/body split but, significantly, does not offer any solution to this problem.

For this reason the play issues a challenge to anti-humanist (or anti-Cartesian) approaches which either promote a harmonious balance between mind and body or disavow the split altogether. Whilst the possibility of a reconciliation of the split is explored, ultimately the play suggests that the problem cannot simply be overstepped. Rather than purging the Cartesian subject of its problems, the conjoining of mind and body at the end of *Cleansed* signals, instead, the death of that subject.

Theoretically however, and from an anti-humanist perspective, the death of the subject is considered a precondition of social change: the death, that is, of the subject conceived as locus of meaning, as containing some innate, pre-given essence. In contrast to such an idealist conception of subjectivity, anti-humanists emphasise the importance of material conditions in the development of the subject. This fundamental contrast between idealist and materialist conceptions of subjectivity constitutes the heart of the debate and division between humanists and anti-humanists (see Soper, 1986, and Dollimore, 2004). If the category of the individual character is taken as 'the most apparently reassuring category of the humanist aesthetic' (Dollimore, 2004: xxix), then Kane's experimentation with character, or dissolution of character, simultaneously signals a challenge to humanist principles of subjectivity by destabilising the idea of the 'I'-centred subject. Nevertheless, formal experimentation in Kane's next play, *Crave*, along with her comments on certain features of it, illuminates the problems of merely substituting an idealist conception of subjectivity for a materialist one.

In *Crave*, Kane resists the forces of a new form of determinism whereby meaning is still located in the human, albeit in material categories such as skin colour, sex or genetic makeup rather than in the human mind. Kane's strategic use of letters to denote archetypes rather than fixed, embodied characters serves to undermine such material determinism. Although A, B, C and M are the bearers of specific meanings for Kane – which also indicate their likely age and gender – the formal absence of specificity testifies to an aversion regarding the very notion of fixed identity (Saunders, 2002a: 104). If the body has become the new object of criticism, the marker of identity so to speak, then Kane's refusal to provide any directions as to bodily specificities reveals an effort to escape such determinations. Not only does Kane experiment with theatrical conventions but she also attempts to open up a space in which identity can be thought of differently – outside boundaries of current thinking in which identity may already be prescribed by, or inscribed on, the body.

Following on from the formal innovations in *Crave*, *4.48 Psychosis* dispenses altogether with individual characters. As in *Crave*, this does not mean that characters do not emerge in the performance or reading of the play. Although a cast of three performed the first production, the number of actors and the specificities of the actors (such as age, gender and race) are not delimited by the play-text. This point is significant, as the play is not 'about' a specific character but, as already indicated in the title, more about a state of mind. On the one hand, the play foregrounds the isolated nature of this mind. 'Do you think it's possible for a person to be born in the wrong body?' asks the voice (215). The 'person' or the 'I' is thus cut off, or separated, from the body. This is emphasised toward the beginning of the play through the monologues, which express the voice's separation not only from its own body but from the bodies of others (206–7). This separation becomes a source of desperation for the voice that speaks lines such as 'I cannot be alone / I cannot be with others' (207). Separated from being, the disembodied consciousness has been rendered incapable of relating not only to self but also to others. At the same time that the split between consciousness and being is foregrounded, it is, however, simultaneously called into question by other elements of the play. The mind's implicit claim to absolute autonomy is shown to be an illusion through the multiple discourses in the play. The monologues of the 'isolated' mind are interwoven with other forms of expression such as doctor/patient conversations, medical records, fictional and biblical references. Instead of standing outside these discourses, the mind is shown to be formed within, and in relation to, these discourses. Although *4.48 Psychosis* is ostensibly about the retreat of a mind from the world, it is a play which, through the interweaving of these multiple discourses, simultaneously emphasises the mind's interrelatedness to the world.

The feeling of self-estrangement, which is explored throughout *4.48 Psychosis*, is captured in the closing lines of the play: 'it is myself I have never met, whose face is pasted on the underside of my mind' (245). The 'myself I have never met' is, however, shown to be constituted by the very 'I' that speaks, as it is the voice of the mind that produces the split or creates its own other. The paradoxical relationship between this other and the self that produces it is visualised by imagining the 'other' as a face 'pasted on the underside of my mind'. This image captures the key feature of consciousness as something which simultaneously relates to and distinguishes itself from something else. On the one hand, by distinguishing itself, consciousness posits its own autonomy. Yet, at the same time, in positing its own autonomy it subjects itself to a violent splitting. The question of the splitting of the subject is discussed at length by Hegel in the *Phenomenology of Spirit* where he describes the process of this split as both violent and inevitable: 'consciousness suffers this violence at its own hands: it spoils its own limited satisfaction' (Hegel, 1977: 51). In other words, to reflect on consciousness, to assert the freedom of human consciousness, is not just a liberating process but also brings with it a sense of being constantly estranged from one's true self (however illusory this 'true self' may be).

The process of asserting one's freedom has further implications in so far as this 'freedom' also implies a level of responsibility which, as illustrated in another section of *4.48 Psychosis*, represents a potentially unbearable burden on the individual. The most barbaric acts committed against human beings by other human beings during modern times are invoked at one point by the passage which begins, 'I gassed the Jews, I killed the Kurds, I bombed the Arabs' (227). The use of the first person pronoun is highly significant and prompts the audience or reader to wonder who this 'I' refers to which appears to take responsibility for all the atrocities accounted. The references to entirely different but equally atrocious incidents suggest a recurrence of the barbaric which is articulated in the subsequent lines 'when I die I'm going to be reincarnated as your child only fifty times worse and as mad as all fuck I'm going to make your life a living fucking hell' (227). The composition of this passage not only presents a temporary breakdown of the distinctions between different historical events but also disavows a position which would allow for the clear identification of perpetrators and victims, or innocent and guilty. The final lines of this passage capture the revulsion that this evokes: '… I REFUSE I REFUSE I REFUSE LOOK AWAY FROM ME / It's all right' (227).

The refusal to acknowledge the inhuman and the temptation to look away from it is contrasted here with a quieter voice, which simply offers a reassurance, that 'it's all right, I'm here' (228). The struggle is perhaps indicative of two different approaches to the inhuman: one which refuses to own up to it, or insists that it is always other (reproachable) humans who are guilty of inhumanity;

and another which acknowledges a collective responsibility for keeping 'our' inhumanity in check.

Although, as I have argued, Kane's writing is fundamentally concerned with questions of the human, the formal presentation of these questions avoids reinstating an essential human at its centre. Instead of being taken as a given, the question of what it is to be human is constantly explored in her writing. At the same time, this exploration illuminates the point that to think the human is simultaneously to think the inhuman. By maintaining a strong sense of the inhuman, and by undermining the oppositional logic which would insist on a strict division between the human and inhuman, Kane's work opens up a space in which posthumanist identities can be imagined and in which thinking the human can become a radically ethical process.

12

Neither here nor there: theatrical space in Kane's work

Annette Pankratz

Sarah Kane's plays pull the rug out from under our feet. They confront us with disconcerting worlds full of suffering, existential despair and violence. Critics and scholars normally attribute the disturbing intensity of the plays to their 'startling theatrical imagery' (Saunders, 2002a: 16). However, it is not the imagery alone, nor is it the plots and their succession of shocking events; it is primarily the theatrical spaces, which unsettle preconceived notions about the 'real' world, dramatic worlds and the world of the theatre.

The 'landscapes' of Kane's plays, 'landscapes of violation, of loneliness, of power, of mental collapse and, most consistently, the landscape of love' (Greig, 2001: ix), are set 'neither here nor there': *Blasted* and *Phaedra's Love* fuse present-day England with nightmarish elsewheres; the university in *Cleansed* comes across as a space between transhistorical real and fictional torture, real and imagined love; in *Crave* and *4.48 Psychosis* fixed settings give way to fragmented mind-spaces and to vast voids filled only with words.

Theatrical space

Three components contribute to the construction of theatrical space: first, the relationship between the world of the play and the 'real' world; second, the relationship between onstage and offstage, and, third, the performance space. Like all fictional texts, a play is always read against the 'real' world. We compare what we see on stage with the world as we know it, expecting the dramatic world to function according to the same physical laws and social norms (Elam, 1980: 100–6). These expectations can be either fulfilled or undermined. By means of special markers, which refer to real people, places or objects – Michael Issacharoff calls them 'definite references' (Issacharoff, 1987: 85) – plays suggest that they reflect 'real' reality. A different choice of references will create 'alternate worlds and destabilisations of superficially realistic ones' (Richardson, 2000: 68).

Specific to dramatic worlds is their division into a visible realm on stage and merely implied spaces offstage. Narratives and visual or acoustic signs connect the 'here and now' of the mimetic space, which is directly visible and which is constituted by all objects, characters and actions onstage, to a 'then and there' in the diegetic space, the more diffuse areas offstage only alluded to by words, sounds or lighting (Issacharoff, 1981; Carlson, 1994; Richardson, 2000: 69–70). The scenic re-enactment by means of iconic signs is contextualised by indexical signs pointing to areas outside of the stage. The iconic objects and characters more or less resemble the objects and people they represent. References to the area outside – by words, acoustic or visual signs – lend them a life outside of the confines of the three walls of the stage. Offstage usually functions as extension of the world on stage (Carlson, 1994: 6). Owing to the implicit focus on the 'real' world, the audience conventionally assume that the diegetic space more or less resembles their reality.

Deictic markers such as personal pronouns or adverbs help to maintain the illusion that what we see on stage is part of a dynamic, complex and complete world. The actors on stage clarify who is meant by 'I' or 'you' (Elam, 1980: 140–1). Moreover, the actors' bodies on stage and the liveness of the performance create a performance space, which is both real and virtual. A play represents an 'as-if' world, but the actors who represent it are actually present in the 'here and now' of the stage. Hence, the theatrical performance oscillates between indexicality and iconicity, between presence and representation (Pavis, 1988: 61; Lehmann, 1999: 175). The living, breathing human beings on stage share the same space as the audience. And yet, they pretend to be someone else and someplace else. We usually know how to distinguish between reality and fiction. In special cases, however, be they accidents (someone falling into the orchestra pit, for instance) or intentional textual or performative irritations, we are no longer certain.

Kane's plays manipulate theatrical space on all three levels of signification: they use diverse, often contradictory frames of reference and deconstruct deictic structures. Archaic rituals are set against contemporary sophistication; transhistorical moral values are countered with postmodern cynicism and despair. The shifting of time and space can be brought about by sudden frame breaks as in *Blasted* or it can oscillate between several positions as in *Phaedra's Love* – in both cases creating an uncomfortable balance between the known and the unknowable, challenging norms and conventions of perception. *Blasted*, *Phaedra's Love* and *Cleansed* deconstruct clear-cut relationships between their dramatic worlds and non-literary reality. The narratives and textual fragments in *Crave* and *4.48 Psychosis* explore the divisions between inside and outside, between the bodies of the actors and the narrative mindspaces of the play.

Blasted and *Phaedra's Love*: changing referentials

Blasted and *Phaedra's Love* confront the audience with eerie dramatic worlds which shift between realism and alienation. During the performance, the audience see one room whose meanings constantly vary. The '*expensive hotel room in Leeds*' (3) becomes an 'undisclosed war-zone' (Saunders, 2002a: 38), which later turns into a nightmarish 'dreamscape' (Saunders, 2002a: 45). The first part of the play situates Ian and Cate in contemporary England; the setting in the hotel room, however, already blurs the boundaries between domestic and public (Iball, 2005: 324). With the entrance of the Soldier, the mimetic space literally explodes (39) and the referential points towards all places torn by civil war. The wall separating inside from outside becomes permeable (Saunders, 2002a: 45) and '[t]he boundary between a British location and the images of a war both present in every household and kept at a safe distance by the television screen' (Berns, 2003: 65) breaks down.

By means of the Soldier the violent world offstage moves centre-stage. The indexical signs of far-away killing from the first part of *Blasted* become iconic signs. Similarly, Ian's brutality and his sexual assaults attain global and universal significance (Sierz, 2001a: 101–2; Wallace, 2004: 122–3). When the Soldier demands that Ian should write about the incredible carnage of the civil war, the journalist claims that 'I don't cover foreign affairs' (48). This distancing attitude is no longer tenable, though. The Soldier rapes Ian and sucks his eyes out. With this act, both shockingly real and symbolic, the space on stage comprises all war zones: from the blinding of Gloucester in *King Lear* to domestic violence in Britain and the war in the former Yugoslavia (Schnierer, 1996: 106; Saunders, 2002a: 54; 58–64).

After the Soldier's suicide (50), the mimetic space moves away from the specificity of the first two parts into an existential dreamscape. Rain falling through the roof of the hotel room serves as an intruding indexical sign, pointing to the natural cycles of birth and death, growth and decay. Analogous with this circularity, it is Cate and Ian again who inhabit the mimetic space just as they did at the beginning of the play. But in contrast to the first two parts and their congruence with the 'real' world, the theatrical space now transcends verisimilitude. For instance, Ian's suffering and resurrection allude to metaphysics and transcendence (Saunders, 2002a: 64).

Phaedra's Love takes up this move into the mythical and anti-transcendental. While *Blasted* works with abrupt frame breaks – from British normality, to an uncanny zone of global war, to a place of timeless suffering – to change the meaning of the mimetic space, *Phaedra's Love* is set in an ambivalent space neither wholly archaic and distant nor completely contemporary. The play blurs the boundaries between ancient Greece and Britain in the 1990s. The beginning of *Phaedra's Love* resembles that of *Blasted*: a realistic contemporary setting inhabited by someone sitting '*in a darkened room watching television*' (65). Just as *Blasted* undermines any referential stability to a hotel room, which '*could be anywhere in the world*' (3), the figure in front of the television exists in a world in-between as the title of the play, the character's name – Hippolytus – and the initial stage direction – '*A royal palace*' (65) – indicate.

The dramatic world oscillates between ironical topicality and mythical universality. Television, a radio-controlled toy car, references to 'Oxfam' (75) and the news (74) as well as the Doctor's diagnosis 'He's depressed' (65) anchor Hippolytus in the culture of young shoppers and fuckers. Likewise, the reactions of the crowd outside the palace point towards life in modern Britain. Man 1 from 'Newcastle' (98) enjoys his outing complete with barbecue and kids. Man 2 complains that 'We pay the raping bastard' (98) and claims that members of the royal family are 'nothing special' (98). The moments of death at the end of the play change the referential: Phaedra's suicide, Theseus' vow for revenge and the brutal slaughter of Hippolytus belong to the worlds of myth and ancient drama with their relentless logic of catastrophe (Brusberg-Kiermeier, 2001: 168).

The fusion of the Phaedra myth with contemporary culture at first leads to a strong sense of irony. The world of an ancient royal family in turmoil blends in with the scandals surrounding the

British royals (78; 95; Brusberg-Kiermeier, 2001: 168) and, in the light of modern mores, Euripides' and Seneca's pretexts are turned upside down. Hippolytus metamorphoses from the chaste young man of the Phaedra-myth to a blasé, over-sexed 'asshole' (Tabert, 1998: 13; see Saunders, 2002a: 74–6). His father Theseus becomes a manipulative power politician. Instead of Greek gods, who control the lives of the mortals, *Phaedra's Love* presents a God-forsaken world of coincidences and accidents. However, the merging of archaic and modern also adds a transhistorical dimension to the characters' existential angst and it lends them an anachronistic heroic grandeur.

Similarly to *Blasted*, *Phaedra's Love* makes use of the dynamics between mimetic and diegetic space and between myth and contemporary culture. At the outset, iconic signs construct the mimetic space as representation of contemporary western culture, while indexical signs allude to a mythical world offstage, in which Theseus rules absolute as 'God on earth' (96). Theseus' appearance imports this mythical realm into the mimetic space. The burning of Phaedra's body and the king's vow of revenge introduce archaic standards of behaviour, which culminate in the slaughter of his son. Situated in a space in-between, Hippolytus accepts his impending punishment (95–7) without acknowledging the morals attached to it: 'Fuck God. Fuck the monarchy' (95). Facing his end by a British lynch mob, he becomes a secularised Messiah (99) who willingly embraces death. His insistence on 'free will' (97) posits him outside the mythical world of fate induced by divine rules, while his death realises the very same fatality – created on the meta-level by the classical pre-texts. The tension between these contradictory spaces culminates in Hippolytus' paradoxical wish at the end of his life, 'If there could have been more moments like this' (103).

Cleansed: claustrophobic symbolic spaces

Cleansed zooms in on the death-scapes which occur at the end of *Blasted* and *Phaedra's Love*. In contrast to the shifts of referentiality in the first two plays, *Cleansed* operates with a continuous and enclosed 'as-if' world, in which the everyday is relegated to the space offstage. Quotidian life happens '*on the other side of the fence*' (109), occasionally intruding acoustically as the '*sound of a cricket match*' (109), '*sound of a football match*' (129) or a child singing '*Lennon and McCartney's "Things We Said Today"*' (136). In contrast to the playfulness and the rules of fair play implied by these sounds, the mimetic space is controlled by Tinker's relentless Old Testament tests and punishments. The fenced-in university thus comes to represent all places of inhuman trial and torture: concentration camps, asylums and Room 101 from George Orwell's *Nineteen Eighty-Four* (1949). At the same time, it also serves as space in which the characters experience extreme forms of love (Tabert, 1998: 16). Owing to the unspecific referential, the dramatic world attains a strongly symbolic quality, in which the characters act out the essence of the modern *conditio humana* (Rubik, 2001: 134).

The structure of the mimetic space enhances the claustrophobic atmosphere. The space on stage consists of a series of boxes within boxes – from the area inside the perimeter fence surrounding the building, the different rooms inside – white, red, round, black – to the peep-show booths in the Black Room. In this arrangement which resembles a Foucauldian panopticon (Wald, 2007: 199) the inmates cannot or do not leave the premises; moreover, most of them are entrapped in their respective environments. Rod and Carl stay in the patch of land '*inside the perimeter fence*' (109). Grace and Graham share the spaces of the White Room and the Round Room; while the Woman seems to live inside one of the peep-show booths in the Black Room.

Moving between the rooms signifies acts of transgression and/or transcendence associated with death, love and madness (Saunders, 2002a: 94–5; Wallace, 2004: 124). Tinker's mobility emphasises his godlike position, his power to observe, control and above all punish the others. When he brings characters to the torture chamber of the Red Room, they enter the realm of the inhuman, unimaginable and 'unspeakable' (Urban, 2001: 43). In this room, Tinker both punishes and creates transgressions: in order to test Carl's vows to Rod ('I'll always love you … I'll never betray you … I'll never lie to you', 110), Tinker shoves a pole up his anus, until Carl betrays his lover ('Rod not me don't kill me', 117). Tinker then cuts out Carl's tongue. Later on, he has Grace beaten up and raped by '*an unseen group of men*' (130) for her violation of the incest taboo.

Cleansed correlates mobility not only with Tinker's sadistic power but also with Robin's attempts to get closer to Grace. He intrudes into the Black Room. Furthermore, his love for Grace even makes him venture 'outside' and buy a box of chocolates (139). These contrast with Robin's inability to enter Grace's mind-space. Spatial transgressions converge with insurmountable personal distance. In the Black Room Robin *'goes into the booth that* **Tinker** *visits'* (133), watches the Woman dance, and breaks down (134). Grace also rejects his love. Afterwards Tinker has Robin eat the chocolates until he wets himself. When he is made to burn the books in the White Room, Grace ignores his distress (141). Unable to express his love, unable to break down the barrier between him and Grace and stunned by the remaining time of supposed imprisonment, Robin commits suicide (144).

Cleansed juxtaposes Tinker's ubiquitous violence and Robin's isolation with a space of transcendence associated with Grace and Graham. The sexualised relationship between Grace and her dead brother creates a mind-space in which the borders between life and death and/or between inside and outside, psyche and body disintegrate. While Graham remains mostly invisible to the other characters, Grace and the audience encounter him as 'corpo-real', as living body on stage. In her love for Graham, Grace wants to go further than resurrecting him and being physically and sexually close to him. She yearns for a total fusion with her brother, wanting to become 'Graham outside like Graham inside' (126). This wish bears ambivalent results. Tinker's electroshocks, which burn out *'bits of her brain'* (135) cannot remove 'Graham inside'; the projection of her mind remains present on stage. Turning into 'Graham outside' by means of Tinker's rather clumsy sex-change operation cannot remove Grace inside. Although Tinker calls her 'Graham' (146) and although Grace *'now looks and sounds exactly like Graham'* (149), in the mimetic space Grace remains Grace, a person separate and separated from Graham (149–51). Although the siblings speak with one voice, they continue to exist in limbo (150).

Parallel to the not-quite merging between Grace and Graham stands Tinker's relationship with the Woman. Grace and Graham's *'dance of love'* (119) and their having sex (120) are mirrored by Tinker and the Woman in scene nineteen. The erstwhile physical distance between the two breaks down. The Woman *'opens the partition* [of the peep-show booth] *and comes through to* **Tinker's** *side'* (147). This leads to sexual and mental intimacy (148–9). Mutual closeness again ties in with ambiguous identities. Tinker had addressed the Woman as 'Grace' (123; 130; 138), using her as a field of projection for his desire. Now the Woman claims that her name is indeed Grace (149), taking over the position of the other Grace, who has now become more or less Graham. Grace's changing identities, the changing Graces, and Tinker's transfer of emotions put the efficacy of the dissolution of spatial and personal boundaries in doubt.

An alternative to these attempts at moving across borders is a life in the 'here and now'. Graham and Grace attain this state after their lovemaking (120). Later in the play, Tinker and the Woman explicitly link a comparable situation with their existence in the 'here and now' (149).

The most detailed eulogy of a life in the 'here and now' comes from Rod. He tells Carl 'I love you *now*./ I'm with you *now*./ I'll do my best, moment to moment, not to betray you./ Now' (111). As soon as Rod extends the 'now' into the future ('I will always love you./ I will never lie to you', 142), he falls prey to Tinker's ruthless testing and dies. The emphasis on absolute moments of being in the 'here and now' implicitly also refers to the 'here and now' of the performance space – accentuated, for example, by Graham's resurrection in the mimetic space.

Crave and *4.48 Psychosis*: mind-spaces and performative spaces

In *Crave* and *4.48 Psychosis*, scenic re-enactment is replaced by fragmented narratives, which dissolve the distinction between onstage and offstage, between here and there, now and then. Both plays do not offer a stable referential. Tales of contemporary life, of love, rape, betrayal and loss, are juxtaposed with ahistorical narratives and intertextual fragments (Voigts-Virchow, 2001). Words, and here above all deictic markers, construct dramatic worlds, which are difficult to grasp, for the outside world is filtered through subjective consciousnesses.

In *Crave* the labels for the speakers – A, B, C and M – do not designate characters in the conventional sense. Accordingly, there are no clearly discernible relationships between them (Voigts-Virchow, 2001: 211). The dissolution of character ties in with the deconstruction of time and space. Specific references – 'This place. **C**: ES3' (187), the psychiatric wing of the Maudsley hospital in London – are juxtaposed with vague allusions to 'this city, fucking love it' (165). Passages in German, Spanish and Serbo-Croatian give the play an additional 'international consciousness' (Urban, 2001: 43). In *Crave* no one enters, and no one leaves the mimetic space. The narratives frame it as an unstable inside, which ranges from the characters' psyche and the interiors of buildings (165; 167; 181; 185; 187) to a cityscape (165; 169–70). While the inside continually alters, the complementary outside remains a blur. 'Somewhere outside the city' (155) can be almost anywhere. Hence, the pending question, 'Out, out into what?' (189) cannot be answered. The narratives import the outside and export the inside. Thoughts and memories become audible. The positions of the speakers constantly shift from past to present or from here to there. The play elegantly moves its narratives from mimetic space to diegetic space and back just with the help of words. C's first sentence, 'You're dead to me' (155), indicates a direct representation in the 'here and now' (although it remains open who the 'you' is). Later narratives transpose this to a somewhere else and a some time ago: 'Somewhere outside the city, I told my mother, You're dead to me ... Three summers ago I was bereaved. No one died but I lost my mother' (155). The dramatic world disintegrates into patches of stories set in an indefinite diegetic space. At the same time, the speakers seldom inhabit the same 'here and now'. Their monologues situate them in separate worlds. Occasional dialogues depend more on the constructions of the audience than on a stable frame of reference for all the characters. It is only in the choral passages that the speakers share the same temporal and spatial setting: 'A: What do you want? / C: To die. / B: To sleep. / M: No more' (158).

However, by speaking in unison A, B, C and M evolve into disindividuated voices: voices which furthermore echo the voices of Shakespeare's Hamlet or Eliot's Prufrock, thereby losing any sense of time, place and authenticity. The unstable narrative settings of the dramatic world take up the characters' inability to communicate and their loss of self (Wallace, 2004: 120). Either they maintain their identities as individualised 'I's, then the communication with a 'you' on the same spatial and temporal plane is hardly ever possible. Alternatively, the situation on the same spatial and temporal level coincides with the dissolution of discernible identities.

With the disintegration of characters and of a precisely defined dramatic world, the performance space and with it the actors' bodies, their voices and the rhythm of their speeches remain as the very few anchors of meaning (Saunders, 2002a: 101; 106). In the performative space, every 'here' refers to the place on stage, every 'now' to the moment of performance. Hence, some of the statements gain a metatheatrical dimension. 'You're dead to me' (155), for example, points to the conventions of fourth-wall realism, which shut the actors off from the world of the audience. 'And if this makes no sense then you understand perfectly' (159) can be read as address to the audience trying to make sense of the play; providing them with the craved-for meaningfulness of the text and simultaneously refusing to guide them meaningfully along the jumbled narrative. Some passages deliberately rely on the performative dimension of words. The succession of 'yes' and 'no' (163; 166; 186; 190), and of 'why' and 'what' (161–2; 182; 185) serve as beats in a rhythm, they do not transport any meanings apart from the meaninglessness and impossibility of all communication (Saunders, 2002a: 101).

4.48 Psychosis operates with the same post-dramatic principles as *Crave*: no clearly defined characters, no specific setting and textual fragments instead of a consistent plot line (Zimmermann, 2002). Kane's last play moves further into the mind- and memory-spaces already prominent in *Cleansed* and *Crave*. As the title indicates, it focuses on psychoses, the dissolution of the psyche and the separation of body and mind, as well as on the treatment of these states of seeming abnormality (Saunders, 2002a: 111–12; Wallace, 2004: 127). The narratives turn the mimetic space into a sequence of 'torture chamber[s]' (239), which, in contrast to *Cleansed*, are situated inside the speakers' (and the audience's) minds. The speakers torture themselves with self-doubts; they undergo therapeutic torture and they (re)present this torture as theatrical act. Reality and fiction, sanity and insanity are deconstructed and eventually become interchangeable.

In contrast to *Crave* and its plethora of ambivalent mind-spaces, one finds – or, following the argumentation of Blattès and Koszul (2006: 109), a reader or viewer can construe – references to three interrelated spaces in *4.48 Psychosis* (this would also tie in with the three speakers conventionally cast for the play; Urban, 2001: 44). The most easily discernible is the realm where therapist and patient(s) meet; the second is made up of references to the Passion of Christ; the third is a fragile mind-space or 'psychological space' (233) full of memories, thoughts and self-analyses. With this mind-space as abstract symbolic centre, *4.48 Psychosis* stages a *psychomachia*, a search for sanity, and the search for someone, which ends with the realisation that the yearned-for 'you' is a 'me': 'It is myself I have never met, whose face is pasted on the underside of my mind' (245). Recurrent metaphors of spatialisation construct the mind as a building with a 'consolidated consciousness' living 'in a darkened banqueting hall near the ceiling' (205; 227). It is possible to isolate recurring themes: the search for an 'Other', the contemplation of suicide, a reckoning with God and commentaries on the futile procedures of therapy.

The fragmented associations of the mind-space are offset by passages which recall therapy sessions. A doctor's 'smooth psychiatric voice of reason' (209) admonishes a patient not to commit suicide (210–12), not to mutilate 'hermself' (205; 216–18) and not to be emotionally attached to the therapist (236–8). Instead, the therapist offers to cure 'this state of desperate absurdity' (220) with the help of medication (219–21). Concomitant to the straight-forward representation of the sessions without interruptions from outside or inside (by a commentator or the articulation of thoughts, say), the medical discourse focuses on the patient's body and on empirically observable phenomena. In contrast to the mind-space with its welter of symbols, similes and metaphors, the space controlled by the doctor acknowledges only physical truths. In this world, metaphors are not real and mental pains are considered an illness which can be healed (211–12).

This realm of pathology differs from the pathos of suffering in the Christological space. The signs of insanity and despair from the mind-space are projected on to a saviour figure, either the sought-for significant Other and/or a metaphysical instance. The speaker can take on the role of prophet declaring what 'shall come to pass' (228). Suicide, one of the options available in the mind-space (208), here turns into a beneficial sacrifice, which fuses Gethsemane (241), the locus of Jesus' despair and fear before his arrest and trial, and Golgotha, the place of the crucifixion. The associations connected with Gethsemane correlate with the repeated emphasis on '4.48' as a moment in the hours of the early morning between 'desperation' (207) and 'sanity' (229; 242). They link the Christological space with the mind-space, setting both off from the space of therapy, which mainly focuses on the patient's body. The anxieties about fitting into the rigid pattern of sanity are rewritten as 'horizon of the soul that eternally recedes' (229). The search culminates in paraphrases of Christ's words on the cross: 'My love, my love, why have you forsaken me?' (219) and 'It is done' (242; 243). This heightens the suffering of the speaker(s) in the psychological space. At the same time, God is still dead, Biblical words belong to the many 'beautiful lies' (229). The Passion regresses into a theatrical gestus and creates an ironical distance between sufferer and suffering (215).

The three metaphoric spaces overlap and merge: the anger with God, 'for making me love a person who does not exist' (215), correlates with the adoration of 'my doctor, my saviour, my omnipotent judge, my priest, my god, the surgeon of my soul' (233) and the despair about his or her rejection (238–9). The therapeutic dialogue continues in the mind-space as ironical record of medications – from 'Sertraline' (223) to '100 aspirin and one bottle of Bulgarian Cabernet Sauvignon, 1986' (225) – as catalogue of contradictory self-analyses ('I can't make decisions … I have decided to commit suicide', 206–7) or the enumeration of aims to be achieved during therapy ('to defend my psychological space … to draw close and enjoyably reciprocate with another', 233–4).

At the same time, the soul-searching presents itself as text, as 'solo symphony' (242), made up of incoherent fragments arranged by the 'last in a long line of literary kleptomaniacs' (213). Despair and fury in the mind-space give way to a re-enactment of Christ's Passion and to a detached representation of the conversations between doctor and patient. In the end, everything is a piece of theatre, the public replay of privacy: 'Just a word on a page and there is the drama' (213). As in *Crave*, the performance space becomes the main locus for the open-ended realisation of the text. The circularity of the *psychomachia* and the ongoing performances merge in the last words, 'please open the curtains' (245).

Conclusion

The theatrical spaces in Sarah Kane's plays are constantly shifting. They take the spectators on trips to strangely familiar places. The shifts of referential and the destabilising deictic markers lead to the direct experience of the Self as Other and to an alienation of the 'normal' and 'common-sensical'. *Blasted* and *Phaedra's Love* operate with changing referentials. *Cleansed* with its series of enclosed spaces moves into anti-realistic symbolic spaces. *Crave* and *4.48 Psychosis* further withdraw from stage realism, zooming in on polyvalent mind-spaces, in which 'the outside world is vastly overrated' (189). The bodies of the actors and the public character of theatre and drama counter this narrative move inside. The performative space serves as a counter-balance to the interiority of *Crave* and *4.48 Psychosis* and enhances the dynamics of 'experiential theatre' (Sierz, 2001a: 6). These later plays force the audience to collaborate in mapping out strange territories without hope for closure; lost and 'obscure to the point of' (223) …

13

'Victim. Perpetrator. Bystander': critical distance in Sarah Kane's Theatre of Cruelty

Hillary Chute

Sarah Kane never played safe. Her plays include stage directions like *Cleansed*'s '[the] *rat begins to eat Carl's right hand*' (130) and '*Tinker produces a large pair of scissors and cuts off Carl's tongue*' (118) – as well as verbal images like the following: 'I fucked small children while they begged for mercy, the killing fields are mine, everyone left the party because of me, I'll suck your fucking eyes out and send them to your mother in a box' (227). Kane's drama is modelled on the question of *distance*: the critical distance negotiated between the ostensible 'object' – the performance – and the spectator's gaze in relation to that performance. Kane's project reinvents a process of looking; it negotiates the process of representation and spectatorship by an insistence on a collapse of comfortable critical distance. Is what and how Kane represents in her theatre *too close* for comfort? Kane's performances insist that the horror they depict is not distant, not 'only' metaphoric – or, to put it another way, as a *4.48*'s speaker maintains: 'The defining feature of a metaphor is that it's real' (211).

4.48's speaker drops, in the middle of a staccato procession of language, the determined statement, 'Victim. Perpetrator. Bystander', which well summarises – in its implied conflation of these three terms – Kane's ontology.[1] Kane not only rejects the idea of 'the world being divided up into ... victims and perpetrators' but, even more fascinatingly, she disrupts the easy position of the bystander; she rearranges the fraught process of looking at performance (Stephenson and Langridge, 1997: 133). Kane maintained that the response her first play elicited 'wasn't about the content ... but about *the familiar being arranged in such a way* that it could be seen afresh' (131, italics mine). Kane posits that her spectators are themselves victims, perpetrators and – literally, perhaps quite uncomfortably, as they watch her performances – self-conscious bystanders. Kane's plays demand a performative response to their violence but do not suggest what that response should be, navigating afresh the approach to an art object as a distant spectacle of otherness. Kane's work poses ethical challenges to its spectators or bystanders, in the sense of the ethical as 'an attitude toward what is other to oneself' (Cornell, 1995: 78). Kane performances are uncomfortable because they refuse to 'comment' neatly on the atrocities they represent. Her work is not 'kitted out with signposts indicating meaning', as the director James Macdonald puts it; Kane's theatre '[presents] material without comment and [asks] the audience to craft their own response', as she described *Blasted* (Stephenson and Langridge, 1997: 131). This is especially threatening since Kane's ethic of representation implicates us as viewers through her work's self-aware contiguity with the historical Real.

The problem of distance

Cleansed is both structured by the complicated problematic of correct distance and also about this correct distance. 'Love' is the content of *Cleansed*, and it is also the play's *form* as a performance object conscious of its spectators. Roland Barthes highlights the lover's immersion in 'the present': 'I am wedged between two tenses, that of the reference and that of the allocution; you have gone (which I lament), you are here (since I am addressing you). Whereupon I feel that the present, that difficult tense, is: a pure portion of anxiety' (Barthes, 1978: 15). *Cleansed* insists on making its spectators aware of temporality; the present that Kane metonymically represents is indubitably an encounter with anxiety. Indeed, in the sense of cruelty being both the 'blood', to use Artaud's phrase, and 'rigour', to further draw on his lexicon, Kane's oeuvre qualifies as a 'theatre of cruelty' (Artaud, 1958: 79).

Cleansed renders 'realistic' a present where the boundaries – and sadism – of a concentration camp are at large: in culture, in every spectator. The present tense of *Cleansed* refuses to register as distant – as a contained, gazed-upon object. It resists a metaphoric discourse that would fail to recognise the play's presentation of the historical Real in the now-time of performance. Since I assert that Kane's violent theatre disturbs comfortable critical distance precisely because of its *metonymic* representational ethic, it is worth pausing on my use of metonymy and metaphor. Kane's own language, the 're-arrangement of the familiar', is an apt way to describe her work as metonymic. Further, I draw on Peggy Phelan's theorising of the term; she writes, 'metonymy is additive and associative; it works to secure a horizontal axis of contiguity and displacement'. In contradistinction, metaphor 'works to secure a vertical hierarchy of value and is reproductive; it works by erasing dissimilarity and negating difference; it turns two into one' (Phelan, 1993: 150). Phelan associates the unfortunate 'cultural work' of metaphor with stubborn self-reproduction: 'the joined task of metaphor and culture is to reproduce itself' (Phelan, 1993: 151).[2] Performance, specifically, is able to resist the 'claims of validity and accuracy endemic to the discourse of reproduction' and approach the Real by moving from the aims of metaphor, reproduction, and pleasure, to those of metonymy, displacement, and pain (Phelan, 1993: 147; 152).[3] My focus here will be on Kane's disruptive, metonymic representational ethic – how her theatre '[replots] the relation between perceiver and object, between self and other' (Phelan, 1993: 165).[4] Pinter does credit to the efficacy of Kane's replotting by confessing when he read her work, 'the act of turning the page was violent' (Hattenstone, 2000).

This problematic of 'correct distance' as discussed by Hal Foster is an approach to apprehending the cultural other – here, for my purposes, the art object as other.[5] In raising the question of spectatorship and correct distance, Kane analyses the way culture talks about itself through the metaphorising act. The 'university' setting in *Cleansed*, with its explicit emphasis on borders and boundaries – where all scenes take place within a perimeter, either within a specific room of the university or, as a repeating stage direction reads, 'just inside the perimeter fence of the university' – mocks a critical discourse, rendering it virulent.[6] Tinker, the brutal dealer and 'Doctor' of *Cleansed*, is also a critic, an arbiter of culture: he reigns over a literally enclosed university, violently monitoring the discursive habits of its residents. The character Tinker, reportedly and believably, earned his name from the journalist Jack Tinker – the ultimately official 'bystander' or spectator – who first catapulted *Blasted* into a news story with his review titled 'This disgusting feast of filth'.

In demanding the displacement of correct distance, Kane's theatre claims its relevance. When he discusses spectacle, Foster appropriately names the question of correct distance one of '*critical distance*' (Foster, 1993: 18, italics mine). *Cleansed*, 'regarded as

the bleakest and most difficult of Kane's plays to date and ...
[also] certainly a punishing theatrical experience', foregrounds
the concept of spectatorship delineated by Artaud, whereby the
spectator is barraged and seized (Greig, 2001: xii). *Cleansed* works
against the gulf implied, as Foster writes, in the 'negotiation of
distance, the home culture, and the culture of study' (Foster,
1993: 13). Kane offers a performance spectacle that is not *like* the
worst aspects of a sadistic culture, but is rather contiguous with it
– to recall Phelan's most basic example of metonymy, 'the kettle is
boiling *because* the water inside the kettle is' (Phelan, 1993: 150).
'How could one speak', Foster writes, 'as Frantz Fanon might ask,
of correct distance when colonialist domination had overcoded
both bodies and psyches of colonized and colonizer alike?' (Foster,
1993: 14). Here one thinks of Kane's figure of 'Victim. Perpetrator.
Bystander', which collapses 'correct distance' and blurs 'overcoded'
bodies and psyches. The categories of spectator and object, past
and present, history and performance flow into one another in
the temporal space of Kane's performances, in which the now of
performance is metonymic of an unseeable present.

'There's been a failure by the critical establishment to develop
an adequate language with which to discuss drama', Kane accused
as she completed *Cleansed* (Stephenson and Langridge, 1997:
132). Kane's work problematises the idea of a correct distance by
presenting her theatre as a confrontation with discomfort – even for
her directors. As Greig writes, *Cleansed*'s 'physicalisation of lyrical
imagery raises the same question that dogs Kane's first three plays:
how do-able are they? ... By demanding an interventionist and
radical approach from her directors she was forcing them to go to
the limits of their theatrical imagination' (Greig, 2001: xiii). This
suffering is part of Kane's violent and *ethical* economy: it refuses the
idea of the body as metaphor through demanding its conspicuous
suffering – both psychical *and* physical, both hopeful (Grace's
crude penis graft) and pointless (Carl's punitive amputations).
Cleansed demands a performative response from its viewers in
presenting this material suffering. In a discussion applicable to
Cleansed, Phelan addresses critical distance in the work of the
performance artist Angelika Festa, who 'asks the spectator to
undergo first a parallel movement and then an opposite one.
The spectator's second "performance" is a movement of accretion,
excess, and the recognition of the plenitude of one's physical
freedom in contrast to the confinement and pain of the performer's
displayed body' (Phelan, 1993: 163).[7] The brute pain in *Cleansed*,

as in Festa, further makes the spectator feel masterless over the image presented, and in this manner halts the declarative claims of the critic (Phelan, 1993: 158).

As Beckett crucially maintains, artistic expression is such that there is 'nothing with which to express, nothing from which to express, no power to express, no desire to express, together with the obligation to express' (Beckett, 1949: 103).[8] The obligation to express, then, in *Cleansed*, is itself violent action. 'A violent and concentrated action is a kind of lyricism', Artaud proposes. 'It summons up supernatural images, a bloodstream of images, a bleeding spurt of images in the poet's head and in the spectator's as well' (Artaud, 1958: 83).

The theatre of cruelty, according to Artaud, is one in which 'violent physical images crush and hypnotize the sensibility of the spectator seized by the theater as by a whirlwind of higher forces' (Artaud, 1958: 83). Kane contextualises the motive behind the whirlwind of violence in her plays with the following simple bottom line, which we may understand to invoke Brecht's notion of excess as functional in the theatre: 'There's only the same danger of overdose [of horror] in theatre as there is in life. The choice is either to represent it, or not to represent it.' Here too Artaud's sense of the spectacle having an ethical function properly describes Kane's desire to represent 'despair and brutality' (Stephenson and Langridge, 1997: 133). As Kane put it, *Blasted* suggests 'a paper-thin wall between the safety and civilisation of peacetime Britain and the chaotic violence of civil war. A wall that can be torn down at any time, without warning' (Stephenson and Langridge, 1997: 133). Kane's articulation of how her spectacle aims to make incontestably certain the possibility of the collapse of distance between historical horror and complacent 'reality' recalls, in urgency and even in tone, Artaud's imperative call for a theatre of cruelty: 'We are not free. And the sky can still fall on our heads. And the theater has been created to teach us that first of all' (Artaud, 1958: 79).

Clearly, the vitriol of the critical attack on *Cleansed* (the syndrome of 'it has nothing to do with me; but it made me feel bombarded and disgusted') illustrates the complicated manner in which this 'theatre of cruelty' operates to comment on modes of, and discourses generated by, the interpretation of culture.[9] Kane's dismayed sense of a metaphorising critical discourse that would focus on unpacking, categorising, and hierarchicalising content (as a 'gross pageant of horrors') prompted her crucial rejections of critical discourse. 'Much more important than the content of the play', Kane asserts, 'is the form ... the form and the content attempt to be one – the form is the meaning' (Stephenson and Langridge, 1997: 130). Form *as* content is itself an anti-metaphoric ontology of performance.

A metonymically driven performance demands of its viewers a displacement of the distance that keeps a violent spectacle safely far away, consumable as other. *Cleansed*'s power draws on its rearrangement of the familiar; Kane's content, she adamantly and politically insists, is not 'new' – as in novel, easily consumable, or, most importantly, detached from any pre-existing system of violence. Moreover, Kane's work insists on a performative response to its efficacious, excessive and yet linguistically economical parade of cruelty.

Metonymy as ethic of representation: history and violence

History is indeed the horizon of Kane's work, and as such fuels its cruelty. Kane aims to represent the historical horror that Pinter describes but realises, as Jameson argues, cannot be 'represented' as such; Kane realises, as Beckett argues, that there is nothing with which to express.[10] Thus, the unseeable present is represented metonymically through performance that calls attention to its own temporalities; to invoke Hal Foster's concept of parallax is helpful for reading Kane in that it denotes a sense of occupying different temporalities in one given moment (Foster, 1993: 5).[11] The parallax in Kane's work revolves around historical representation: history is both directly inaccessible and profoundly present.

Kane's plays produce the effect of what Foucault calls 'effective history', which 'divides our emotions, dramatizes our instincts, multiplies our body and sets it against itself'. This is because, as Foucault claims, 'knowledge is not made for understanding; it is made for cutting' (Foucault, 1977: 154). Violence alone – and violence as metaphor – would not achieve the alarming cultural perspicacity that Kane's plays communicate. Kane's work depicts a deliberate, political conflation of 'everyday' violation coupled with violation on a grand scale. Violence in Kane is not anchored solely in the everyday, nor solely in the horizon of history (it is not a metaphor for either), and thus this violence is able to *mean* afresh. The audience has the protection of theatre, but history's sense of injury. *Blasted* offended, Kane says, because 'it implied a direct link between domestic violence in Britain and civil war in the former

Yugoslavia' (Stephenson and Langridge, 1997: 130–1). *Cleansed* also posits the imbrication of the everyday and history, but less explicitly than *Blasted* at the level of content.

'Love', the subject of *Cleansed*, is its content, but is itself form, is metonymy. Barthes contends that the discourse of the lover 'is a horizontal discourse': 'Tenderness ... is nothing but an infinite, insatiable metonymy; the gesture, the episode of tenderness ... can only be interrupted with laceration: everything seems called into question once again: return of rhythm' (Barthes, 1978: 7; 224). (*Cleansed*'s emphasis on rhythm, as we will see, is crucial to its cruelty.) 'If you want to write about extreme love you can only write about it in an extreme way', Kane maintained of *Cleansed* (Sierz, 2001a: 116). Indeed, Barthes's suggestion, 'Is it not indecent to compare the situation of a love-sick subject to that of an inmate at Dachau?' feels appropriate to the university-cum-concentration-camp setting of *Cleansed* (Barthes, 1978: 19). Yet 'love' in *Cleansed* directs us not to the stuff of love but to love's metonymic ontology; using the figure of love, Kane asserts the inextricability of form and content. Beckett's writing on Joyce recalls *Cleansed*: 'Here form *is* content, content *is* form ... It is not written at all' (Beckett, 1929: 14). Invoking, then, a written text's performative dimensions, Beckett continues, 'It is not to be read – or rather it is not only to be read. His writing is not *about* something; *it is that something itself*' (14).

Events and details in *Cleansed* are exaggeratedly *literalised*. This dramatic literalisation, which foregrounds Adorno's concept of a 'surplus of reality', moves against a metaphorising discourse that secures its own stable reproduction in a critical economy (45).[12] Most vividly, the scene in *Cleansed* where Grace is raped as well as beaten, and finally machine-gunned by 'Voices' on stage, which are not bodily represented, literalises the penetration of subjectivity by language. The act of speaking made *spatial* is made explicit here – 'literal', in fact – and sounds, language, speech, words enter us, enter our subjectivity and enter Grace through rape. The pairing, doubling or mutability of Grace and Graham, which ends in Grace 'becoming' Graham when Tinker surgically attaches a penis to her crotch and cuts off her breasts, is another powerful example of literalisation. The play tracks this movement from inside to outside in a self-reflexive blurring of such divisions. In the end, it does not matter if Grace becomes her (br)other, just as it does not matter if Graham is 'dead' or dead. The dissolving of inside/outside, self/other, subject/object oppositions is crucial to *Cleansed*, and one way the play makes us aware of this blurring is through the anti-metaphorical feature of literalisation.

As in Beckett, Kane represents psychic trauma as *the* cultural condition – one on a par with physical trauma. The manner in which pain is inflicted on bodies is so swift – for instance, Tinker simply lopping off limbs – that in comparison, the protraction of the time of the performance of language through spatialisation and temporalisation, coupled with its anxious inability to 'express', is an equal violation at work. For all the violence inflicted on bodies in *Cleansed*, language is possibly the most violent agent, although the division between physical violence and the psychic violence of language (as *Not I* also dramatises) is not even particularly productive: violence on all levels is pervasive, and here represents metonymically a larger present which cannot be directly accessed in theatre but must still be expressed through performance.

Robin's excruciating counting aloud in *Cleansed* has the effect on spectators of violation, a brutal detachment of temporality from history (this detachment itself is a historical signifier). Just as Pinter reminds us that the page of a play as expression is violent, so is the play's young character Robin counting on an abacus, slowly articulating, in time, the number of days he has left in his prison-sanatorium (143–4). After Robin counts again, this time to thirty, he investigates if he has provoked any response. 'Gracie?' Robin finally asks an indifferent, presumably drugged Grace, repeating, his head in the noose, 'Grace. Grace. Grace. Grace. Grace. Grace. Please, Miss', before the chair is pulled out from under him, and Grace remains utterly impassive (144). Tinker, leading Grace off, says, in the scene's last line, 'Say goodnight to the folks, Gracie' (145).

This scene is, I argue, the most punishing in *Cleansed*. The inability to express, the having, as Beckett put it, nothing *with which* to express, except the dead and flat pleading of sequential numbers (rattled off in time, spatialising and temporalising speech); the sheer repetition of a person's name; and finally, a last-ditch injection of protocol ('Please, Miss') highlight the sheer cruelty of the scene, the blunt, bouncing knife of language, the emptiness of attempts at expression, the virulence of language in its manifest forms. In *Cleansed* there is no effective way to 'express', a fact that Carl's empty idioms of love and Robin's slow, violent counting forcefully underscore. *Cleansed* is a parodic rejection – as is, in a sense, *Not I* – of John 15:3's 'You are already clean because of the word which I have spoken to you'. This biblical notion is one of which Kane, who struggled with her own intensely Christian upbringing and adolescence, was surely aware. In *Cleansed* 'the word' does not 'clean'. Rather, language often has the opposite effect, muddying, or effacing the subject. Kane forces spectators to register the numbing in-timeness of counting before the pain of the death of Robin, whose last plea, after 'Gracie' and 'Grace' both fail to work, is an alienated 'Miss'; she forces spectators to apprehend the violence of 'saying goodnight to the folks'. Like 'lovely', a word consistently punctuating both *Cleansed* and *Blasted* (often closing scenes), 'folks' is a slap in the face: Robin sways from the ceiling, and Graham, himself already dead, sits beneath him.

Through an emphasis on the embodiment and spatialisation of language, Kane demands our constant attention to the pain of observing horror *in time*. Kane's plays utilise, mobilise, redirect, redeploy, make rhythmic and make violent the designified 'flatness' of language in its range of cultural locations, dramatising and performing its lack, and the layers of language that constitute, represent, enact and violate subjectivity. Both repetition and rhythm (recall Barthes's lacerating 'return of rhythm') are pervasive in *Cleansed*. Kane's metonymic representational ethic foregrounds repetition – of language, of actions – and thus empties them of their subjective meaning, enacting an anti-metaphorical movement, as words ('Lovely'), phrases ('I love you') and even violations (the constant hacking away at body parts in *Cleansed*), are shown as repeated and repeatable. In this way, her work breaks out of 'a vertical hierarchy of value', as Phelan describes the theoretical product of metaphor, which would lend itself to a less cruel theatre, one with more easily apperceptible morals (150). *Cleansed*'s repetition exceeds attempts to 'mean' in the sense of a reproductive critical discourse that identifies metaphoric meaning.

Rhythm in the play – from the very first scene – insists on the temporality of the spectator.[13] Kane calls attention to rhythm through song and dance: Grace and Graham dance to 'You are My Sunshine'; and Carl's dance is precipitated both by Lennon and McCartney's 'Things We Said Today' and by the singing of a child. Graham and Carl, as well, do '*a dance of love*' (as the stage directions read) for Grace and Rod, respectively. Graham's '*dance of love*' spurs Grace to copy his movements, and, when they subsequently have intercourse, they find '*each other's rhythm is the same as their own*' (120). During Carl's dance, he '*loses rhythm – Carl jerks and lurches out of time, his feet sticking in the mud, a spasmodic dance of desperate regret*' (136). Kane presents us with the violence of loving bodies; and then literalises this violence as Tinker cuts off Carl's feet.

Kane's work – in part through her attention to repetition and rhythm – ritualises the everyday as the horizon of history. Kane approaches the vast, horrific present through a necessarily metonymic performative. 'This relationship of domination is no more a "relationship" than the place where it occurs is place', Foucault writes; and *Cleansed*'s university-cum-concentration-camp comes to mind (as does *Blasted*'s hotel-room-cum-bombed-out-shelter). 'For precisely this reason, it is fixed, throughout its history, in rituals, in meticulous procedures that impose rights and obligations. It establishes marks of its power and engraves memories on things and even within bodies' (Foucault, 1977: 150). This is the purview of Kane's oeuvre. Even through attention to such seemingly prosaic rituals as 'I-love-you', Kane's work alludes to a domination-threaded totality of history. Kane's spectacle of cruelty, producing powerful images of suffering, mandates a performative revelation; a rearrangement or renegotiation of looking that collapses distance yet does not posit transcendence or didacticism. Rod fittingly declares, 'I'm with you *now*. I'll do my best, moment by moment, not to betray you. Now' (111). Performance 'addresses its deepest questions' to the now, as Phelan reminds us (Phelan, 1993: 146). Yet as Kane's history-driven theatre insists – to draw on Foster's language – 'there is no simple Now: every present is nonsynchronous, a mix of different times' (Foster, 1993: 5).

Kane's metonymic performances stand in for, as Foucault puts it, 'a new cruelty of history' (Foucault, 1977: 143). Pinter's take on Kane is redolent of this 'cruelty of history': 'Everyone's aware, to varying degrees, of the cruelty of mankind, but we manage to compromise with it, put it on the shelf and not think about it for a good part of the day ... I think she had a vision of the world that was extremely accurate, and therefore horrific' (Hattenstone, 2000). One is reminded here that Kane reportedly based Robin's abacus-counting suicide on an apartheid-era incident involving an imprisoned black activist on South Africa's Robben Island (hence the character's name), and that Carl's anal impalement is said to be modelled on a Serb method of crucifixion. Jameson, while he differs from Foucault, also posits a powerful concept of history apt for Kane's work:

> History is what hurts, it is what refuses desire and sets inexorable
> limits ... History can be apprehended only through its effects, and

never directly as some reified force. This is indeed the ultimate sense in which History as ground and untranscendable horizon needs no particular theoretical justification: we may be sure that its alienating necessities will not forget us, however much we might prefer to ignore them. (Jameson, 1981: 102)

Kane dares us to disagree. Her theatre confrontationally insists that despite the fact that history hurts – desperately, horribly, fatally – we must not distance ourselves from its cruelty.

Notes

1 Describing the anatomy of any one entity, this concept is crucial to a reading of Kane's plays, where brutes, like Cleansed's Tinker, are themselves shown to be victims –and voyeurs.

2 Roman Jakobson's article 'Two aspects of language and two types of aphasic disturbances' (Jakobson and Halle, 1956: 53–82) set the terms for the distinction between metaphor and metonymy; here metaphor is associated with selection and substitution, while metonymy is associated with combination and contexture. I name Kane's theatre metonymic because it focuses, for instance, on the contiguity and proximity of violence.

3 In comments specifically apposite to Cleansed, Phelan asserts that this shift to metonymy is often enacted through the staging of dramas of misrecognition – involving twins, doubles etc. (Phelan, 1993: 152).

4 Phelan's specific critical focus, on the other hand, is on how performance employs the body metonymically. As I do, she believes that performers and their critics must redesign the reigning stable set of assumptions about the positions of theatrical exchange, in which the spectator has an easily located point of view.

5 Foster's working definition of 'correct distance' is from Catherine Clément's discussion of the question of the other for the European in the mid-1930s, namely Lacan's sense of negotiation of distance between the fledgling ego and its image in the 'Mirror Stage'; and Lévi-Strauss's various readings of 'correct distance' from the cultural other – such as in the fascist extreme of non-identification, and the surrealist tendency to over-identify and appropriate. Foster's focus is twentieth-century theory, while I am interested in how the collapse of correct distance demanded by Kane's work signifies a valuable politics of art (Foster, 1993: 13).

6 Kane claimed that her MA in Playwriting at Birmingham University 'nearly destroyed her as a writer' (Stephenson and Langridge, 1997: 129).

7 Festa creates 'hardship art' or 'ordeal art', as we may understand Kane, in a sense, also did.

8 This is an explicit theme of Kane's work. For instance, she asserts of

Phaedra's Love that there was something 'about the inadequacy of language to express emotion that interested me' (Stephenson and Langridge, 1997: 132).

9 One critical response deems viewing *Blasted* 'like having your face rammed into an over-flowing ashtray' (Stephenson and Langridge, 1997: xvi). 'In 100 minutes of suffering time *Cleansed* quite indiscriminately bombards you with a gross pageant of horrors and suffering', Nicholas de Jongh of *The London Evening Standard* spews, constructing a critical narrative whereby *Cleansed* was a bad dream that *happened to him*, an active force working on a passive appraising agent. This response recalls Benjamin on the Dadaists: their art 'became an instrument of ballistics. It hit the spectator like a bullet, it happened to him, thus acquiring a tactile quality' (Benjamin, 1968: 238).

10 Jameson writes, 'history is not a text, not a narrative, master or otherwise, but that, as an absent cause, it is inaccessible to us except in textual form, and that our approach to it and to the Real itself necessarily passes through its prior textualization' (Jameson, 1981: 35).

11 The *OED* defines parallax as 'difference or change in the apparent position or the direction of an object as seen from two different points'. Another dictionary definition (*Webster's*), importantly for this discussion of spectatorship, indicates 'the parallax of an object may be used in determining its distance from the observer'.

12 Adorno's phrase discussing Beckett. This is created through the 'disproportion between all-powerful reality and the powerless subject … where … the experience of reality is beyond the grasp of the subject' (Adorno, 1970: 45).

13 The *Cleansed* director James Macdonald recalls Kane's insistence on rhythm: 'The only thing she would get narked about was actors not observing her punctuation. "If they don't get that fucking comma right, I'm going to kill them"' (Macdonald, 1999).

14

Sarah Kane's *Phaedra's Love*: staging the implacable

Peter A. Campbell

To critics of the original 1995 Royal Court production of *Blasted*, who claimed that her images of rape, mutilation and cannibalism were too disturbing and nihilistic, Sarah Kane responded: 'There isn't anything you can't represent on stage. If you are saying that you can't represent something, you are saying you can't talk about it, you are denying its existence. My responsibility is to the truth, however difficult that truth happens to be' (Stephenson and Langridge, 1997: 134). Kane insisted that the images, or 'truths', of which she spoke must be represented, and believed that these images could lead spectators to experience something unique and perhaps even dangerous – and in so doing learn from that experience. She felt the images needed to be realised according to the demands of the stage directions; those stage directions, however, demand a strong interpretative act to stage them convincingly and effectively. As Sean Carney suggests, 'her work attempts to occupy a position in theatrical representation that is potentially impossible', and the attempts provoke 'theatre to raise questions about its own nature' (Carney, 2005: 288). For Kane, the fallout from *Blasted* forced her to consider how the impossible via theatrical staging could be most effectively represented.

Kane's second play, *Phaedra's Love*, based on the Seneca version of the Hippolytus and Phaedra story, is usually dismissed in discussions of Kane as a minor play interrupting her truly innovative original work. However, it was a vital transitional piece for Kane, especially as she directed its premiere in 1996 at London's Gate Theatre. Here she was forced to consider not just the intention behind her theatrical vision but the most effective ways to stage her theatrical ideas. The audience's reaction to the staging of violence and sexuality in the original productions of *Blasted* and *Phaedra's Love* was sometimes shock, sometimes disgust and, most problematically for Kane, sometimes distraction or laughter at the images because they were not seen as convincing or 'real' enough. *Phaedra's Love* served as a liminal phase for Kane's dramaturgy, as she tested a more hybrid staging aesthetic that combined the known techniques of cinematically influenced stage realism with the yet unknown (for Kane) yet more suggestive, theatricalised representation that she exploits in her third play, *Cleansed*. With *Phaedra's Love*, Kane as director confronted Kane as writer as she struggled to stage sexuality and violence in a theatre context dominated by what Stanton B. Garner, Jr calls the 'materiality and corporeality in the realist tradition, with its essentially conflicting loyalties to verisimilitude and illusionism' (Garner, 1994: 10). By analysing Kane's work as director, along with other directors' difficulties and staging choices in working on *Phaedra's Love*, I hope to demonstrate the hybrid staging demands of the play and its significance in Kane's oeuvre as a metatheatrical exploration of the limitations of stage representation.

It is not simply coincidence that this transformation takes place as Kane adapts a classical tragedy, as many of her own concerns about violence and its representation in the theatre are explicit in classical tragedy. *Phaedra's Love* rejects many of the classical conventions of Euripides and Seneca and the even more restrictive rules of the neoclassical Racine, especially in showing the acts of violence that occur offstage in earlier versions. While Phaedra's suicide does take place offstage, Kane's play otherwise attempts to represent the acts of violence that affect the story, most of which occur when Theseus returns in the climactic final scene. His discovery of Phaedra's suicide and Hippolytus' refusal to deny her claim of rape leads him to bring together the people on the street to a scene of mob violence: here Theseus himself rapes and kills Phaedra's disguised daughter Strophe and inflames the crowd to kill Hippolytus. They continue to eviscerate Hippolytus and barbecue his genitals and innards, feeding them to dogs. As Brusberg-Kiermeier points out, 'Kane prefers the power, not only of the visual, but the visible' (Brusberg-Kiermeier, 2001: 169), a point she makes clear when stating: 'I mean, if you're not going to see what happens, why pay ten pounds to not see it? The reported deaths in Seneca are incredibly strongly written, conjuring the image really well, but personally I'd rather have an image right in front of me' (Benedict, 1996). This preference for the image prompted Kane to attempt to find ways to make these actions visible. However, her experience with undesirable audience responses led her to consider less realistic staging as a means to lead the audience to consider the violence and sexuality as serious and consequential, thus avoiding reflexes such as laughter or shock, which could lead to a dismissal of the content, as it did at times with the original productions of *Blasted* and *Phaedra's Love*.

Kane's production of *Phaedra's Love* 'concentrated on breaking down barriers between audience and actors where seating was dispersed throughout the theatre, and no single playing space selected' (Saunders, 2002a: 80). The spectators were very close to the playing space, and in the final sequence the members of the crowd, who had been sitting in the audience, got up from their seats to participate in the murder of Hippolytus, which included 'bleeding body parts chucked over the audience's head' (Hemming, 1996). The action was so close to the audience that Kate Basset in *The Times* wrote that the 'violence does not reach us by word of mouth. It is in our faces, almost literally as the cast thwack between clumps of seats'. Bassett also commented that the 'lashings of stage violence are not really shocking, just hard to believe' (Bassett, 1996). The audience's incredulity became laughter at, for example, Hippolytus' bloody body parts being thrown around the stage. This would clearly not have been Kane's intention, although it did occasionally happen in her initial production (Sierz, 2001a: 108). These kinds of staging problems exemplify how Kane's images can be ineffective because of their lack of verisimilitude. The serious result is that the audience dismisses the action entirely as it recognises that what is occurring on stage is inadequately formulated and unconvincing on any level.

While *Phaedra's Love* offers some of the same staging challenges as *Blasted* in its depictions of oral sex, rape, mutilation and killing, it also hints at more suggestive possibilities. This potential for less realistic images has been demonstrated in productions of the play, beginning with Kane's own, which tend to mix the realistic bloodshed and sex of *Blasted* with the more symbolic and ritualistic representations of sex and violence that Kane and the director James Macdonald gave *Cleansed* in its original 1998 production. Kane described her direction of *Phaedra's Love* as a way of exploring her own theatrical language, to make herself more effective as a theatre writer: 'Sometimes during *Blasted* I wasn't seeing exactly the image I'd written and I couldn't understand why. I thought I should find out just how hard it is to realize my own images, because it's one of those things I can never make any concessions about' (Stephenson and Langridge, 1997: 134).

Kane recognised that the audience's response to the action before them is more important than the representation itself achieving some sort of arbitrarily 'real' or 'cinematic' representation. *Phaedra's Love* is, in a sense, Kane's response to the critical response to *Blasted*. While *Blasted* begins as a metaphor for the war in Bosnia and becomes a war, with *Phaedra's Love* Kane found herself in a real 'war with the substance of theatre itself, provoking theatre to raise questions about its own nature' (Carney, 2005: 288). As directors (including Kane) approach this text, they also find themselves in this war, which becomes a battle of differing styles of representation.

Through her own work directing *Phaedra's Love*, Kane realised both the difficulty of staging her own writing and the potential in finding a truly theatrical language that was not limited to cinematic realism in either its staging or its dramaturgy. She wanted to give the audience a visceral experience, not necessarily just bombard them with visceral images. The specific difficulty of this is evident in productions of *Phaedra's Love*; unlike *Blasted*, which has graphic images of sex and violence that are difficult to represent, *Phaedra's Love*'s demands for dogs and a vulture are practically impossible without using directorial strategies of suggestion or symbolism. Other directors working on *Phaedra's Love* since Kane's original production have also seen it as a challenge of staging technique. As Jonathan Herron, who directed *Phaedra's Love* at the 2004 Edinburgh Festival, explains, *Phaedra's Love* falls somewhere in between the realistic and symbolic in its staging needs: 'I think the moments [of sexuality and violence] operate symbolically *and* realistically and I didn't want to weaken them by plunging too much in one direction. So we developed a style that would allow the audience to really believe in the actions and also interpret them symbolically' (Herron, 2005). This hybrid strategy has been used by several recent directors to create their productions of *Phaedra's Love*. While some of these directors have attempted extreme cinematic realism in production, even they ended up settling for some more suggestive stagings simply because the demands of the play went beyond their production capabilities.

While the Hippolytus character is traditionally virginal and vigilant in his indifference to women, with his allegiance in Euripides to the virgin goddess Artemis, Kane's Hippolytus is excessive in every aspect of his life, especially his sexual activity. In the play's first scene, Hippolytus masturbates in front of the television. Beyond his obvious gluttony and laziness, Hippolytus is also immediately identified with violence and sex, as he reaches climax into a dirty sock as the televised action in the unnamed 'Hollywood film' becomes '*increasingly violent*' (65). In the New York City premiere production of *Phaedra's Love* that I directed in May of 2004, the film on the television screen was *Backdraft*; flames filled the screen and screaming fire-fighters tried to put them out and avoid suffocation and burning themselves. The film provided a visual image of flames, which spoke directly to the images of burning that Phaedra brings with her from Seneca. It also provided juxtaposition to the lack of heat generated by Hippolytus' sexual excitement and climax, a coolness that Hippolytus carries with him throughout the play. The 'cool' verging-on-cold Hippolytus with the desperately 'hot' Phaedra is a fundamental theme of the mythological story and its many adaptations that makes its way quite explicitly into Kane's retelling.

This dichotomy of cool and hot has also played out in the staging aesthetic of productions of *Phaedra's Love*. Kane reacted against productions of her work that were too emotionally cool, like a production at Schauspiel Bonn in 1998, in which 'they had Phaedra coming back on stage after her death, narrating the last scene, including the stage directions, like in a dream' (Saunders, 2002a: 136). This type of production can create too much distance between the audience and stage, and make the effect of the work too intellectualised. Kane also reacted against productions that were too 'hot' and bloody, as seen by her comments about the 1996 German premiere production of *Blasted* in Hamburg, which she found 'too in your face – it lacked sensitivity, fragility, and subtlety. It was more about the physical violence than the mental, emotional violence' (Saunders, 2002a: 138). This kind of production reflected the violent images but in ways that prevented the audience from recognising their deeper implications. Especially since Kane's suicide in 1999, Kane's agent, Mel Kenyon, is hesitant to give performance rights to directors and producers whose connection to the material is 'one of subjective emotion – a depressive empathy'; she finds this type of relationship neglects the form of the work and can lead to productions that are more about the actor's emotional experience than the audience's (Saunders, 2002a: 144). Kane's work in production, especially in Continental Europe, has often been classified as having a '"rawness" in acting style that stimulates real emotional pain from the performer', which even before her death produced a cliché of raw emotional acting in many productions of Kane's work (Saunders, 2003: 101).

Kane's Hippolytus maintains the stubbornness of his character in Seneca and most of the mythological tradition, but it involves the *refusal* to deny him any excess of the flesh. He has an almost arbitrary embrace of all that is perceived as extreme. He is a contemporary rock star instead of a classical hero, famous and worshipped not merely because of his connections to the gods but because of his glamorous, decadent lifestyle. He is a natural performer, acting in his role with confidence and skill and refusing to give in to anyone else, which is what makes him so attractive. He even allows himself to believe, occasionally, that his indulgences are simply a result of his honourable and myopic pursuit of honesty.

When it comes to staged acts of sex, the scene where Phaedra performs oral sex is more often than not suggested by some sort of re-enactment that just (sometimes barely) avoids the actual act. As Singer observes, 'The stage directions that involve murder and dismemberment must be "modified" to be staged, but directions involving sex need not be. Pornography is common, but Kane declined to reap the benefits of that spectacle. The sex staged in Kane's work was unremarkable' (Singer, 2004: 166). In my production, we attempted to make the act of spectatorship a vital element, forcing the spectators to make decisions about what they were watching in order to make them conscious of their role as spectators. In *Phaedra's Love*, as with *Blasted*, Kane uses acts of violence and sexuality to force the audience into recognising their own complicity in the violence of the contemporary world, even if it is simply through their complacency as passive spectators. To create a theatrical manifestation of this idea, visual designer Brian Rogers set up a series of surveillance cameras throughout the large loft space used for the production. These cameras connected to monitors in two rows, one on the floor and one hanging from the ceiling, several feet in front of the audience. The scenes in Hippolytus' room, which comprise a good portion of the action of the play, took place in the back corner of the space, far away from the audience. However, the scenes were also visible to the audience on the monitors from several camera angles in close shots, focusing especially on Hippolytus sitting on the couch, and making his facial gestures very clear. There were also microphones in this space, making even the soft, intimate conversations between Phaedra and Hippolytus audible. The audience watched these scenes in the close frames of the monitors directly in front of them while at the same time watching the 'live' action far away, which was visible and discernible, but always obstructed. This obstruction was the solution I found not only to suggest the sexual acts but also to create a mediated distance from them, to make the audience experience them viscerally without bombarding them.

Jason Nodler, who directed the play for Infernal Bridegroom Productions at the Axiom Theatre in Houston in 2002, describes his staging of this scene:

> H [Hippolytus] sat facing forward on his couch and P [Phaedra] knelt in front of him, her back to the audience. He held her head and gagged her once or twice. When she finished, she rolled away into a seated profile, face three quarters forward to the audience so as not to look at H and H turned his attention to the television. (Nodler, 2005)

However, it is the violence of the final scene that has led to staging difficulties in *Phaedra's Love*. Violence generally presents different problems from sex in terms of the actual staging, and the limitations of representations are more significant. A realistic representation of violence has to include artificial elements, like fake blood; it is much more difficult to 'suggest' such things, as audiences expect to see them when, as in this scene, Hippolytus' stomach is supposed to have been cut open and his penis has been cut off and thrown on to a barbecue. In Nodler's production, this scene was staged with great detail to the realistic elements of the violence, with cinematically real blood and props (Nodler 'used F/X guys who usually work in film to achieve realistic blood and guts effects') in close proximity to an audience. In this way, it is very similar to Kane's own staging of the final scene, and some of the same problems that Kane confronted are repeated:

> We didn't use children as indicated and we didn't roast the phallus. We did use a dog, but she didn't eat the penis. She just ran around and barked. At the end of the day we just couldn't afford to make a new phallus for each show. That, the absence of children (we just felt it would be too scarring), and the absence of a live vulture were my main regrets about the production. (Nodler, 2005)

Nodler says that 'Virtually no liberties were taken with the script' and that 'Nothing was stylized' (Nodler, 2005). However, as is true of most productions, the vulture is not staged, nor does the dog follow the stage directions. Nodler did decide to use suggestive lighting and sound for the vulture instead of leaving it out entirely. The refusal to use children because of the fear of psychological damage is not mentioned by other directors, but the clichéd danger of working with children or live animals is tested by Kane in *Phaedra's Love*, and, with the exception of the rats in *Cleansed*, she doesn't use either again. In the US premiere of *Phaedra's Love*, at Chicago's Defiant Theatre in 1998, the director Lisa Rothschiller also used cinematic techniques and effects for much of the violence, and emphasised the bloodiness of the final scene by having an all-white set, which served as a palette for the gore of the killings of Strophe and Hippolytus. This production also tried to stage a vulture, beginning by showing a video of vultures against the white backdrop and then using a 'fantastic puppet controlled by two actors' designed by a horror film special effects artist. Despite Rothschiller's ambitions, again the dog was not done according to the script; there was a moving dog puppet manufactured, but it 'got cut after final dress, as it was simply too distractingly funny' (Rothschiller, 2005).

In my production, the acts of violence, in contrast to the obscured sexual acts, were staged in full view of the audience, although some of them did take place at some physical distance: Hippolytus is mutilated near the back of the space, allowing for the blood and entrails that are taken out of him to seem real but preventing the type of close observation that would reveal them as mere theatrical effects. The entrails, which were actually pieces of raw, bloody meat, were then, as per the stage directions, thrown on to a grill, where they sizzled and smoked as they cooked. The audience then could see an image of a bloodied, disembowelled Hippolytus on the monitors. The violence was also put into a ritual and community context, as I transformed the unnamed men and women that Kane calls for in the script into a chorus that helps Theseus rape and murder Strophe and then mutilate and murder Hippolytus. The acts of violence themselves became somewhat ritualised and were thus made to represent, as in the actions and text of a tragic Greek chorus, the actions and thoughts of a community. In this case, it was a numbed, dulled community brought easily and quickly to terrible action by a misled Theseus. The coolness of the staging of these violent rituals, in silence with deliberate and specific choreography, took the action out of the realistic realm; still, the staging highlighted the horror of the actions without providing an emotional context other than the spectators' own with which to judge the violence they had observed.

I was unable to solve the staging of the vulture, which I attempted to suggest merely by directing Hippolytus' gaze to the ceiling as he says the line 'Vultures' (102). This line was delivered directly into a camera, and the audience then saw him on the monitors looking up. However, this was clearly not as strong as a physical representation of them, and was difficult for the audience to read clearly. I considered using the video monitors already present and showing a video of vultures, but, as the camera had been used only for live feeds, it seemed a choice that would have been more confusing than illuminating. There were also no dogs or children, as I chose to reassemble the crowd as a chorus in part because I could not conceive of a theatrically viable way to stage the dogs and children. While Hippolytus' dismembering was not easy to see, as it was done at a distance, the strongest audience reactions were to the rape and murder of Strophe and the smell of meat cooking on the grill. For the rape, Strophe's face was visible on the monitors as Theseus pushed up her dress and forced her over the side of Hippolytus' couch. He then tore off her underwear and began thrusting at her from behind as the audience could see her face in close-up. Theseus thrust for almost a minute before taking the knife in his hand and pulling it across Strophe's throat, again in close up. He then let her head drop onto the side of the couch; it remained on the monitors to the end of the play. The grill, on the other hand, was downstage and almost centre, close to the audience. It was an electric grill that heated in silence, and there were visible gasps when the chorus dropped the meat on and it sizzled sharply. The smoke it generated stayed in the space through the end of the piece, with some audience members responding so viscerally that they had to leave because of nausea.

This final scene depends upon finding the right balance to create a visceral reaction in the audience without overwhelming them so they only turn away in disgust or refuse to consider the disturbing images. In retrospect, my staging of the violence in the final scene was a little too distanced, and too mediated, reducing some of the power of the violent images by falling back on the suggestive. But this 'coolness' was offset by the grill and the very real smoking meat, which gave the audience an experience that then complemented and enhanced the acts being suggested on the stage. This sensory experience is what Kane and others were trying to achieve by staging the play in close proximity to the audience, in hopes that the shared space would create shared emotional and sometimes physical elements, generating actual heat and at least the potential for contact between performers and audience. This close connection can function, as did the smoking meat, to enhance the suggestion that audience members are reacting not just to what they are seeing and hearing but also to what they are feeling through their other senses.

While it is the final scene that contains the majority of the violence and staging difficulties, the brief scene before it most clearly shows how the elements of the play lead to its grisly conclusion, and how Kane frames and justifies her vision. Scene seven is the return of Theseus, which in Seneca is the central plot event, when Phaedra tells Theseus that Hippolytus has raped her. Kane's scene echoes Seneca, but makes it a visceral event instead of an intellectual one. Theseus already knows of Phaedra's accusations, and, since she is already dead, there is no exposition, only the presence of Theseus and his self-flagellation. The scene eliminates the language of classical discourse, focusing completely on image and emotion. Theseus is not here to recognise or realise something. He is simmering with anger and hatred and a desire for blood. In Seneca, Theseus responds to Phaedra's accusations by believing her and saying of his son and his society:

> What has become of us? What kind of age is this
> when such outrage can walk among us, smile,
> and assume that the smiling faces of others conceal
> at least a like depravity? (Seneca, 1992: 117)

This is a critique not just of Hippolytus, but of the culture that spawned such a creature.

Phaedra's Love makes Theseus the object of this criticism as well, and even more representative of his culture than Hippolytus. Kane's scene shows how Theseus is ruled by immediate, instinctive emotion and judgement, which lead to a scene of climactic violence. Theseus' response parallels the reaction of some critics to *Blasted*, who without taking the time to process what they had seen evaluated it nevertheless and immediately presented it to their audience. The result of this action in the play is, as with Kane post-*Blasted*, a misguided sacrifice. For Kane, however, the criticism led her to a further examination of the limitations of the theatrical form in which she worked. It did not lead her to stop her attempts at a theatre that affected an audience viscerally, but to experiment with different methods of achieving her goal. Kane said that she was attempting in *Phaedra's Love* to 'subvert the convention of everything happening offstage and have it on-stage and see how that works' (Saunders, 2002a: 80). She was doing more than that, however. By showing what was traditionally spoken, and by taking away the revelation of Phaedra's lie, which causes Theseus' recognition, the play subverts the expectations of tragedy. Moreover, by choosing to explore the limits of theatrical staging by using the known mythological and tragic structure of the Phaedra myth, she makes her subversion not just about staging the offstage events of tragedy but about the theatre itself. Furthermore, as the violence, dogs and vulture of the final scene test the limits of theatrical representation, the play demands consciousness by both the creative producers and the audience of the manner in which these acts are performed in the theatre. *Phaedra's Love*, then, was clearly and primarily a metatheatrical investigation of the act of theatre for Kane. It remains so both for those producing it and for audiences viewing it.

After *Phaedra's Love*, Kane's work did not become less violent; *Cleansed* is perhaps her most violent work. However, her later dramaturgy allowed for more suggestive and symbolic manifestations of that violence. The experience of writing and directing *Phaedra's Love*, then, was a key factor in Kane's move away from the naturalistic or cinematic as she recognised the limitations of naturalistic representation and the theatrical efficacy of using suggestion and symbolism to achieve the kind of visceral and critical responses she desired from her audience. *Phaedra's Love* is a self-conscious battle about theatrical staging and dramaturgy that compelled Kane to attempt new forms to engage her audience.

15

Under the surface of things: Sarah Kane's *Skin* and the medium of theatre

Mateusz Borowski

The evolution of Sarah Kane's oeuvre could be said to reflect concisely the development of twentieth-century theatre. As the playwright herself admitted, the opening scenes of her debut *Blasted* draw on the tradition of late nineteenth-century naturalism and psychological realism (Saunders, 2003: 41). Indeed, the description of the hotel room in Leeds with which the play begins seems to herald a realistic action in the Ibsenite style. However, Kane painfully disappoints these expectations, when the Soldier enters the stage and the logic of nightmare imposes its rules on the theatrical world. The final series of images, separated from one another by blackouts, shares more affinities with Beckettian metaphors. A similar merging of sordid naturalism with metaphoric, exaggeratedly cruel imagery can be found also in *Phaedra's Love* and, even to a much larger extent, in *Cleansed*. Both these plays, criticised by the press for their explicit representation of sex and violence, earned Kane the title of 'a naughty schoolgirl desperately trying to shock an increasingly bored and languid audience' (Morley, 1998). However, on closer investigation, in her third play one can detect a significant formal shift that marks the playwright's transition to a different style of writing and testifies to her changed approach to theatrical means of expression. If in *Blasted* and *Phaedra's Love* violent images described in the stage directions seem all too literal, in *Cleansed* bodily suffering openly manifests its theatricality. For example, when Carl is being beaten by an invisible group of men, the spectators hear only the sound of blows and see the reaction of the victim's body; they are not presented with a detailed, naturalistic scene of torture (116). Similarly, when Tinker cuts Carl's hands off, the stage directions inform the reader that the character *'tries to pick up his hands – he can't, he has no hands'* (129). This description, smacking of black humour, seems to indicate that it is unnecessary, even undesirable, to literally reproduce the scene of cutting hands by illusionistic means. Rather it should be turned into an overtly theatrical, metaphoric image, as was the case in the premiere of that play, directed by James Macdonald, in which red ribbons represented blood; little bags were used to stand for rats and an orange-lit cloth symbolised fire (Sierz, 2001a: 114).

Moreover, if *Blasted* and *Phaedra's Love* contained clues suggesting that the action takes place in contemporary Britain, *Cleansed*, set in a cross between a concentration camp and a university campus, lacks any references to the external world, which would allow anchoring it in a specific, socio-cultural context. These tendencies towards an abstract, poetic and overtly theatricalised form became even more visible in Kane's later texts. *Crave* and *4.48 Psychosis* not only lack the brutal images associated with her previous work; more importantly, with their lack of unified characterisation, linear action, and their vestigial dialogue, poetic language and overt intertextuality, they contain no explicit references to the situational context in which the spoken text could be placed. Cruel and vivid imagery, so prominent in the early work, is entirely ousted in these later texts, or, to put it more accurately, rendered in verbal descriptions and not in stage directions that could be later reproduced by theatrical means or embodied by actors.

What could account for this change in Kane's style of writing? What initiated her growing departure from the traditional, dialogue-based dramatic form? Why did she altogether abandon the visual means of expression, concentrating exclusively on the verbal? There is, as I conjecture, one missing link in the development of Kane as a playwright.

This missing link, typically overlooked in critical analyses of her oeuvre, is *Skin*, the only one of a number of screenplays written by Kane which was made into a film and subsequently published together with the other play-texts. It is not certain when exactly it came into being, but, according to her agent, Mel Kenyon, Kane worked on it after finishing *Blasted* and perhaps simultaneously during the writing of *Phaedra's Love* (Saunders, 2002a: 150; 193). It certainly shows clear affinities with her earlier plays in which she made use of explicit, naturalistic scenes of bodily suffering. On the other hand, the play with which *Skin* shares most of its thematic concerns and literary influences is *Cleansed*, staged a year after Kane's screenplay had been produced and broadcast by Channel 4 in June 1997. Destruction of identity caused by unfulfilled love, the motif of androgyny and a number of motifs borrowed from Strindberg's chamber plays are the most obvious parallels that both these texts evince. The major difference stems from them being written with two different media in mind. Significantly, it was about *Cleansed* that she commented: 'I made a deliberate decision to write something that couldn't be a film or television' (Saunders, 2002a: 13–14). Indeed, on closer reading, it becomes clear that in this play she heavily relies on the means of expression available only in the theatre, and does not try to create a naturalistic copy of external reality. The technical advancements offered by film allowed Kane to show scenes of bodily mutilation in the minutest detail and with a degree of imitative accuracy that she could never achieve in the theatre. But even if this text may on the surface bear all-too-clear marks of being a modern descendant of the naturalist tradition, in fact it elicits from the spectator an entirely different type of response. Outlining the terms of this new contract with the spectator in Kane's screenplay requires taking a closer look at the structure and the function of particular representational strategies used in *Skin*. However, I would like to go beyond the scope of an analysis of this particular text and hypothesise how the experience of working on *Skin* became a significant step in the development of the original poetics of Kane's later texts. By focusing on chosen motifs from *Crave*, I would like to demonstrate that the striking stylistic differences in fact conceal a hidden continuity which testifies to a consistent development of moving further and further away from traditional methods of creating a stage world and producing reality effects for the sake of a deeper engagement with spectators.

Skin is by no means a socially engaged short film, or a naturalistic or Dogma-like documentary that presents a slice of life about a neo-Nazi hooligan from South London, although such an interpretation might be suggested by the title. Kane is not in the least interested in investigating the reasons for the revival of nationalistic movements which Europe faced in the latter part of the 1990s. Even if she shows in her screenplay a group of young skinheads, she does not do it in order to fathom the psychological causes and social consequences of hatred towards foreigners. Rather she uses racism and violence as material for metaphors to talk about one of the central themes that operate throughout her entire oeuvre: how irresistible longing for another person leads to destruction of self and ruins the inner life of the protagonists. Also, in *Skin* the central topic is the havoc wreaked on Billy's life by his obsessive fascination for an unknown, black woman who lives in a house opposite his and whom he observes from his window.

Already in the first scene of *Skin* the representation of reality bears visible traces of its dream-like character. The first image that the viewers can see is a messy, sunlit room in which Billy sleeps, covered by a floral duvet. The first words are spoken by Billy's voice recorded on the answerphone: 'Hello, I'm asleep' (249). The same line resounds at the very end of the scene, enclosing the first sequence of the play within a type of a frame. This parenthesis may be treated as a signal suggesting that the represented reality has in fact oneiric provenance. What could also support this reading of the opening scene is the metaphoric image of cannabis plants in the garden surrounding the house in which Billy lives. Although in the next scenes the viewers accompany the protagonist when he performs such everyday activities as taking a shower, putting on clothes and eating with his friends, Kane clearly structures *Skin* in such a way that one can never be sure whether the events in the play take place in objective reality or in an imaginary vision.

Just as in many Freudian interpretations of dreams, throughout the whole film Billy constantly meets his own doubles. In the opening scene we can see a cuddly polar bear standing next to Billy's bed. The same toy appears in the next scene, held by a small black boy who stares at the group of skinheads through the window of a café, laughing at Billy's threatening gestures. A similar doubling occurs in one of the following scenes. First, we can see Billy wearing 'tight blue jeans, white tee-shirt, red braces and cherry red docs' (256). When he is called by Marcia, he changes his clothes and runs to her flat, but the person who opens the door for him is a young white woman with a shaven head, dressed exactly the same as he was a few minutes before (257). Clearly, Billy, as if caught in the web of some long, tiring dream or a narcotic vision, constantly meets his own doubles, each of them being a projection of his own infantile fears and feminine traits of character, the suppression of which conditions the formation of a mature and coherent male self.

The entire action of the film, composed of short, metaphoric scenes, depicts the main character's gradual loss of selfhood caused by overpowering feelings that break out of his control and arouse in him a fervent and unfulfilled wish of absolute corporal and spiritual unity with his beloved. Moreover, when Billy finally plucks up the courage to visit Marcia, she makes him undergo a kind of purification ritual in which he is methodically deprived of all that established his identity as a white male English supremacist. Marcia forces him to have sex, beats him, feeds him with dog food, shaves his body, scrubs his tattoos with bleach and a stiff brush, and cuts her name into his back with a knife. In the last sequence of this cruel rite, Billy, dressed in Marcia's clothes, is sitting at her feet and utters only one word: 'Mum' (263). Two similar scenes that frame the action of *Skin* very clearly mark the beginning and the end of this process involving the destruction of a sense of identity. In one of the first sequences of the film, Billy looks at himself in the mirror, smiling, then making faces and finally kissing his reflection. Towards the end of the film, he examines his face, disfigured by Marcia, then breaks the mirror with his fist and looks at his face again, this time fragmentarily reflected on the cracked surface. Before he takes an overdose of painkillers, in an attempt to commit suicide, he says only 'No more Billy' (266).

The representational strategies adopted in *Skin* undoubtedly trace back to expressionist poetics. However, Kane modifies them to a large extent in order to increase the impact exerted by the fictional reality on the viewer. The function of the scenes of physical suffering, which abound in *Skin*, is not restricted to evoking shock that could be more striking and engaging for the recipient than a typical reality effect. The series of physical tortures that Marcia performs on Billy's body significantly changes the nature of the process of the loss of identity. In a typically expressionist drama, such as Walter Hasenclever's *Die Menschen* (1917), the scenes are not linked causally, and they do not combine into a single, logically developing chain of events. Each of them is a unity in itself and they are connected only by the presence of the central character who goes through an alien world trying to fathom its mystery and find the meaning of his or her identity. In *Skin* Kane very profoundly changes the rudiments of this model. She manifestly marks the represented world with the stamp of Billy's subjective point of view, but she uses entirely different means of expression to show his change. In *Skin*, the evolution of the protagonist is not depicted in the form of a series of events and encounters with other characters. Here the process of the erosion of identity has a primarily corporeal dimension, while its consecutive stages are illustrated by the physical changes that Billy's body undergoes. If in the typical expressionist drama action is set inside the protagonist's mind, in *Skin* it takes places literally on the main character's skin. By the same token, Kane much more effectively than the expressionists undermines the illusion of a coherent and stable self, demonstrating that a sense of integrity is not built on any internal, mental conviction but merely on a set of external traces, bodily features and behaviours. When these traces, one after another, cease to exist for Billy, his sense of an unchangeable identity wanes, too.

Therefore one can posit that although *Skin* draws on expressionist poetics, it also turns inside out the basic expressionist convention of eliciting identification of the spectator with the main character. Billy is not a typical expressionist Everyman whose feelings the spectators should share and understand. In order to prevent this type of emotional identification with the protagonist, Kane introduces yet another character who takes on the role of the classical *meneur de jeu*, who controls and manipulates the events in the film. After all, it is not at all obvious that in *Skin* the young neo-Nazi is the only protagonist. The character who seems to be equally significant in the development of action is Neville, a black lodger sharing the same building in which Billy lives. He constantly watches over Billy; speaks to him like a father to a naughty child; appears out of thin air in his flat; and, finally saves his life, bringing him back to consciousness after his suicide attempt. He is also the one who tends the cannabis plants. He seems to control the course of events in the play, which thus cannot be treated as dream vision inside Billy's head. The only point of identification for the spectators is the impersonal eye of the camera which relentlessly registers all images and presents them to the viewer, who, as one might suspect, should on their own explain the dream vision shown on the screen. This is indicated not only by the structure of the action and the relationships between the characters but also by a prominent self-reflexive element introduced by Kane.

After the breakfast at the café, Billy and his friends go to Brixton to interrupt the wedding of a black couple. During a fight when the skinheads provoke one of the guests, a teenager who was recording the ceremony gets entangled in the middle of the fighting crowd. Although he no longer controls his camera, it still haphazardly registers bits and pieces of reality that surrounds him. By making in this short sequence the working of the camera her theme, Kane suggests that the scenes out of which her film is composed resemble an aleatory mosaic rather than a firmly constructed plot. The viewers of *Skin* have no choice but to follow the camera, which presents them with increasingly violent images that do not lead to any conclusive denouement. Therefore, it is none of the fictional characters but the spectators themselves who have to become dreamers, trapped in a delirious vision, which should draw them inside the fictional world. One could thus conclude that Kane's screenplay, although on the surface similar to the expressionist plays, is in fact a descendant of Strindberg's *Dream Play*. In the preface, Strindberg emphasises that the oneiric action is not a vision of any of the characters, but that it is encompassed only by the consciousness of the author-poet. Similarly, in *Skin* the surreal fictional world should exert an impact on the audience because it addresses the viewers directly, without the mediating presence of any of the fictional characters, which in an expressionist play provided a prism for the represented world.

In order to clarify this difference in more theoretical terms one could have recourse to the typology of the dramatic interior monologue introduced by the French scholar Joseph Danan in his book *Le théâtre de la pensée*, in which he presents two basic models of the theatrical interior monologue. The more traditional one is monodrama. It turns the stage into a mental space within which the speaking subject constructs its inner theatre, representing itself or others. This is the case of a typical expressionist Everyman who may be disintegrating into a myriad of incompatible scenes, but still their stream of consciousness belongs to the order of the fictional stage reality. Contrary to this are texts which exemplify what Danan calls the interface model of the interior monologue. In these plays, the stage events are not presented from any definite subjective perspective of a single character, but rather unfold on their own, just as a revolving reel projects images on to the cinematic screen. Thus, the interface model structures the represented reality according to a more abstract pattern. Moreover, it gives much more interpretative freedom to the spectators who, for want of any other fictional point of anchorage, have to connect to the stage events and images without the guiding mediation of an epic narrator. Instead of eliciting the auditors' identification with a single character, the interface confronts them directly with an amorphous stage reality and turns them into 'dreamers' of the visions that gradually unfold on stage (Danan, 1995: 336–7).

Reading *Skin* as a type of an interface-script, a visionary rather than naturalist text which by various means elicits the spectator's imaginary identification with the fictional reality, may shed light on the structure of Kane's later texts for the theatre, which to a very great extent depart from the traditional model of drama and all its pertaining methods of addressing the recipient. *Crave* and *4.48 Psychosis* seem so much emancipated from the formal requirements of a play-text that they do not require any theatrical image to accompany them. They could simply be delivered on an empty stage, since the only material that they draw on is spoken language. The extremely vivid and complex imagery that these texts contain does not need to be transposed on to other theatrical sign systems, since it reaches the audience in the form of verbal descriptions. This claim might be corroborated by the fact that during the rehearsals for *Crave*, directed by Vicky Featherstone, Kane came up with the idea that the whole stage should be dark throughout the entire performance, providing an empty space in which no visual element would distract the listeners' attention from the quality and materiality of the four speaking voices (Saunders, 2002a: 131). Featherstone and Kane ultimately decided to inscribe the text of the play in a sketchy situational context, and put it on stage in a chat show format, with four speakers seated on movable chairs. However, the idea of turning *Crave* into an installation constructed out of pure voices resounding on an empty stage suggests that the play even more heavily than Kane's earlier texts relies for its effectiveness on the direct contact with the spectators and on their imaginary engagement.

Again, as in *Skin*, one of the major topics in *Crave* is the dissolution of self within a puzzling, internal landscape. Already at the beginning, the voice marked by the letter M says: 'Sometimes the shape of my head alarms me. When I catch sight of it reflected in a darkened train window, the landscape passing through the image of my head' (160). This image, in which the scenes of Billy looking at himself in the mirror reverberate, when treated as a metatextual metaphor can provide a clue to the interpretation of the text. Just like the images that move through the reflection of the head by the window, the disconnected lines spoken by four anonymous voices, marked only with the letters A, B, C and M, seem to be flowing freely from the stage, addressing the audience directly, and combining into a dynamic, kaleidoscopic mosaic. Listening to the text spoken from the stage is like watching a landscape during a train journey, and should necessarily inspire the audience's imagination to make up for the absence of pictures on the stage. What is more, Kane in an altogether ironic way returns to the medium of film, using it as a metaphor that explains the structure of the text. 'My thoughts race in glorious technicolor' (174), announces C, while the reference to the cinema adds another element to the self-reflexive dimension of the play. Listening to the text can also be compared to watching a film, the movement of the consecutive lines of the text in front of the reader's eyes resembling the continuous succession of frames wound past a lens in a cine projector that emits the multitude of images, like those described in the numerous narrative passages of the play. What contributes to this entire imagery of the text is the presence of the lines which evoke an impressionistic, dynamic mosaic of colours: 'A Blue into green / C All blue' (172); 'C I crave white on white and black' (174) and 'A A pale gold sea under a pale pink sky' (197) are only a few examples which make direct appeals to the recipient's imagination.

Perhaps then the words 'Look./ Listen' (162; 171) appearing twice in the play are not only part of a dialogue between the voices, but also address the listeners, guiding their reception of the text and directing their attention to the visual and the auditory qualities of language. Apart from the complex visual design, the play also operates with musical codes, activating the acoustic qualities of words: 'I don't have music, Christ I wish I had music but all I have is words' (172), says C, as if suggesting that the musical dimension and the rhythmic pattern of the play should not be overlooked, either. After all, full potential of the text can be activated only when the play meets an audience who agree to co-operate in giving the final shape to the text. The oxymoronic phrase 'the stain of scream' (179) provides another self-reflexive metaphor which most succinctly describes this combination of the richness of visual elements with an elaborate rhythmic pattern of *Crave*, whose fragmentary structure, allowing a multitude of interpretations, resembles a blot of colourful paint with no clearly established outline. This concoction must be injected into the listener's eye, on whose retina it will always generate new images. Their final shape depends on the active co-operation of the audience, whom the text not only addresses but also positions, especially by means of deictic devices woven into it. Such is probably the function of the short dialogue: 'B Here / ... / M Inside. / A Here' (165). The use of the deictic adverb points to the existence of the imaginary place, a dark, empty space, where the text and the listener meet, while the word 'inside' once again indicates that *Crave* presents the audience with a mental landscape, a look inside somebody's head. Who this person is becomes clear when the line spoken by A, 'You're losing your mind in front of my eyes' (185), is treated as another deictic address to the audience. In a reversal of the train window metaphor from the beginning of the play, the one who is looked at is not a fictional character and his or her psyche but the theatrical spectators themselves. When the recipient acquires the prerogatives of the co-author, the whole play becomes partly their own creation. Listening to the flow of sentences in the text equals looking at one's own thoughts.

The ultimate outcome of this strategy of reception is the blurring of the borderline between the text, its author and its recipient, an aim that Kane tried to achieve by abandoning the stage image altogether. Therefore the structure of *Crave* is another attempt at giving account of how a stable, unified self falls apart into a myriad of incoherent pieces. This time, however, Kane tried to make the audience turn their eyes away from the surface of reality and look inside their own heads in which the fictional stories told by anonymous voices interweave with the listeners' imagination. The flow of words and images programmed in *Crave* escapes the audience's need for a coherent meaning, since the play represents a subject who can no longer put the bits and pieces of their internal life into a coherent whole, thus assuring a sense of a stable identity. The text itself explicitly points to this impossibility of establishing any firm interpretation: 'What's anything got to do with anything?' asks C, to which M answers: 'Nothing' (163–4), while at another juncture M mentions 'a private iconography which I cannot decipher' (183). It is not the matter of describing the split identity in objective terms or representing it in the form of a visual stage metaphor of the grotesque Androgyne. Perhaps the self-reflexive structure of *Crave*, exposing and deconstructing the codes of fiction constitution, bringing the processes of perception into focus, and drawing the listener inside the text, allows the recipients, and notably those who agree to co-operate with the text, to experience at first hand the moment when identity collapses and meaning fades away.

Skin is a borderline between the outside and the inside of the body, but also between the external reality and the inner world. It is also the screen on which marks of identity are projected, a surface on which the characters' past is inscribed in the form of scars and bruises that reflect their psychic traumas. Skin can also be adorned with tattoos or covered with clothes, thus marking the body with additional attributes that ascribe it to a specific type of identity, like 'male' or 'Nazi'. Also, skin holds the body together, but at the same time imprisons it in a definite shape and does not let internal structures merge with the outside world: 'Brain and bollock, innard and eyelid, toenail and teeth, all wrapped up in pig's foreskin' (253), says Billy, squeezing meat out of a sausage, this metaphor announcing his future lot, when he himself will be deprived by Marcia of all the signs that assured the stability of his own self-hood. Skin, and the body that it holds together, become for Billy the ultimate, impassable borderline that prevents absolute union with his beloved.

It is this borderline that Kane obsessively tried to erase on the stage and on screen, especially in her later plays, looking for such representational strategies that could give account of the falling apart of identity and expose audiences to the experience of loss of self. She was also very clear about her insistence to work in theatre, refusing to adapt her plays for television or film. She even refused to grant permission to adapt *Crave* as a radioplay, although the form of this text, deprived of stage directions and composed only of lines spoken by four voices, might seem to be suitable material for this medium (Saunders, 2002a: 150). She always stressed that her texts, although very often eschewing traditional dramatic conventions, have to be embodied on stage in order to achieve their full force of impact on the spectators or listeners. This directness of contact between the stage and the audience is irretrievably lost whenever a human voice is electronically modified or when the living embodiment of a theatrical performance becomes mercilessly framed and captured on film. For it is only in the theatre that unmediated voice can acquire the necessary dimension of corporeality and materiality that will reach the imagination of the audience.

Looking for novel ways of exposing the audience to an authentic theatrical experience was the primary aim of Kane's formal experiments. When asked about the reasons why she decided to write for the theatre, she answered that only theatre allowed her to observe the reaction of the audience (Tabert, 1998: 16). Maybe for this reason her later plays relied on the co-operation of the audience who have to make an effort to put together scattered bits and pieces of language and create out of them the missing images. However, regardless of all the innovations that she was introducing in her works, Kane always concentrated on this uniquely theatrical suspension between fiction and reality. And taking advantage of this tension, immanently inscribed in theatre, between the real and the imagined, the actor and the character, the body and the costume, she continually tried to prove to her audience that an authentic, although artificially induced, theatrical experience is still possible.

'We are anathema' – Sarah Kane's plays as postdramatic theatre versus the 'dreary and repugnant tale of sense'

Eckart Voigts-Virchow

On the very first night of *Blasted*, the play became a *succès de scandale*. Yet to some extent the very fact that *Blasted*, *Cleansed* and (less so) Kane's subsequent plays remain anathema to mainstream theatre in Britain enables me to argue that they break down the boundaries between dramatic writing in Britain and the post-dramatic theatrical scene. Furthermore, Kane's success in France (particularly with Isabelle Huppert's performance of *4.48 Psychosis* at the Bouffes du Nord, directed by Claude Régy) and, above all, in Germany, seems to indicate that her work is compatible with 'European' forms of post-dramatic theatre. One might attempt an unsophisticated syllogism involving the terms 'Sarah Kane', 'German theatre' and 'post-dramatic theatre', which produce the following conclusions: (1) Kane's plays are successful in Germany; (2) post-dramatic theatre is successful in Germany; (3) it follows that Kane wrote post-dramatic theatre.

While this syllogism is far too neat, it is true that Sarah Kane's plays have been tremendously successful in Germany. Arguably, she found her most receptive audience on the European mainland, whereas revivals in Britain are relatively rare. In Germany, translations of her plays were rapidly published, for instance in the influential journal *Theater Heute*. Renowned German authors such as Durs Grünbein, Marius von Mayenburg and Elisabeth Plessen have been translators of her work, which have been available in a German-language omnibus edition since 2002 from the prestigious publisher Rowohlt. In 1999 (for *Cleansed*) and 2000 (for *Crave*), she was voted best foreign playwright on the German stage, and *4.48 Psychosis* was almost equally well received in 2002. Even in recent years, her plays have continued to be shown regularly on stages of regional repertory theatres all over Germany, not only in Berlin, Hamburg, Munich and Bonn, where her plays received their often star-studded German premieres.[1] In the first years of the new millennium one could see not only every play by Kane at the Berlin Schaubühne, but also a great number of regional German productions of her plays, and particularly of her final two works *4.48 Psychosis* and *Crave*. Whilst Vicky Featherstone's and James Macdonald's British productions of *Crave* and *4.48 Psychosis* were brought to Germany for the Bonn Biennale in 2002, Thomas Ostermeier presented his Kane productions at the Barbican, London, in 2006. According to the Rowohlt representative Nils Tabert, Kane is 'considered to be the most important British playwright of the 1990s, definitely the most radical' (Saunders, 2002a: 134). Probably with the stale and underfunded theatrical scene in Britain in mind, one German critic called her a 'queen among dwarves' (Höbel, 2000: 278), and Michael Merschmeier opined in the leading German theatre journal *Theater Heute* that 'Kane is still cult' (Merschmeier, 2002: 25). When Michael Billington came to the Berlin Schaubühne to discuss her work in 2005, he was surprised to find she had best survived the demise of the late 1990s craze for British 'in-yer-face' theatre on German stages (Behrendt, 2005: 9).

Where does this success place Kane's work in relation to the various versions of post-dramatic theatre in Germany and Europe? The theory of 'postdramatic' theatre was formulated by the German theatre researcher Hans-Thies Lehmann at the beginning of the 1990s with reference to the transnational performance scene, but with special emphasis and impact on Germany (Lehmann, 1999; 2006). As Lehmann's seminal book is now available in English, the label 'post-dramatic' will arguably stick in English-language research as well.

It is likely that Sarah Kane's plays thrive in a theatrical climate which is conducive to 'post-dramatic' theatrical forms and theories. Kane's overwhelming success in Germany is arguably due to the closeness of her aesthetics to this kind of theatrical practice, or, in other words, what Nils Tabert suggests is the German 'obsession with form' (Saunders, 2002a: 136). In my own experience, the 'Giessen School' of theatre students – out of which the idea of 'post-dramatic theatre' emerged under the auspices of Andrzej Wirth and from influences by visiting professors of the American and European avant-garde[2] – are not at all averse to addressing the work of Kane.[3]

I remain rather hesitant, however, about asserting that Kane's theatre fully embraces the forms and theories of post-dramatic theatre. After all, the term is largely absent from the plentiful discussions of her work to date, and Graham Saunders's monograph mentions neither the concept nor its theorist, Hans-Thies Lehmann. This essay will be devoted to assessing my opening remarks rather than to yet another reading of Kane's plays. My key concept will be the claim that her work is 'anathematic' to the notion of dramatic theatre, and I will also touch upon differences between representations of violence on stage and the 'body art' or 'live art' approach to stage violence.

The point of departure for Lehmann's label 'post-dramatic' is Peter Szondi's analysis of theatre up to the 1950s, which held that Aristotelian theatrical form could no longer be compatible with expressing the contemporary experience of the modern world. Roughly, post-dramatic theatre may be defined as a set of theatrical means that transform the Aristotelian formula (mimetic illusionism, narrative, impersonation and dialogue) in performance spaces. This kind of theatre turns the normative dramatic text into a loose Theatertext (i.e. non dramatic texts used on stage), which simply triggers off an autonomous performance seeking to go beyond dramatic action, beyond impersonation, beyond dialogue and, finally, beyond illusionism, referentiality and representation. These features are replaced with an 'energetic' theatre (with reference to Lyotard) in which affects are disentangled from representations. This includes experiments with 'live art', which replaces the re-enactment of a text with 'work that broadly embraces ephemeral, time-based visual and performing arts events that include a human presence and broaden, challenge or question traditional views of the arts' (Live Art Archive), to quote a necessarily sketchy definition from the Live Art Archive at the University of Bristol. 'Post-dramatic' theatre and 'live art' have become rather influential in the state-funded theatrical scene in Germany – probably in terms of setting the agenda for 'cutting-edge' theatre rather than in terms of quantity. Lehmann's term 'post-dramatic' evolves from a reference to Brecht's dismissiveness about 'dramatic theatre': as a kind of theatre which claims to contain a 'world model' – not necessarily a complete or continuous one, but one in degrees of mimetic forms which may or may not be suffused with epic or poetic elements. He concedes, however, that the weak prefix 'post' implies that the dramatic traditions still constitute the key reference point for this newer theatrical practice, which nevertheless eschews the pathos of 'newness'. Lehmann dissociates his usage from passing remarks by Richard Schechner (apropos of 'happenings' and even Beckett, Genet and Ionesco). Interestingly, he argues that the mass media have cued theatre to evolve towards post-dramatic forms since the 1970s (Lehmann, 1999: 22). His 1999 list of core post-dramatic *Theatermacher* (literally, 'theatremakers', from Heiner Müller and Einar Schleef to Robert Wilson and Suzan-Lori Parks) is characteristically low on British names (Tim Etchells's Forced Entertainment and the Anglo-German Gob Squad are two notable exceptions). Kane's name, of course, is missing from his 1999 book.

Sarah Kane: Playwright

Never cared much for playwrights. (Tim Etchells, 1999: 105)

On a most basic level, post-dramatic theatre in Britain has been weak because of scant state funding. Besides, post-dramatic theatre is necessarily about risk and experiment. London theatre audiences for example (tourists, schools, urban professionals) pay high prices for tickets and tend to dislike the idea of being unpleasantly surprised by a show. In terms of theatre aesthetics even many of the celebrated 'in-yer-face' dramatists of the 1990s kept to the mainstream in that they created 'colliding' characters (characters in conflict), told stories, aimed at variants of catharsis and suspense (objects of particular derision for Lehmann, 1999: 49–51) and re-enacted them in ways which in the final analysis conform to various degrees of mimeticism. To put it bluntly: in terms of expected box office returns in London it is less of a risk to call one's play *Shopping and Fucking*, simulate adventurous forms of sexuality and spill blood over the stage than to abandon 'as-if' representation, character or story. If one needs historical precedents one merely has to look back (in anger) to 1956, when theatre aesthetics evolved largely independently of, one might even say in spite of, John Osborne's scandalous transformation of the drawing-room. Consequently, critical attention to post-dramatic theatre from Britain has been minimal. For instance, David Ian Rabey's overview of *English Drama since 1940* chooses to disregard non-dramatic theatrical forms in spite of claims that seem to reflect a post-dramatic aesthetics. According to Rabey, theatre 'can demonstrate the unique power of the fully articulate physical presence' (Rabey, 2003: 2).

One of the most obvious areas in which Kane and post-dramatic theatre seem incompatible, however, is the notion of writing. Kane grew out of the particularly English culture of 'Theatre in Education'. She directed plays in school, directed and acted while studying for a BA in Drama at Bristol University, and subsequently enrolled in an MA course in David Edgar's playwriting programme at Birmingham University. This contrasts sharply with the director-driven theatrical scene in Germany. Here, *Theatermacher* such as Frank Castorf or René Pollesch have become notorious for their destructive approach to dramatic traditions. The plea by commentators such as Gerda Poschmann, who has called upon writers and directors to cease the traditional competition between them, is not surprising in the German context but almost unintelligible in a context of the playwright-driven theatre in Britain (Poschmann, 1997: 346). Consequently, a lot of what has been termed 'postdramatic' theatre has been assigned to the work of collaborative groups who may not even credit a 'writer'. In fact, Tim Etchells, the writer/director of the Sheffield-based Forced Entertainment has criticised the focus on 'writing' in British theatre in no uncertain terms, deploring young writers' 'long long pontifications on the understanding of a comma' (Etchells, 1999: 104) – a criticism that might be addressed directly to a play such as *Crave* in which Kane exhibits a Beckettian preoccupation with punctuation. In the decisive category of the 'fragment' however, both Etchells and Kane are back in agreement, and Kane's statement that she increasingly found 'performance more interesting than acting; theatre more compelling than plays' is on record (Saunders, 2002a: 17). In view of recent crossovers from British playwrights and directors to film one must emphasise that London is (culturally even more than geographically) much closer to Hollywood than are Berlin, Hamburg or Frankfurt, and as a consequence British training (of writers, actors, directors alike) tends to result in a compatibility with mainstream 'dramatic' theatre-making (and, therefore, television and film). Arguably, the words and text of her plays were of supreme importance to Sarah Kane. Most of Kane's plays came out of writing workshops. She ran workshops with visiting writers at the Royal Court, she worked as Literary Associate at the Bush Theatre and first produced *Crave* in a public reading. Kane was also dismissive of star director Peter Zadek's version of *Cleansed* and kept an ironic distance from the pretensions of total directorial freedom one associates with *Regietheater* (i.e. the director-doninated theatre in Germany).

One may argue that Kane, at least up to *Crave*, adhered to basic categories of dramatic writing, to the 'as if' mode: she introduced characters, such as 'Ian' or 'Cate', impersonated by actors, and she involved them in a narrative, however disruptive it may seem. *Crave* and *4.48 Psychosis* subsequently moved beyond this mode, but still adhered to the Beckettian, minimalist, open aesthetics, which includes story fragments, character sketches, immobilised plotting and a dense, precise and rich language beyond the limits imposed by 'realist' impersonation. According to the Beckett scholar Ruby Cohn, Kane moved from 'violent' to 'linguistic' plays (Cohn, 2001: 39).

Mutilations, sexual aggression, suicide and anthropophagia: *Blasted, Cleansed,* and *Phaedra's Love* as theatre of excess and hyperbole

In contrast to Kane's final plays, her first three texts, *Blasted, Phaedra's Love* and *Cleansed*, seem to stay within the dramatic framework of impersonation, dialogue and representation. In the first three plays, it is in the excess and hyperboles required, above all, by the stage directions, that the dramatic concept is subverted from within. It is clear from the reaction to *Blasted* that the major complaint of the critics was directed not against the play's violence – after all, audiences have become used to that – but against the fact that the contingent lack of structure of a violent world spills over into the dramatic form. Kane's violence disconnects affects from representation because it erupts spontaneously and inexplicably. Hans-Thies Lehmann suggests a number of terms that usefully describe Kane's first plays. His ideal is a transgeneric, affective 'theatre of risk' (Lehmann, 1999: 471), against the conventions of sense making. He calls for a theatre of transgression, or, as he terms it, *Überschreitung* (Lehmann, 1999: 456), beyond all sense of order, measure and appropriateness, because these parameters express a political hegemony. Against the adaptability of art, an art within the 'rules' or a 'law and order' art, theatre must remain exceptional. In one of his few essays that address Sarah Kane, he names her (along with Heiner Müller) as a proponent of a reformulated political theatre (Lehmann, 2002: 170).

Because politics means war and terror, Kane's phantasmagoric, illogical horror is a political expression of an 'identity Bosnia'. For Lehmann, both Müller and Kane reintroduce the category of the

political into post-dramatic theatre, a category which was alleged
to be absent from the postmodernist theatre of Jan Fabre, Robert
Wilson, Jan Lauwers or René Pollesch. Regardless of whether or
not one highlights the political agenda of Kane, the key word, of
course, is hyperbole. Kane uses a hyperbolic disfiguration in order
to disrupt the dramatic order in her plays. In 1995, Kane single-
handedly succeeded in breaking theatrical law and order and
in reintroducing seemingly absent taboos into British theatrical
discourse. A brief look at the stage directions of *Blasted* illustrates
Kane's attack on the human body in an excess of sexualised
violence, mutilation and anthropophagia, which contrasts sharply
with moments of tenderness: '[Soldier] *kisses* **Ian** *very tenderly on
the lips ... He pulls down* **Ian**'s *trousers, undoes his own and rapes
him – eyes closed and smelling* **Ian**'s *hair*' (49).

Stage directions such as these make clear that Kane participates
in an interest relating to the body in performance, which has
been fostered above all by female performance artists (Lehmann,
1999: 251). *Phaedra's Love* has fellatio, rape, vultures, and
genital mutilation and disembowelment. *Cleansed* offers various
amputations, rats carrying away body parts and a pole forced a few
inches through an anus. These monstrosities have a potential for
covering up 'meaning' under the affective impact of what is done
by and to the characters on stage. If performed as 'naturalistic'
representations of violence, these enactments will come across as
either shockingly brutal or as extremely silly – after all, no one
is really hurt by the goings-on. One convincing way of staging
these directions is to abandon their 'as-if-ness', to not even pretend
that the audience has just witnessed the sucking out of eyes or
eating of babies. One may, for instance, read the stage directions
out on stage.[4] Reading out the stage directions (or, in Lessing's
terminology, didascalia) instead of (or at the same time as) acting
out these monstrosities and thus highlighting their nascent state
as mere preparatory notations might help in adding a cognitive
dimension to their affective potential to generate shock (or, in
the worst case, laughter). Articulating the stage directions makes
Kane's *Blasted* at the same time more meaningful and (on the
surface) more post-dramatic – but ultimately less controversial.

Kane's didascalia read like an intensified, compressed and
radical version of Shakespeare via Bond via Beckett, complete
with the blinding of Gloucester in *King Lear*, the victimised baby
from *Saved* and the incapacitated talking heads in *Endgame*, *Play*
or *What Where*. Kane fits in perfectly with Lehmann's 'hellish

bodies' (my translation), and the 'panorama of moral depravity and millennial debasement' (Lehmann, 1999: 395). Kane, however, stops short of the ritualistic damaging of the performing self in the body art of Chris Burden, Marina Abramovič and others, which Lehmann conceptualises as an 'afformative' act – an act without meaning or aim beyond itself. Intentional suicide as an expression of depression – a means to an end – might be regarded as meaningful and performative outside of the realm of art, whereas an aimless, meaningless suicide might be, perversely, seen as performance art. In spite of Lehmann's claim that a 'public suicide' would mark the ultimate (and unrepeatable) transformation of selfhood and the final negation of conventional representation and theatricality, Kane's suicide was always perceived as the private result of an illness rather than as the ultimate work of a performance artist, as a public statement of self-transformation. Kane's theatre, therefore, keeps the idea of aesthetic distance, of theatre as a signifying process – in clear contradiction to that old dream of the traditional avant-garde (oxymoron intended) according to Peter Bürger: of art spilling over into life and *praxis* (Bürger, 1974: 66). If Kane's plays fail to hurt the spectator in performing this signifying process, however, their nucleus of pain is likely to have been mediated through other current (and painless) representations of violence (such as the films of Quentin Tarantino). In fact, the textual hints at her impending suicide in *4.48 Psychosis* go some way towards publicising Kane's self-transformation. *4.48 Psychosis*, then, 'performs' her death, albeit in reverse order.[5] Certainly 'the shadow of Kane's death', as David Greig put it in his introduction to the *Complete Plays*, crucially changes the way *4.48 Psychosis* is read (Greig, 2001: xvii) and there is ample evidence how Kane's suicide changed the way her work was received by critics and audiences alike (Saunders, 2002a: 109–11). It follows that, even if Kane's death was never intended to become an ultimate statement of the 'body art' kind, it obviously determines the way her work is perceived. The sacrifice of one's life is incompatible with ironic distance, and in this sense Kane succeeded in substantiating her work with a statement of absolute freedom. Tabert confirms this cynical truth when he argues that 'her death kind of verified that she was absolutely serious' (Saunders, 2002a: 135). A case in point is the reaction of the critic Benedict Nightingale, who felt 'deeply troubled' by her suicide, withdrawing his earlier accusation that Kane used 'mere theatrical shock tactics' (Wengrow, 2000). Similarly, Ruby Cohn prefers Kane's later plays and speaks about a strange 'obligation' to her work: 'Those of us who did not know Sarah Kane owe her the tribute of examining her drama dispassionately' (Cohn, 2001: 40). Surely, theatre research cannot merely offer tributes. As a result of willing herself to become a victim, Kane's violent scenes were eventually taken seriously.

The critical reaction to *Blasted* suggested a helpless and half-hearted attempt at rationalising a gut response of disgust and revulsion – impressions of horror that will stay in the memory of audiences. The main reason why they will stay with audiences is that it is a kind of horror that one cannot come 'to terms' with, that cannot be explained or rationalised. More than the other plays, *Blasted* and *Cleansed* are about affects rather than effects; they are about excessive violence free of irony which provokes responses unadulterated by rational distancing – but whether these affects are generated resides ultimately with the performance, not with the text. In a sense, then, the disruptive and alienating violent power of *Blasted* makes it even more incompatible with theatrical convention than the formally more daring *Crave* and *4.48 Psychosis*. The critical reaction shows that Kane's final plays could be much better incorporated in a theatrical tradition. In a more general perspective, a verbal, Beckettian aesthetics goes down better in academia than gross mutilation, sexual aberrance, mental illness and suicidal Satanism.

Sarah Kane and the theatre text: *Crave* and *4.48 Psychosis*

In an earlier essay, I suggested that Kane's stance on violence sought to re-establish Artaudian holiness in spite of, or even against, the casual casualties of ironic violence *à la* Tarantino *et al.* (Voigts-Virchow, 2001). This is confirmed by Kane's remark to Nils Tabert after writing *Crave*, that she was 'past violence', which to her had become 'so marketable and boring'. I also examined *Crave* for its content of 'emotional plagiarism' of authors such as Beckett or Eliot. Clearly, Kane saw herself as the last 'in a long line of literary kleptomaniacs (a time honoured tradition)' (213) as she put it in *4.48 Psychosis*. She seems to have suffered from, rather than delighted in, the intertextual awareness in the vein of a Joycean 'Plurabelle'. For her, drama became a 'dreary and repugnant tale of sense' (214, again in *4.48 Psychosis*). Investing acts of extremities, sex and violence with hyperbolic meaning was Kane's strategy up to *Cleansed*, but after deeming this strategy a failure she experienced her 'linguistic turn', reinvented herself as Marie Kelvedon (complete with her cat Grotowski) and produced theatre texts that intersect even more precisely with preoccupations of post-dramatic theatre. It is clear that Kane's experiments with the theatrical text hold the key to her final plays, *Crave* and *4.48 Psychosis*. In her paraphrases of Kane's plays, Ruby Cohn, somewhat inappropriately at least for the 'linguistic' plays, speaks of 'dialogue' and 'plot' (Cohn, 2001: 44; 46).

The approach to character, language and structure in these plays is clearly Beckettian in that it bares these theatrical elements, reducing them to mere figments, which ironically reinvigorate their theatrical power. The abstract voices of *Crave* constitute the same timeless, almost bodiless and increasingly wordless existence that Lehmann and others may find particularly in the late works of Beckett. Of course, the voices indicate specks of identity, such as gender, age or ethnicity, and, as is frequently the case with Beckett, the issues of gender and race are likely to erupt in casting. The category of character has been disfigured and the category of language corroded, so much so that characters and their language have been dissociated and language has become autonomous. This is nowhere more evident than in *Crave* when B utters the numbers '199714424' (188) – part of Kane's personal mythology, which she sought to keep private (Saunders, 2002a: 105). 'We're not beginning to mean something?' (Beckett, 1986: 108), reads Hamm's concerned question in *Endgame*, and numbers without a recognisable referent in *4.48 Psychosis* are a clear antidote for the 'repugnant tale of sense' (214). This is not to say that the elliptic, structural but allusive language of *Crave* and *4.48 Psychosis* is meaningless merely because it embraces the aesthetics of ambiguity, which is arguably the hallmark of modernism. On the contrary, the elliptic ambiguity adds layers of subtextual meaning to the language. Particularly in *Crave*, it is marked by collage, fragmentation, repetition and intertextuality. One of its chief referents, again derived from Beckett, is its 'theatereality', its deictic reference to the stage itself. Kane's final words written for the stage in *4.48 Psychosis* are 'please open the curtains' (245). This is a metatheatrical gesture reminiscent of *Endgame*, as well as an inversion of 'the world is a stage', the *theatrum mundi* ironically indicating the subject's suicidal loss of the world. The London production, directed by James Macdonald, nicely captured this in opening the shutters of the theatre building to the street scenes and noises, although this is clearly another inversion of Kane's use of metaphor to indicate a rejection of life.

Kane's texts, therefore, disfigure the notion of character but do not abandon the concept entirely. Other than in the fragmentary performance texts by Tim Etchells and Forced Entertainment, for instance, speech is still assigned to performers whose identity is tied to a role, even if this role has faded from 'Ian', 'Cate', 'Grace' and 'Tinker' to the sketchy figures of 'A', 'B', 'C' and 'M', or even to implicit voices in the text of *4.48 Psychosis*, which moves furthest away from the theatrical 'as-if'. True, *Cleansed* is an extremely fragmentary accumulation of sketchy episodes in the tradition of the *Stationendrama* ('station drama', composed of small scenes). True, Tim Etchells has also written about his own intertextual plagiarism because he sees himself as a 'thieving machine' and writing as 'collecting, sifting and using from bits of other people's stuff' (Etchells, 1999: 101). Neither *Cleansed* nor *Crave*, however, is a collage of fragments or a disparate list of '2,334 Filthy Words and Phrases' (*Pleasure*, by Forced Entertainment, 1997). Nor do they use inaudible language or an open improvisation of confessions by role-less performers, as in the truly post-dramatic (sometimes durational) pieces such as Forced Entertainment's *Speak Bitterness* (1994) or *Quizoola* (1996). A residual notion of 'fiction' may be detected even in the narration of *4.48 Psychosis* – a patient talking to a doctor. Some passages are obviously a satire on medical language or amateur psychology, some adapt the language of the Book of Revelation, some appear as emanations of a 'lyrical I', expressing disgust, despair, and loss of identity.

This is not to say that the Kane texts cannot be turned into 'post-dramatic' theatre. The Frankfurt production of *4.48 Psychosis*, for instance, is an excellent example of a Kane production with a post-dramatic sensibility.[6] Significantly, the director Wanda Golonka is a former assistant of Pina Bausch and has a record of successful dance pieces, and therefore she concentrated her production on the bodies in performance – the body of both the spectators and the performer. It preserves its multi-vocal set-up in a single performer (Marina Galic, in a red, frayed dress, with additional off-voices). Golonka has Galic share the performance space with the audience (as did Kane in her own direction of *Phaedra's Love*), who spent their time suspended on swings, the chains of which were fastened to the flies. This clear theatrical metaphor of the precarious nature of identity and existence is intensified by the performer's courses through the audience maze. While she keeps writing chalk numbers on the boards along her way, thus spatialising the numbers in a way similar to Kane's page layout, she shakes the chains, sending out tremors as bodily signals to a 'shaken' audience.

Kane clearly dissolves the link of impersonated character and dramatic text, and, thus, via Martin Crimp's *Attempts on Her Life*, exhibits an awareness of the post-dramatic concept of *Theatertext*. Taking Brecht, Beckett and Artaud to task, and influenced by the American avant-garde of Wilson and Foreman, Andrzej Wirth has called for a move away from analysing 'dialogue' to analysing 'discourse'. In this context, the term 'drama' seems to limit the reach of analysis within the realm of figurated and impersonated (dialogue) speech in the representative 'as if' mode or the role-playing within the mainstream theatrical practice which is often referred to as 'naturalistic' in the English-speaking world. Speech in *4.48 Psychosis* is free in the sense that it is not assigned to a performer (even if the presence of 'dialogues' is at times indicated by dashes) and hardly predetermined in the way it should be performed. It is 'disfigured' speech in that it is not bound by the requirements of characterisation or situation.

In conclusion, I would like to state the obvious – that *Crave* and *4.48 Psychosis* are clear emanations of a post-dramatic theatrical sensibility on the part of Sarah Kane. In her work there is a clear tendency towards more experimental theatre texts, and this is where I would locate her post-dramatic theatrical maturity. In the true spirit of post-dramatic theatre, she asserted that she thought of *Crave* 'more as a text for performance than as a play' (Saunders, 2002a: 17). There is, however, another, more controversial conclusion to be drawn from her work. Kane herself argued that her later works were more despairing and radical than her first plays, and *Blasted* and *Cleansed* in particular. She said that *Crave* and *4.48 Psychosis* express a non-interventionist attitude towards life, and are therefore an uncompromising statement of rejection and denial. Ironically, however, this seems to have resonated with audiences as a non-confrontational theatrical practice. Certainly, productions of Kane's plays, at least in Germany, have recently focused on her later works, and, as has been amply shown by a number of commentators, her reputation in the theatre has shifted since *Crave* and now rests chiefly on the intertextual richness and 'maturity' of her final two plays. If viewed from the perspective of audience response, therefore, both *Blasted* and *Cleansed* (and not her final plays) remain 'anathematic' and rest uneasily with current theatrical practice. It is in fact in her confrontational, antagonistic and demanding stage directions, rather than in their almost complete absence or graphemic transformation into dashes and 'poetic' indentions in *Crave* and – more particularly – *4.48 Psychosis*, that a post-dramatic otherness is preserved. Having said this, I concede that *Crave* and *4.48 Psychosis* may stand the test of time as richer or more 'avant-garde' texts. Kane's later plays constitute an abstracted rather than enacted pathology, a merely verbal violence. Whereas *Crave* and *4.48 Psychosis* confirm the status of theatre as an 'oral' institution (*oralische Anstalt*, Ginka Steinwachs, punning, of course, on 'moral' institution), the (literally) unspeakable acts of *Blasted* and *Cleansed* cannot be tamed in interpretation but merely avoided as performances. Within the work of Kane, the audience has changed from being uneasy 'witnesses' of uncanny practices to being mere 'auditors', which is arguably a far less threatening and precarious position. Kane has claimed for her theatre an 'anathematic' position, that is, according to ecclesiastical usage, the position of what has been excommunicated, damned and consigned to perdition (ironically, however, the word 'anathema' referred initially to 'a thing devoted', see the *OED* etymology). If, therefore, post-dramatic theatre is chiefly about devoted, anathematic theatrical practice, then Kane's declaration 'We are anathema / the pariahs of reason' (228) from *4.48 Psychosis* is best expressed in *Blasted* and *Cleansed*.

Notes

1 Hamburg (*Blasted*, dir. Anselm Weber, 1996; *Cleansed*, dir. Peter Zadek, 1998), Munich (*4.48 Psychosis*, dir. Thirza Bruncken, 2001), Berlin (*Crave*, dir. Thomas Ostermeier, 2000), or Bonn (*Phaedra's Love*, dir. Ricarda Beilharz, John von Düffel, 1998).

2 Visiting professors included Richard Schechner, Robert Wilson, Richard Foreman, John Jesurun, Heiner Müller, George Tabori and Julia Kristeva. Former Giessen students who have become influential in German theatres include René Pollesch, Tim Staffel, Moritz Rinke, Stefan Pucher, Rimini Protokoll (Stefan Kaegi, Helgard Haug, Daniel Wetzel), She She Pop, Showcase Beat Le Mot.

3 For instance, *4.48 Psychosis* was directed by Ina Annett Keppel in 2002 and shown at the Twentieth Anniversary of the Theatre Studies program at Giessen University.

4 This was done with the ending of *Phaedra's Love* at the Schauspiel Bonn (1998) and in Armin Petras's Schauspiel Frankfurt version of *Blasted* (2003/4).

5 Written in the autumn and winter of 1998/99, *4.48 Psychosis* was not staged until June 2000.
6 More than thirty performances of the play directed by Wanda Golonka were given in the 2003/4 season at the Schauspiel Frankfurt in Durs Grünbein's translation.

Epilogue: 'The mark of Kane'

Edward Bond

To understand Sarah Kane you must understand the origin and logic of drama, which is also the logic of imagination and humanness. The exordium is necessary before her plays can be understood. She is the crisis of modern drama.

Theatre is not drama. There are many sorts of theatre. Kitchen sink, propaganda, 'drawing room' (academically respectable because it may be written about without touching on reality, its signs are existential angst and 'silence'), 'after dinner speaker' (also academically respectable, its object is to exhibit the writer's cleverness), and various forms of junk art-theatre – ritual, rite, performance, happenings, symbolic (all these exploit reductive effects and claim transcendence but are sub-real). Theatre rearranges furniture but there is no house.

Van Gogh wrote of the anxiety of the white canvas. It is without conventional and ideological marks. Not all painters see the white canvas. For these others the dead-hand has already scrawled its graffiti on it. The white canvas is the barrier between plagiarism of the past and creativity of the future. All creativity creates new reality. In drama the barrier may be called 'the terror of the white canvas' – terror because drama destroys and creates reality. The terror of the white canvas divides theatre from drama. To create drama the actor crosses the barrier to find the Invisible Object.[1] Writers and directors may point to the site of the invisible object. Only the actor may enter the site and the object visible.

Creativity originates in the new born, the infant, the neonate. The self is not genetically determined. Genes order the possibility of self but not its creation. The difference between genes and self is close to that between brain and mind. Genes cannot think or experience. The mind knows it has a brain, the brain cannot know it has a mind. The neonate is the pre-self. It creates a self by becoming consciousness: *self*-consciousness is the creation of

209

self. For the neonate, it and the world are one. Nothing is external. The neonate is in – *is* – infinity and eternity. This primordial 'infinity-eternity' experiences pain and pleasure. It is aware of them. Repetition leads to awareness not just of experience but of structure. Awareness of structure necessitates a consciousness of it (since structure is not immediately present to awareness). Consciousness must be aware that it is aware. In this way the pre-self creates the self. Structure is conceptual, reasoning not sensing. The self conceives pain and pleasure as the Tragic and the Comic. These are the self's first concepts: they establish the self. The Tragic and the Comic are not sensations of pleasures and pain but concepts of their meaning. The 'I' is created by entering the Tragic and the Comic.[2] The relationship derives from the self and its site, the world. Drama does not merely search for meaning, it creates it – creates human reality.

Imagination is cause not effect. We are aware not of imagination but what is imagined. The pre-self receives the world in imagination. When the pre-self conceives the self, and the Tragic and the Comic, imagination finds reason. Thereafter, imagination seeks reason, it is the mode of its existence. It *might* seek the solipsistic imaginary but cannot because it is in the site. Creativity is imagination seeking reason in its site – the world, society. Imagination has the two stipulating, structuring values: the Tragic and the Comic. It could almost be said that the self is the site's particular relation between the two. The Comic and the Tragic are the passage into the human. They are the only two existential structural concepts in which reason and imagination cannot be separated. Their logic – on site – is absolute. It is the logic of drama, which is also the logic of humanness. Human meaning is human reality.

Drama's subject is not justice but the *creation* of justice. Self-consciousness is a singularity. An object does not need a 'right to be', it just *is* in the natural order. Self-consciousness is not an object but an act. To act it must be able to act, but as its act is just to *be* this must itself enable its *being*, so that its *is* is its *ought*: self-consciousness must be the self's right to be. If blocked, the mind and consciousness are traumatised and dysfunctional. The self structurally instantiates its right to be in the moment of consciousness. The right to be is the human imperative. The right implicates that its site – place – should be the right place for 'the right to be' to be in (but not because consciousness is the site – place – of itself). In sum, that the world should be its home. All and whatever the infant and later the child does is intended to make its world its home – the child is massively dominated by the drama of the Tragic and the Comic, and only later is the domination temporised by the circumstantial and trivial.[3] This is the child's radical innocence.[4] When the neonate creates a self it divides itself from the world and enters it. In time it enters society. There the right to be becomes the imperative to justice. Its origin is egotistic, but its effect is altruistic. That is, it is rational – I cannot have my justice at the expense of others without creating chaos. But humanness is more than this. The first creation of the self is an act of radical innocence – the entry into primordial justice, inscribed in the relationship between the Tragic and the Comic. This is the human text, the text of the self (animals have no text). Thereafter, humanness is the search not for the utilitarian Utopia but for primordial justice founded in the Tragic and the Comic. It is the human paradox, the origin of our self-enmity and our freedom. Justice is personal, political and ontological. If this were *not* so, violence would be the sum of humanness so long as it were, in Hobbes's meaning, effective.[5] Humanly, Auschwitz would not have been unjust but only too small-scale to be effective. But that it *is* so makes justice the *object* of drama.

Society is unjust. The self enters injustice. The self has two needs, one is to survive, the other is to live justly. They clash. Justice has no objective, determined description but it needs one. It is not an essence, for instance, but a relationship of the imperative to the possibilities of the situation on its site. The determination is logical. Justice in society cannot be what it is in the neonate-monad. Existentially the determination should relate the relationship of the Tragic and the Comic to the site – here, society. Instead, in unjust society the description of justice must legitimise injustice. Ideology does this. It does it partly by relating the social to a historical interpretation of the ontological. Ultimately ideology's power depends on its proprietorship of two things, the economy and nothingness. Ideology must administer society efficiently. To do this it creates morality. Morality is intended to administer injustice. If I do not steal (am good) I support unjust society. I survive and may prosper by being unjust. All mortality is corrupt. I live which is the human imperative working through the Tragic and the Comic. The law cannot give justice. If it ever tried society would collapse. The law administers injustice for the advantage of administration. Culture is intended to make ideology coherent and plausible. Culture may be divided against itself. It is a lie but it must also command enough truth to make society adminsterable and to a degree to express the human imperative (historically in art and religion). Culture is the lie-truth – the truth had at the expense of lie.

The human imperative is to seek justice but what justice is must be determined, be created, in each historical site. It is not a matter of adapting noble everlasting aphorisms to circumstances. That would be too clumsy for humanness. The logic is deeper, it creates human reality. All that is permanent is the human imperative working through the Tragic and the Comic. Seeking justice is not an ideal. It is not genetically determined, on the contrary: it is the logic made possible by Nothingness. The logic is structural in the self, coterminous with conscious being. But ideology turns it into systematic immorality. To be moral I offend my humanness. The social consequence is chaos. I am my own enemy, and I seek revenge on my enemy. Ideology's redescription provides for this: the redesription provides victims, it is a structural support of society. Often the victims are moralised into unknowing complicity and reify their phantom role. So I act out my craving for revenge on others, but I intend it against myself. My motive for my vengeful injustice is not that I am evil or animal-atavistic – I am motivated by the sublimest human need, by the *imperative for justice*. My motivation to justice is realised in my act of injustice. Conversely, the criminal is motivated not by revenge on a society which may have deprived him – the motive for crime is *radical innocence*, the enactment of the imperative to make the world just. It is not even the Freudian desire for condign punishment. If you stand on your head long enough the world turns upside down. The white canvas must be very broad to conceal such contradictions between reality and existence, between meaning and understanding. The law can never understand the paradox, but deciphering it is the logic of drama and humanness. It is the text of Euripides, of Lear and Hamlet. But now a collapsing society can no longer be held together by the disintegrating self. In modern drama site – situation – takes precedence over character.

Social culture is the historically necessary truth-lie. For long periods of time the truth-lie suffices administration and justifies culture. The human imperative is expressed (covertly to itself) in religion and the transcendental. But there are times such as our own of rapid and extreme change. Then a gap opens between technology and the social order based on it and ideology fails. The *truth*-lie turns into the *lie*-truth and then perhaps into the lie-lie. In modern society this is fascism, the union of legend and rationalism, of mysticism and science. The *lie*-truth does not enable humanness, it becomes fanatical and destructive – it fosters the God-rot and the instrumentalisation of science which are human plagues. But drama seeks reason and enacts it, proves it in the Invisible Object, in which reason and imagination are joined in human meaning. In such times in the past drama recreated itself in a new human subjectivity and a new human reality. This was the drama of the Greeks, Jacobeans, the nineteenth-century *fin de siècle* and early modernity.

It is an empty cliché that human nature does not change. Humanness has no nature. The slightest knowledge of history shows that human *behaviour* changes prodigiously. Constant is the human imperative – I recognise myself in the cave artists' images, they enact my need for humanness, they are drawn for me. The origin of the cliché is this – we become more human but increased technological power gives greater violence to our decreasing humanness. It is the Faustian Trap.[6] Humanness is materialism, we are in material nature. *In* it but not *of* it, we are *of* history. We do not change as animals or natural objects do. We translate material change – and initiate material change – within the logic of our subjectivity. We redramatise ourselves. There is nothing transcendental in religion, art or ourselves. Transcendentalism is just imagination in a meaningless cosmos seeking meaning that enables administration to administer and gives hope to humanness entangled in historical injustice. Imagination must have a gap – a nothingness – in which to be free – but in which it is also liable to fantasise, to amend existential failure in daydreams, utopias or even madness. Some animals have elementary reason. No animal has imagination. Animals are shut close to their environment. In humans there is a gap between the self and its environment. It is the gap of nothingness. It is the site of history, of the drama-stage and of absolute human logic.

The logic derives from the structure of creativity. It is as near-as-can-be innate in the self. It is the human imperative to justice implicit in the right to be, the radical innocence of the pursuit of justice in the changing site (our situation), and the concepts of the Tragic and the Comic and their relationship. Together these things are the self. Because for the Greeks the earth was still sacred they kept the Tragic and the Comic apart. For them reason was reverence. The Jacobeans prepared the earth for trade, they rejoined the Tragic and the Comic. For them reason was practical. Post-modernity abandons reason. There is no meaning. In its place it puts the theatres of the tragic-comic, the Absurd, postmodern primitivism, reactionary spiritualism, Beckett and the other clowns of Auschwitz not justified by their pathos, illuminated by their irony or exonerated by their bitterness. Postmodernism retards reason to linearity. To free ourselves from this chaos we must recover the Tragic and the Comic and their relationship. The relationship must be stable, but to be sensitive to change it must also be precarious – being human is dangerous and the greatest danger comes from the self. The relationship is either a new reality or a new destruction. Reason and imagination cannot be divided in the Tragic and the Comic. That is why their relationship can only be enacted – recreated – in the Invisible Object. Together they enable the human, but the human does not know itself. In this Hegel is right – as yet the owl of Minerva flies at dusk.[7]

But something – provisional and inadequate – must be said of the Tragic and the Comic and their relationship. The Tragic is meaning in the face of the meaningless universe, is vulnerability and the lesson of care, is endurance and the willingness to fear, is the pitiless abandoning of illusion and pretence. The Comic is anarchy, derision, treachery, hubris, games of death, panic, nonchalance. The Tragic and the Comic take their stability from each other, and their relationship is the meaning of the self. The relationship may be understood as the situation in the gate. The gate is the site of modern drama. Tragedy asks who are the dead in the gateway? Comedy asks where does the gate lead? The relationship between the two is the logical situation in the human site, and in drama the situation in the gateway. The relationship is not changed by law or fiat or wish. It is the joint determination of freedom and necessity. The human imperative asserts its freedom not against but in terms of the situation's material necessity. What is dramatised in the gateway is what we will live and how we will die.

Society's psychology – culture – and the self's psychology both express the same logic. So far in history the two logics have sufficiently coincided. In all adversities and disasters the relationship between the Tragic and the Comic has enacted humanness. Society has ensured the self, and the self has engendered humanness in society. There is no guarantee that this is the self, and the self has engendered humanness in society. There is no guarantee that this continues. The self is not an essence but a relationship, not an effect of humanness but a cause of humanness. Historically the self imposes its imperative on society and society returns it to the self. What happens if society is powerful enough to abandon not the self, of course, but its human imperative? That happens when administration has sufficient power and means to totally impose its ideology on the imperative. Such a society stops creating culture and instead administers means without ends. At first this is not apparent because it lives off past culture, using up the remnants. Human dissatisfactions and problems are not redramatised to create new humanness. Instead they are made sterile – paralysed by technology and linear science. The new economic power replaces necessitousness with consumption. But to do this – to silence the imperative – morality must be made fundamentalist. Increasingly social misfits and social outsiders are made victims of revenge which is increasingly severe and may become total – a postmodern form of human sacrifice. Revenge and consumption become the new morality. Consumers do not notice they live the lie-lie. How can they notice? In the working out of human logic a new reality has been created, with a new human subjectivity as part of it. That's how one day death camps become necessary institutions of their creator's administration, worthy institutions of justice. Over the gateway of Auschwitz was written *Arbeit Macht Frei*, they did not dare to write *Zum Deutschen Volk* – the human imperative had not been totally destroyed, exterminated. Nazism could not do it, yet democracy might.

This is not yet our situation, but we are the first society that does not create a culture. We live off the past. And as humanness is a relationship between self and society, we are dying out. To an objective observer from another world we are already dead. Our society is not postmodern, it is posthumous.[8] The situation is not unanticipated. Some hundred years ago Freud sensed death – the Thanatos – in the beginnings of modernity. He saw it as a death-instinct in the self. But Thanatos is a characteristic not of self but of societies, it is in their logic not our instincts. The problem is not that we are evil, or have lost our religion or reverted to the beast. On the contrary, we believe in extravagant transcendentalisms and the super-rationality of science (itself a vicious combination). The problem is that we do not understand ourselves. Yet our understanding of ourselves is the meaning we give ourselves – we create the meaning, live it and *are* it. We must understand the logic of humanness and rediscover drama – it is the fatal necessity of our age.

We can now understand *Blasted*. It has two halves and between them is the barrier of the white canvas. The first half is the shabby day-to-day which is also society's day-to-day. For the most part the characters are from a B movie. *Blasted* crosses the barrier. Posthumous society cannot cross it – certainly its reality is on the far side of the barrier, but it can bring it on to *this* side of the barrier. There it is sanitised, institutionalised, fictionalised and made normal. The second part of *Blasted* shows posthumous society's reality unsanitised. It also shows the common ontological tragedy – the self abandoned not only in posthumous society but in the meaningless universe: a self that in order to *be* must seek meaning, yet is abandoned in meaningless nothingness. All past ideology incorporated the ontological into the social – it transcendentalised nothingness. But to do that it had to relate the ontological to the human imperative and give it at least some human meaning. That is far beyond the ability of posthumous ideology: its ontological is horror movies. *Blasted* is truly innovative in the directness with which it crosses the barrier to show posthumous society's reality, its Invisible Object. The play is radical innocence talking directly to its corrupt society. It is as if Shakespeare had written Middleton's *The Changeling* (the title reveals its moment in logic; it is why in my play *In the Company of Men* the protagonist has to be an orphan). Shakespeare abstained from putting a play in a madhouse. His creative role was to establish a new administrative order, but as he also enacted the human imperative he had to show that the new order would still not fulfil the imperative and in time would break down. A contemporary dramatist sees that it has broken down into chaos and there is chaos.

We are the dramatic species. Drama takes place in all human institutions and situations. There humanness or destruction may be created. But society must also have institutions which create creation, that enact the original logic that created the self, but in terms of adult minds in the total world. This is necessary because the Tragic and the Comic are concepts and so must impose their imagination-rational interpretation in the site as it changes – it is the existential imperative of the self in change. The self must ask what is the meaning of its situation? For the Greeks the institution was the stage and drama (and its related forms), in the interregnum it was the church and religion. In modernity it is the media. But the media are just another form of consumption. They have no responsibility to the human imperative, they replace its logic with the mechanics of the market. Greek drama enacted justice, modern screens are obsessed with guilt, they reiterate violent revenge and vigilantism. They barbarise without even the spurious beneficence of other forms of consumption. We have no institution to house drama or human meaning, no creative house of creativity. We have the slums of Hollywood and the bureaucracies of television – and the arsenals of our confusion.

It is easy to see how the self acts out of human logic. But how does the social collective act it out as if it had one will? It does not have one will, the logic issues over the conflicts within it. All society's structures, institutions and ideological doctrines interact – creating a logic is their *raison d'être*. The outcome of their interaction is the logic of their interaction. Necessarily society relates to its site as the self does to its. You may war within history but not against it. We can now understand Sarah Kane's role in posthumous society: suicide. When the mutually sustaining relationship of the Tragic and the Comic fails, the reason attached to imagination (in primary and later creation) becomes incoherent. The logic makes its inexorable move. The Tragic and the Comic change places and each takes on the structural dynamic of the other. It is why postmodernism passes into posthumous-modernism. It is also Sarah Kane's trap. She did not *quite* understand *Blasted*. Nor did its first director. The owl of Minerva flies at dusk … The explanation of it she gave in later interviews was one she had been given. Many close to her told her that although she could use language she had no structure. The truth is the opposite … The structure of *Blasted* is awesomely brilliant. It is at the centre of modern drama. But she had not yet learned to introspect her creativity and there was no theatre to help her. The Royal Court's posthumous revival of *Blasted* was irresponsibly incompetent.[9] No theatre should be excused such negligence.

That is why instead of speaking *of* her society she became its spokeswoman and spoke *for* it. She does not write the play, she becomes it. She has no alternative, it is the logic of creation in the meaningless diremption of the Tragic and the Comic. Because of the diremption, what is happening is not at first clear. She sets out to find the perfect lover.[10] She does this on the far side of the barrier because it has become her *site* – she is the play. But the search also takes place on *this* side of the barrier. Dating, mating, matching and escort shows are television trivia, part of the *lie-lie*. But posthumous society plays it at face-value. It keeps (seemingly) the 'tragic' and the 'comic' in their right places by sanitising them as sentimentality and fun: we are lost but know where we are. It is the snake-pit world of Jerry Springer. But when you cross the barrier in posthumous society the Tragic and the Comic are *not* in their right places – the Comic drives the Tragic and meaning is changed. The logic is simple and inescapable; the search for the perfect lover is the search for someone to murder you. The murderer is the invisible object.

The next stage is even simpler. Clearly, on *this* side of the white canvas posthumous society provides consumption. What does it provide on the far side? As the Tragic and the Comic have changed places it must provide the consumption that is destruction. Society's role is to murder Sarah Kane. But the administration of morality has replaced the search for justice.

Medieval society administered a lie-*truth*, it could have killed Sarah Kane for heresy, lese-majesty or treason. Posthumous society has no meaning. It kills diligently – in hecatombs – in wars and induced famines – but never for justice. It kills to sustain the consumer market. Sarah Kane seeks the human imperative where its meaning is changed. But she cannot know that – she is not writing the play but in it. She has become the prophetess of posthumous society – but she is a Cassandra who does not believe her own prophesy: in this society the Holy Grail is poisoned. Society cannot kill her because, finally, the act would be too honest – it would enact the truth of modern society, of posthumous consumption, and posthumous society is incapable of any truth. It is so entangled that it even tells lies to the truth – as a collective self its processes are transparent to all its agencies, yet it can lie even to its *own* desire for truth – a formula already established in the intensity of the self's struggle with itself in unjust society. We have made schizophrenia the art form of the dead.

Sarah Kane is locked in the play on the far side of the white canvas. Ibsen becomes Hedda Gabler. When the Tragic and the Comic change places, the imperative to humanness becomes the imperative to death. It is as it is with the criminal whose crime – however atrocious – is a search for a just world. Humanness loses everything when it loses its meaning. We cannot be human without the concept of tragedy. Whole civilisations have stood at this point. If Sarah Kane cannot find her murderer, she must kill herself. It is now the logic of her existence, the only way she can live. She has for suicide what the religious call a *calling*. Her suicide – for her – is a Comedy. For society it is a Tragedy. And there is one last step in the logic: now she is dead society can kill her. It has become safe. Her drama will be turned into theatre and marketed as a consumer product.

There is no barrier between life and drama. They are one reality, a cause in one is an effect in the other. Saying otherwise is

Philistine aestheticism. Sarah Kane's last play was as total as her first. Our stage finds life only in death. If we cannot create a new drama the experiment of humanness fails. The logic that created it will destroy it.

Notes by the editors

1 This is an important concept in Edward Bond's analysis of theatre. The Invisible Object refers to the actor who has the potential to create meaning that has been obscured by ideological processes. Bond uses the term 'object' because it *objectifies* and gives meaning to a situation or event. The enactment can be produced through an action, sound, word or speech. As Bond outlines here, only the actor has the potential to find The Invisible Object – the writer or director can only assist. For further discussion of the term and its practical application in drama see Katafiasz (2005) and Bond (2005).

2 Bond's ideas about the neonate share similarities with the work of the French psychoanalyst Jacques Lacan who also talks of a primordial state. However, Lacan believed that self-hood was created through the acquisition of language, which he calls *The Mirror Stage*. This allows entry into society, or *The Symbolic Order*. For an introduction to Lacan's ideas see Jefferson and Robey (1986): 151–65.

3 Bond uses the terms Tragic and Comic in a somewhat different sense from how they are generally understood. Whereas Lacan memorably described the unconscious mind as structured like a language, Bond sees the human mind, shaped by its unique property of Imagination, as being based on a dramatic structure. In this way the mind creates its sense of self-hood (or 'humanness' as Bond calls it) by the need to not only self-dramatise its situation but to make sense of the world. The Comic and the Tragic to Bond are specific sites in the human imagination by which the development of the child is based around the right for the self and others to be, as well as being at home in the world. For a detailed account of the process see Bond, 'The reason for theatre', in Bond (2000): 113–61; Roper (2005).

4 Bond believes that this prelinguistic state is summoned up when we experience a situation that is completely unexpected, which can be described through language alone. See Bond (2003): 95–122; Katafiasz (2005) and Roper (2005): 134–9.

5 Bond is referring to the philosopher Thomas Hobbes (1588–1679) who in his book *Leviathan* (1651) saw the laws that govern society arising from a human fear of violence and desire for self-preservation.

6 Bond gives this term to a paradox whereby changes in culture and technology from the twentieth century onwards have brought 'civilising' benefits to humankind yet have also created or have

potential for destruction on a scale unrealisable say to the Greeks or Jacobeans. See Bond, 'The Faustian Trap' (2005): 106–12.

7 G. W. F. Hegel (1770–1831), German idealist philosopher. Bond's term comes from the following passage in *Philosophy of the Right* (1821): 'When philosophy paints its grey on grey, then has a shape of life grown old. By philosophy's grey on grey it cannot be rejuvenated but only understood. The owl of Minerva spreads its wings only with the falling of dusk.' Hegel takes his allusion from Roman mythology. Minerva was the goddess of wisdom and associated with the owl, which Hegel uses as a metaphor for philosophical knowledge. Here he argues that philosophy itself can interpret reality only after an actual event. Bond applies Hegel's observation to drama, where often meaning can be interpreted only after the event has taken place.

8 For Bond the two terms are frequently synonymous and interchangeable where he believes that technology, globalisation and consumerism have rendered humankind as a species 'dead' as we are ceasing to create our humanness. Enactment through self-dramatisation has the potential to counter these forces.

9 Bond is referring to the 2001 revival of *Blasted* at the Royal Court.

10 Here it is likely that Bond is referring to moments in Kane's final play *4.48 Psychosis* where one of the speaker(s) talks about their search for a lover (214–15; 218–19).

References

Adorno, T. (1970), *Aesthetic Theory*, trans. C. Lenhardt (New York: Routledge and Kegan Paul).

Aristotle (1954), *Poetics*, trans. I. Bywater (New York: Modern Library).

Armand, L. (2006), 'The organ grinder's monkey', in L. Armand (ed.), *Avant-Post: The Avant-Garde under 'Post-' Conditions* (Prague: Litteraria Pragensia Books), pp. 1–17.

Artaud, A. (1958), *The Theater and Its Double*, trans. M. C. Richards (New York: Grove Press).

—— (1964), *Lettres*, in *Oeuvres complètes*, vol. V (Paris: Gallimard).

—— (1970), *The Theatre and Its Double*, trans. V. Corti (London: Calder and Boyars).

—— (1974), *Lettres à propos de* Pour en finir avec le jugement de dieu, in *Oeuvres complètes*, vol. XIII (Paris: Gallimard).

—— (1984a), *Cahiers de Rodez*, in *Oeuvres complètes*, vol. XX (Paris: Gallimard).

—— (1984b), *Cahiers de Rodez*, in *Oeuvres complètes*, vol. XIX (Paris: Gallimard).

—— (1988), *Selected Writings*, ed. S. Sontag (Berkeley: University of California Press).

—— (1993), *Theatre and Its Double*, trans. V. Corti (London: Calder).

—— (1999), *Collected Works*, vol. IV (London: John Calder).

Aston, E. (2003), *Feminist Views on the English Stage* (Cambridge: Cambridge University Press).

Badmington, N. (ed.) (2000), *Posthumanism* (Basingstoke: Palgrave).

Bakhtin, M. (1968), *Rabelais and His World*, trans. H. Iswolsky (Cambridge MA: MIT Press).

Balme, C. and P. M. Boenisch (2001), 'Re-play. Wiederholung der Welt / Welten der Wiederholung im zeitgenössischen britischen Drama', in J. Felix, B. Keifer, S. Marschall and M. Stiglegger (eds), *Die Wieder-holung* (Marburg: Schüren), pp. 269–84.

Barfield, S. (2006), 'Sarah Kane's *Phaedra's Love*', *Didaskalia*, 6: 3, http://www.didaskalia.net/reviews/2006/2006_12_21_03.html.

Barker, H. (1985), *The Castle* and *Scenes from an Execution* (London: John Calder).

—— (1993), *Arguments for a Theatre* (Manchester: Manchester University Press, 2nd edn; 3rd edn, 1997).

Barry, P. (1995), *Beginning Theory: Introduction to Literary and Cultural Theory* (Manchester: Manchester University Press).

Barthes, R. (1977), *Fragments d'un discours amoureux* (Paris: Éditions du Seuil).

—— (1978), *A Lover's Discourse: Fragments*, trans. R. Howard (New York: Hill and Wang).

Bassett, K. (1996), 'Bloodbath at the court of copulation', *The Times* (23 May).

Bateson, G. *et al.* (1969), 'Auf dem Weg zu einer Schizophrenie-Theorie', in *Schizophrenie und Familie: Beiträge zu einer neuen Theorie von Gregory Bateson et al.* (Frankfurt am Main: Suhrkamp), pp. 11–43.

Beckett, S. (1929), 'Dante, Bruno, Vico, Joyce', in S. Beach (ed.), *Our Exgamination round His Factification for Incamination of Work in Progress* (Paris: Shakespeare and Company).

—— and G. Duthuit (1949), 'Three Dialogues', *Transition*, 5, 101–26.

—— (1958), *The Unnameable* (New York: Grove Press).

—— (1965), *Proust: Three Discourses with Georges Duthuit* (London: John Calder).

—— (1986), *The Complete Dramatic Works* (London: Faber).

—— (1994), *Collected Shorter Plays* (London: Faber).

Beevor, A. (2002), *Berlin: The Downfall, 1945* (London: Viking).

Behrendt, E. (2005), 'Die fünf-Sterne-Folter', *Theater Heute*, 5, 9–10.

Benedict, D. (1996), 'What Sarah did next', *Independent* (15 May).

—— (1998), 'Real live horror show', *Independent* (9 May).

Benjamin, W. (1968), 'The work of art in the age of mechanical reproduction', in H. Arendt (ed.), *Illuminations: Essays and Reflections*, trans. H. Zohn (New York: Harcourt Brace Jovanovich).

Berns, U. (2003), 'History and violence in British epic theatre: from Bond and Churchill to Kane and Ravenhill', in C. Schlote and P. Zenzinger (eds), *CDE Studies Volume 10: New Beginnings in Twentieth-Century Theatre and Drama* (Trier: Wissenschaftlicher Verlag Trier), pp. 49–72.

Billington, M. (1995), 'The good fairies desert the court's Theatre of the Absurd', *Guardian* (20 January).

—— (1998), 'Long walk to freedom', *Guardian* (15 August).

—— (2001), 'Review of *Blasted*', *Guardian* (5 April).

Blackadder, N. (2003), *Performing Opposition: Modern Theatre and the Scandalized Audience* (Westport: Prager).

Blattès, S. and B. Koszul (2006), 'From page to stage. Construction of space in Sarah Kane's *4.48 Psychosis*', in T. Rommel and M. Schreiber (eds), *CDE Volume 13: Mapping Uncertain Territories. Space and Place in Contemporary Theatre and Drama* (Trier: Wissenschaftlicher Verlag Trier), pp. 101–10.

Blau, H. (1990), 'The oversight of ceaseless eyes', in E. Brater and

R. Cohn (eds), *Around the Absurd: Essays on Modern and Postmodern Drama* (Ann Arbor: University of Michigan Press), pp. 279–91.

Bond, E. (2000a), Unpublished letter to G. Saunders (24 July).

—— (2000b), Unpublished letter to G. Saunders (9 November).

—— (2000c), *The Hidden Plot: Notes on Theatre and the State* (London: Methuen).

—— (2002), Unpublished letter to S. Holmes (9 December).

—— (2003), 'Notes on imagination', in *Plays: 7* (London: Methuen).

—— (2005), 'Drama devices', in D. Davis (ed.), *Edward Bond and the Dramatic Child* (Stoke-on-Trent: Trentham), pp. 84–92.

Bourdieu, P. (1979), *Distinction: A Social Critique of the Judgement of Taste*, trans. R. Nice (Cambridge, MA: Harvard University Press).

Boyle, A. J. (1997), *Tragic Seneca: An Essay in the Theatrical Tradition* (New York: Routledge).

Bradby D. (2001), *Beckett: Waiting for Godot* (Cambridge: Cambridge University Press).

Braden, G. (1970), 'The rhetoric and psychology of power in the dramas of Seneca', *Arion*, 9, 5–41.

Brater, E. (1987), *Beyond Minimalism* (Oxford: Oxford University Press).

Brewster, S., J. Joughin, D. Owen, and R. Walker (eds) (2000), *Inhuman Reflections: Thinking the Limits of the Human* (Manchester: Manchester University Press).

Brusberg-Kiermeier, S. (1999), 'Obituary: Sarah Kane', *Hard Times*, 69, 40.

—— (2001), 'Re-writing Seneca: Sarah Kane's *Phaedra's Love*', in B. Reitz and A. v. Rothkirch (eds), *CDE Volume 8: Crossing Borders, Intercultural Drama and Theatre at the Turn of the Millennium* (Trier: Wissenschaftlicher Verlag Trier), pp. 165–72.

—— (2004), 'Absolution erteilen und Erlösen erlernen? Religion im zeitgenössischen anglo-amerikanischen Drama', in C. Wulf, H. Macha and E. Liebau (eds), *Formen des Religiösen: Pädagogisch-anthropologische Annäherungen* (Weinheim: Beltz), pp. 360–9.

Bürger, P. (1974), *Theorie der Avantgarde* (Frankfurt am Main: Suhrkamp).

——(1984), *Theory of the Avant-Garde*, trans. M. Shaw (Minneapolis: University Press of Minnesota).

Buse, P. (2001), *Drama + Theory: Critical Approaches to Modern British Drama* (Manchester: Manchester University Press).

Butler, J. (1995), 'Desire', in F. Lentricchia and T. McLaughlin (eds), *Critical Terms for Literary Study* (Chicago: University of Chicago Press, 2nd edn), pp. 369–86.

Calder, W. M. (1976), 'Seneca: tragedian of imperial Rome', *Classical Journal*, 72, 1–11.

Cardullo, B. and R. Knopf (2001), *Theater of the Avant–Garde 1890– 1950: A Critical Anthology* (New Haven: Yale University Press).

Carlson, M. (1994), 'Indexical space in the theatre', *Asaph*, 10, 1–10.

Carney, S. (2005), 'The tragedy of history in Sarah Kane's *Blasted*', *Theatre Survey*, 46: 2, 275–96.

Cavell, S. (1994), *A Pitch of Philosophy: Autobiographical Exercises* (Cambridge, MA: Harvard University Press).

Christopher, J. (1998), 'Rat with hand exits stage left', *Independent* (4 May).

Churchill, C. (1994), *The Skriker*, London: Nick Hern Books.

Cioran, E. M. (1991), *Anathemas and Admirations*, trans. R. Howard (New York: Arcade Publishing).

Coe, R. N. (1968), *Beckett*, rev. edn (Edinburgh: Oliver and Boyd).

Cohn, R. (2001), 'Sarah Kane, an architect of drama', *Cycnos*, 18: 1, 39–49.

Cornell, D. (1995), 'What is ethical feminism?' in S. Benhabib, J. Butler, D. Cornell and N. Fraser (eds), *Feminist Contentions: A Philosophical Exchange* (New York: Routledge), pp. 75–106.

Curtis, N. (1995), 'Random tour in a chamber of horrors', *Evening Standard* (19 January).

Daniels, S. (1991), *Plays One* (London: Methuen).

Danan, J. (1995), *Le theatre de la penseé* (Rouen: Éditions médianes).

Davis, D. (ed.) (2005), *Edward Bond and the Dramatic Child* (Stoke-on-Trent: Trentham).

Davis, P. (1983), 'Vindicat omnes natura sibi: a reading of Seneca's *Phaedra*', in A. J. Boyle (ed.), *Seneca Tragicus. Ramus Essays on Senecan Drama* (Berwick: Aureal), pp. 114–27.

De Vos, L. (2003), '*4.48 Psychosis* van Sarah Kane door Claude Régy. Over de onvoorstelbaarheid van de voorstelling van het niets', *Documenta*, 21: 3, 200–13.

—— (2005), 'Als een opgebrande kaars. *4.48 Psychosis* door Hollandia', *Documenta*, 23: 2, 124–7.

—— (2006), '"Little is left to tell": Samuel Beckett's and Sarah Kane's subverted monologues', in C. Wallace (ed.), *Monologues: Theatre, Performance, Subjectivity* (Prague: Litteraria Pragensia), pp. 110–24.

Deleuze, G. and F. Guattari (1977), *Anti-Oedipus*, trans. R. Hurly, M. Seem and H. R. Lane (New York: Viking Press); *Anti-Ödipus: Kapitalismus und Schizophrenie I* (Frankfurt am Main: Suhrkamp, 3rd edn, 1981).

Derrida, J. (1998), 'To unsense the subjectile', in J. Derrida and P. Thévenin, *The Secret Art of Antonin Artaud* (London: MIT Press), pp. 59–157.

Descartes, R. (1997), *Key Philosophical Writings*, trans. E. S. Haldane and G. R. T. Ross (Ware: Wordsworth Editions).

D'Monte, R. and G. Saunders (eds) (2008), *Cool Britannia? British Political Drama in the 1990s* (London: Palgrave).

Dollimore, J. (2004), *Radical Tragedy* (Basingstoke: Palgrave, 3rd edn).

Dromgoole, D. (2000), *The Full Room: An A–Z of Contemporary Playwriting* (London: Methuen).

Edgar, D. (1999), *State of Play: Playwrights on Playwriting* (London: Faber).

Edwardes, J. (1995), Review of *Blasted*, *Time Out* (25 January).

Elam, K. (1980), *The Semiotics of Theatre and Drama* (London: Methuen).

Elias, N. (1976), *Über den Prozess der Zivilisation: Soziogenetische und psychogenetische Untersuchungen. Erster Band: Wandlungen des Verhaltens in weltlichen Oberschichten des Abendlandes* (Frankfurt am Main: Suhrkamp, 18th edn, 1993).

Elyot, K. (2004), *Forty Winks* (London: Nick Hern).

Esslin, M. (1987), 'Towards the zero of language', in J. Acheson and K. Arthur (eds), *Beckett's Later Fiction and Drama* (London: Macmillan).

Etchells, T. (1999), *Certain Fragments. Contemporary Performance and Forced Entertainment* (London: Routledge).

Eyre, R. and N. Wright (2000), *Changing Stages* (London: Bloomsbury).

Finter, H. (1997), 'Antonin Artaud and the impossible theatre: The legacy of the Theatre of Cruelty', *The Drama Review*, 41: 4, 15–40.

Fletcher, B. S. *et al.* (1978), *A Student's Guide to the Plays of Samuel Beckett* (London: Faber).

Fletcher, J. and J. Spurling (1972), *Beckett: A Study of His Plays* (London: Methuen).

Foss, R. (1995), Review of *Blasted*, *What's On* (25 January).

Foster, H (1993), *Compulsive Beauty* (Cambridge, MA: MIT Press).

Foucault, M. (1977), *Language, Counter-Memory, Practice: Selected Essays and Interviews*, ed. D. F. Bouchard, trans. B. and S. Simon (Ithaca: Cornell University Press, 1977).

Fowler, A. (1982), *Kinds of Literature: An Introduction to the Theory of Genres and Modes* (Oxford: Clarendon Press).

Fuchs, E. (1996), *The Death of Character: Perspectives on Theater after Modernism* (Bloomington: Indiana University Press).

Garner, Jr, S. B. (1994), *Bodied Spaces: Phenomenology and Performance in Contemporary Drama* (Ithaca: Cornell University Press).

Garton, C. (1972), *Personal Aspects of the Roman Theatre* (Toronto: Hakkert).

Giomini, R. (1955), *Saggio sulla 'Fedra' di Seneca* (Rome: Signorelli).

Glenn, J. (1976), 'The fantasies of Phaedra: a psychoanalytic reading', *Classical World*, 69, 435–42.

Goldberg, S. M. (2000), 'Going for baroque: Seneca and the English', in G. Harrison (ed.), *Seneca in Performance* (London: Duckworth), pp. 209–31.

Gottlieb, V. (1999), 'Lukewarm Britannia', in V. Gottlieb and C. Chambers (eds), *Theatre in a Cool Climate* (Oxford: Amber Lane), pp. 201–12.

Greig, D. (2001), 'Introduction', in S. Kane, *Complete Plays* (London: Methuen), pp. ix–xviii.

Griffin, M. T. (1976), *Seneca: A Philosopher in Politics* (Oxford: Clarendon Press).

Gross, J. (1995), Review of *Blasted*, *Sunday Telegraph* (22 January).

Hal, F. (1993), 'Postmodernism in Parallax', *October*, 63, 3–20.

Hasenclever, W. (1959), 'Die Menschen', in K. Otten (ed.), *Schrei und Bekenntnis: Expresionnistisches Theater* (Neuwied: Luchterhand), pp. 520–46.

Hattenstone, S. (2000), 'A sad hurrah ', *Guardian* (1 July).

Hayman, R. (1970), *Samuel Beckett* (London: Heinemann).

Hegel, G. W. F. (1977), *Phenomenology of Spirit*, trans. A. V. Miller (Oxford: Clarendon Press).

—— (1999), 'Elements of the philosophy of the right', in L. Dickey and H. B. Nisbet (eds), *G. W. F. Hegel: Political Writings*, trans. H. B. Nisbet (Cambridge: Cambridge University Press), pp.118–26.

Hemming, S. (1995), 'Review of *Blasted*', *Financial Times* (23 January).

—— (1996), 'Review of *Phaedra's Love*', *Financial Times* (23 May).

Henry, D. and B. Walker (1966), 'Phantasmagoria and idyll: an element of Seneca's *Phaedra*', *Greece and Rome*, 13, 223–39.

Herrmann, L. (1924), *Théâtre de Sénèque* (Paris: Belles Lettres).

Herron, J. (2005), Unpublished email interview with P. Campbell (27 February).

Herter, H. (1971), 'Phaidra in griechischer und römischer Gestalt', *Rheinisches Museum für Philologie*, 114, 14–77.

Höbel, W. (2000), 'Chorprobe im Leichenkabinett', *Spiegel*, 13, 278–9.

Hobson, H. (1956), *International Theatre Annual* (London: John Calder).

Iball, H. (2005), 'Room service. En suite on the *Blasted* frontline', *Contemporary Theatre Review*, 15: 3, 320–9.

—— (2008), *Sarah Kane's Blasted* (London: Continuum).

Ihde, D. (1976), *Listening and Voice: A Phenomenology of Sound* (Athens: Ohio University Press).

Innes, C. (1992), *Modern British Drama 1890–1990* (Cambridge: Cambridge University Press).

—— (1993), *Avant-Garde Theatre 1892–1992* (London: Routledge).

Issacharoff, M. (1981), 'Space and reference in drama', *Poetics Today*, 2, 211–24.

—— (1987), 'How playscripts refer. Some preliminary considerations', in A. Whiteside and M. Issacharoff (eds), *On Referring in Literature* (Bloomington: Indiana University Press), pp. 84–94.

Jakobson, R. and M. Halle (1956), *Fundamentals of Language* (The Hague: Mouton).

Jameson, F. (1981), *The Political Unconscious: Narrative as a Socially Symbolic Act* (Ithaca: Cornell University Press).

Jefferson, A. and D. Robey (1986), *Modern Literary Theory: A Comparative Introduction* (London: Batsford, 2nd edn).

Kalb, J. (1989), *Beckett in Performance* (Cambridge: Cambridge University Press).

Kane, S. (1993), *Blasted*, unpublished draft typescript.

—— (1997), Unpublished letter to G. Saunders (31 October).

—— (1998a), 'Drama with balls', *Guardian* (20 August).

—— (1998b), Unpublished interview with A. Sierz (14 September).

—— (1999), Letter to A. Sierz (18 January).

—— (2001), *Complete Plays* (London: Methuen).

Kant, I. (1991), *The Moral Law. Groundwork of the Metaphysic of Morals*, trans. H. J. Paton (London: Routledge).

Katafiasz, K. (2005), 'Alienation is the "Theatre of Auschwitz": an exploration of form in Edward Bond's theatre', in D. Davis (ed.), *Edward Bond and the Dramatic Child* (Stoke-on-Trent: Trentham), pp. 25–48.

Kellaway, K. (1995), 'Throwing out the blasted hatred bag', *Observer* (22 January).

Keynon, M. (2000), *Nightwaves*. BBC Radio 3 (23 June).

Kingston, J. (1995), Review of *Blasted*, *The Times* (20 January).

Kleinspehn, T. (1987), *Warum sind wir so unersättlich? Über den Bedeutungswandel des Essens* (Frankfurt am Main: Suhrkamp).

Knapp, B. L. (1980), *Antonin Artaud. Man of Vision* (Chicago: Swallow Press).

Knox, B. M. W. (1979), *Word and Action: Essays on the Ancient Theatre* (Baltimore: Johns Hopkins University Press).

Lacan, J. (1977), 'Desire and the interpretation of desire in *Hamlet*', *Yale French Studies*, 55/56, 11–52.

Lacey S. (1995), *British Realist Theatre: The New Wave in its Context 1956–1965* (London: Routledge).

Leeman, A. D. (1976), 'Seneca's *Phaedra* as a Stoic tragedy', in J. M. Bremer, S. L. Radt and C. J. Ruigh (eds), *Miscellanea Tragica in honorem J. C. Kamerbeek* (Amsterdam: Hakkert), pp. 199–212.

Lehmann, H.-T. (1999), *Postdramatisches Theater* (Frankfurt am Main: Verlag der Autoren).

—— (2006), *Postdramatic Theatre*, trans. K. Jürs-Munby (London: Routledge).

—— (2002), 'Sarah Kane, Heiner Müller: approche d'un théâtre politique', *Études Théâtrales*, 24: 5, 161–71.

Lennard, J. and M. Luckhurst (2002), *The Drama Handbook: A Guide to Reading Plays* (Oxford: Oxford University Press).

Levinas, E. (1985), *Ethics and Infinity*, trans. R. Cohen (Pittsburgh: Duquesne University Press).

—— (1989), *The Levinas Reader*, ed. S. Hand (Oxford: Blackwell).

Lewis, E. (1987), *Ficky Stingers*, in M. Remnant (ed.), *Plays by Women: Volume 6* (London: Methuen), pp. 115–25.

Liebermann, W. (1974), *Studien zu Senecas Tragödien* (Meissenheim/Glan: Hain).

Luckhurst, M. (2002), 'An embarrassment of riches: women dramatists in 1990s Britain', in B. Reitz and M. Berninger (eds), *British Drama of the 1990s* (Heidelberg: Winter), pp. 65–77.

Lyons, C. (1982), *Samuel Beckett* (London: Macmillan).

Macdonald, J. (1999), 'They never got her', *Guardian* (28 February).

McMullan, A. (1993), *'Theatre on Trial': Beckett's Later Drama* (London: Routledge).

Maguinness, W. S. (1956), 'Seneca and the Poets', *Hermathena*, 88, 81–98.

Malkin, J. (1992), *Verbal Violence in Contemporary Drama* (Cambridge: Cambridge University Press).

Malpas, S. (2005), *The Postmodern* (London: Routledge).

Marlowe, C. (1986), *Edward the Second*, in *The Complete Plays*, ed. J. B. Steane (London: Penguin).

Mazzoli, G. (1991), 'Seneca e la poesia', *Fondation Hardt Entretiens*, 36, 177–209.

Mennell, S. (1985), *All Manners of Food: Eating and Taste in England and France from the Middle Ages to the Present* (London: Blackwell).

Mercier, V. (1977), *Beckett / Beckett* (Oxford: Oxford University Press).

Merck, N. (2000), 'Ein post-dramatisches Wortrequiem', *Badische Zeitung* (28 March).

Merschmeier, M. (2002), 'Ruhe im Requiem', *Theater Heute*, 1, 24–5.

Michel, A. (1969), 'Rhétorique, tragédie, philosophie, Sénèque et le sublime', *Giornale Italiano di Filologia*, 21, 245–57.

Miles, G. (1996), *Shakespeare and the Constant Romans* (Oxford: Clarendon Press).

Miller, C. (1995), 'Theatre: is it a tragedy? No! It's a comedy: is *My Night with Reg*: a) an Aids comedy, b) a betrayal, c) yet another gay play, or d) none of the above?' *Independent* (8 March).

Miller, J. (1995), 'You pays your money and they eats their eyes', *Sunday Times* (22 January).

Morley, S. (1995), Review of *Blasted*, *Spectator* (28 January).

—— (1998), Review of *Cleansed*, *Spectator* (16 May).

Morris, P. (2000), 'The brand of Kane', *Arete*, 4, 143–52.

Most, G. W. (1992), *'disiecti membra poetae*: the rhetoric of dismemberment in Neronian poetry', in R. Hexter and D. Selden (eds), *Innovations of Antiquity* (New York: Routledge), pp. 391–419.

Murdoch, I. (1961), 'Against dryness', *Encounter*, 16: 1, 16–20.

Murphy, R. (1999), *Theorizing the Avant-Garde: Modernism, Expressionism and the Problem of Postmodernity* (Cambridge: Cambridge University Press).

Nathan, D. (1995), Review of *Blasted*, *Jewish Chronicle* (27 January).

Nightingale, B. (2001), 'Passion that still blazes: Review of *Blasted*', *The Times* (3 April).

Nin, A. (1966), *Diary of Anaïs Nin. 1931–1934* (New York: Swallow Press).

Nodler, J. (2005), Unpublished email interview with P. Campbell (2 February).

O'Reilly, K. (2002), *Peeling* (London: Faber).

Osborne, J. (1993), *Plays One* (London: Faber).

Pankratz, A. (2001), 'Greek to us? Appropriations of myths in contemporary British and Irish drama', in B. Reitz and A. v. Rothkirch (eds), *CDE Volume 8: Crossing Borders, Intercultural Drama and Theatre at the Turn of the Millennium* (Trier: Wissenschaftlicher Verlag Trier), pp. 151–63.

—— (2005), 'Sarah Kanes *Crave* als multiples Fragment', in P. Csobadi, G. Gruber *et al.* (eds), *Das Fragment im (Musik-)Theater. Zufall und/ oder Notwendigkeit?* (Anif: Müller-Speiser), pp. 236–49.

Parrish, S. (2007), Unpublished email correspondence with E. Aston (3 September).

Pavis, P. (1988), *Semiotik der Theaterrezeption* (Tübingen: Narr).

Peter, J. (1995), 'Alive when kicking', *Sunday Times* (29 January).

—— (1998), 'Short stark shock', *Sunday Times* (10 May).

Phelan, P. (1993), *Unmarked: The Politics of Performance* (New York: Routledge).

Poschmann, G. (1997), *Der nicht mehr dramatische Theatertext* (Tübingen: Niemeyer).

Pratt, N. (1963), 'Major systems of figurative language in Senecan melodrama', *Transactions of the American Philological Association*, 94, 199–234.

Pronko, L. C. (1964), *Avant-Garde: The Experimental Theater in France* (Berkeley: University of California Press).

Quay, C. (2007), *Mythopoiesis vor dem Ende? Formen des Mythischen im zeitgenössischen britischen und irischen Drama* (Trier: Wissenschaftlicher Verlag Trier).

Quinn, A. (1982), *Figures of Speech* (Salt Lake City: Gibbs M. Smith).

Raab, M. (1999), *Erfahrungsräume: Das Englische Drama der Neunziger Jahre* (Trier: Wissenschaftlicher Verlag Trier).

Rabey, D. I. (2003), *English Drama since 1940* (London: Longman).

Rame, F. (1991), *The Rape*, in F. Rame and D. Fo, *A Woman Alone and Other Plays*, trans. G. Hanna, E. Emery and C. Cairns (London: Methuen), pp. 83–8.

Ravenhill, M. (1996), *Shopping and Fucking* (London: Methuen).

Rebellato, D. (1998), 'Brief Encounter Platform', unpublished interview with Sarah Kane, Royal Holloway College, London (3 November).

—— (1999), 'Sarah Kane. An appreciation', *New Theatre Quarterly*, 15: 3, 280–1.

—— (2007), 'From the state of the nation to globalization: shifting political agendas in contemporary british playwriting', in N. Holdsworth and M. Luckhurst (eds), *A Concise Companion to Contemporary British and Irish Drama* (Oxford: Blackwell), pp. 245–62.

Regenbogen, O. (1930), 'Schmerz und Tod in den Tragödien Senecas', in F. Saxl (ed.), *Vorträge der Bibliothek Warburg, Vorträge 1927–1928* (Leipzig: Teubner), pp. 167–218.

Reitz, B. (ed.) (1999), *CDE Volume 6: Race and Religion in Contemporary Theatre and Drama in English* (Trier: Wissenschaftlicher Verlag Trier).

Remnant, M. (1987), 'Introduction', in *Plays by Women: Volume 6* (London: Methuen), pp. 7–12.

Richardson, B. (2000), 'Theatrical space and the domain of *Endgame*', *Journal of Dramatic Theory and Criticism*, 14: 2, 67–75.

Rist, J. M. (1996), *Man, Soul and Body: Essays in Ancient Thought from Plato to Dionysius* (London: Variorum).

Ronell, A. (2002), *Stupidity* (Urbana: University of Illinois Press).

Roper, B. (2005), 'Imagination and self in Edward Bond's work', in D. Davis (ed.), *Edward Bond and the Dramatic Child* (Stoke-on-Trent: Trentham), pp. 124–47.

Rosenmeyer, T. G. (1989), *Senecan Drama and Stoic Cosmology* (Berkeley: University of California Press).

Rothschiller, L. (2005), email interview with P. Campbell (12 March).

Royal Court Press Office (2000), 'Press release: Exposure', Royal Court (September).

Rubik, M. (2001), 'Saying the unspeakable. Realism and metaphor in the depiction of torture in modern drama', in B. Reitz and H. Stahl (eds), *CDE Studies 8: What Revels Are in Hand? Assessments of Contemporary Drama in English in Honour of Wolfgang Lippke* (Trier: Wissenschaftlicher Verlag Trier), pp. 121–38.

Ruch, M. (1964), 'La langue de la psychologie amoureuse dans "la Phèdre" de Sénèque', *Les Études Classiques*, 32, 356–63.

Rudich, V. (1993), *Political Dissidence under Nero* (New York: Routledge).

Sakellaridou, E. (1999), 'New faces for British political theatre', *Studies in Theatre and Performance*, 20: 1, 43–51.

Saunders, G. (2002a), *'Love Me or Kill Me': Sarah Kane and the Theatre of Extremes* (Manchester: Manchester University Press).

—— (2002b), 'The apocalyptic theatre of Sarah Kane', in A. Knapp, E. Otto, G. Stratmann and M. Tönnies (eds), *British Drama of the 1990s* (Heidelberg: Winter), pp. 123–35.

—— (2003), '"Just a word on a page and there is the drama": Sarah Kane's theatrical legacy', *Contemporary Theatre Review*, 13: 1, 97–110.

—— (2004), '"Out Vile Jelly": Sarah Kane's *Blasted* and Shakespeare's *King Lear*', *New Theatre Quarterly*, 20: 1, 69–78.

Scarry, E. (1985), *The Body in Pain. The Making and Unmaking of the World* (Oxford: Oxford University Press).

Schäfer, A. and Wimmer, M. (1998), 'Einleitung: zur Aktualität des Ritualbegriffs', in Schäfer and Wimmer (eds), *Rituale und Ritualisierungen* (Opladen: Leske und Budrich), pp. 9–47.

Schnierer, P. P. (1996), 'The theatre of war. English drama and the

Bosnian conflict', in B. Reitz (ed.), *CDE Volume 10: Drama and Reality* (Trier: Wissenschaftlicher Verlag Trier), pp. 101–10.

Segal, C. (1986), *Language and Desire in Seneca's Phaedra* (Princeton: Princeton University Press).

Seneca (1987), *Phaedra*, ed. and trans. A. J. Boyle (Liverpool: Francis Cairns).

—— (1992), *The Tragedies: Volume I*, ed. and trans. D. Slavitt (Baltimore: Johns Hopkins University Press).

Shakespeare, W. (1984), *Complete Works*, ed. W. J. Craig (Oxford: Oxford University Press).

Sharbutt, J. (2004), 'A kingdom of (brutally) honest men: review of *Phaedra's Love*', www.offoffonline.com/archives.php?id=75.

Sierz, A. (1998), 'Cool Britannia? "In-Yer-Face" writing in the British theatre today', *New Theatre Quarterly*, 56, 324–33.

—— (1999), Unpublished interview with Sarah Kane.

—— (2001a), *In-Yer-Face Theatre: British Drama Today* (London: Faber).

—— (2001b), 'Sarah Kane checklist', *New Theatre Quarterly*, 17: 3, 285–90.

—— (2001c), '"The element that most outrages": morality, censorship, and Sarah Kane's *Blasted*', *European Studies*, 17, 225–39.

—— (2002), 'In-yer-face theatre. Mark Ravenhill and 1990s drama', in A. Knapp, E. Otto, G. Stratmann and M. Tönnies (eds), *British Drama of the 1990s* (Heidelberg: Winter), pp. 107–21.

—— (2003), '"In yer face?" in Bristol', *New Theatre Quarterly*, 19: 1, 90–1.

Simmel, G. (1957), *Brücke und Tür* (Stuttgart: Köhler).

Singer, A. (2004), 'Don't want to be this: the elusive Sarah Kane', *The Drama Review* 48: 2, 139–71.

Skeggs, B. (2005), 'The making of class and gender through visualizing moral subject formation', *Sociology*, 39: 5, 965–82.

Skovgaard-Hansen, M. (1972), 'The fall of Phaethon: Meaning in Seneca's "Hippolytus"', *Classica et Mediaevalia*, 29, 92–123.

Slethaug, G. E. (1993), 'Desire/lack', in I. R. Makaryk (ed.), *Encyclopedia of Contemporary Literary Theory* (Toronto: University of Toronto Press).

Soncini, S. (2004), 'Stage wars: the representation of conflict in contemporary British theatre', in C. Dente and S. Soncini (eds), *Conflict Zones: Actions Languages Mediations* (Pisa: Edizioni ETS), pp. 85–101.

Sontag, S. (1988), 'Artaud', in A. Artaud, *Selected Writings* (Berkeley: University of California Press).

Soper, K. (1986), *Humanism and Anti-Humanism* (London: Hutchinson).

Spencer, C. (2001), 'Admirably repulsive', *Daily Telegraph* (5 April).

Stephens S. (2001), 'Interview with Mel Kenyon', Royal Court Sarah Kane Season: Resource Pack, http://www.royalcourttheatre.com/files/downloads/sarah_kane_edupack.pdf.

Stephenson, H. and N. Langridge (1997), *Rage and Reason: Women Playwrights on Playwriting* (London: Methuen).

Stoppard, T. (1972), *Jumpers* (London: Faber).

Stratton, K. (1998), 'Extreme measures: an interview with Sarah Kane', *Time Out London* (4 January).

Szondi, P. (1971), *Theorie des Modernen Dramas 1880–1950* (Frankfurt am Main: Edition Suhrkamp).

Tabert, N. (ed.) (1998), *Playspotting. Die Londoner Theaterszene der 90er* (Reinbeck: Rowohlt).

Tarrant, R. J. (1978), 'Senecan drama and its antecedents', *Harvard Studies in Classical Philology*, 82, 213–63.

Taylor, P. (1995), 'Courting disaster', *Independent* (20 January).

Thévenin, P. (1998), 'The search for a lost world', in J. Derrida and P. Thévenin, *The Secret Art of Antonin Artaud* (London: MIT Press), pp. 1–56.

Thielemans, J. (1999), 'Rehearsing the Future': *4th European Directors Forum. Strategies for the Emerging Director in Europe* (London: Director's Guild of Great Britain).

Tinker, J. (1995), 'This disgusting feast of filth', *Daily Mail* (19 January).

Tönnies, M. (2002), 'The "sensationalist Theatre of Cruelty" in 1990s Britain, its 1960s forebears and the beginning of the 21st century', in M. Rubik and E. Mettinger-Schartmann (eds), *CDE Volume 9: (Dis)Continuities. Trends and Traditions in Contemporary Theatre and Drama in English* (Trier: Wissenschaftlicher Verlag Trier), pp. 57–71.

tucker green, d. (2003), *dirty butterfly* (London: Nick Hern).

Turner, V. (1982), *The Ritual Process: Structure and Anti-Structure* (New York: Aldine, 9th edn).

Urban, K. (2001), 'An ethics of catastrophe', *PAJ: A Journal of Performance and Art*, 23: 3, 36–46.

—— (2004), 'Towards a theory of Cruel Britannia: coolness, cruelty, and the "Nineties"', *New Theatre Quarterly*, 20: 4, 354–72.

Verhaeghe, P. (1999), *Love in a Time of Loneliness. Three Essays on Drive and Desire* (New York: The Other Press).

Vernon, B. (1995), '*Blasted*: a savage play looks beyond indifference to a savage world', *Guardian* (23 January).

Vinopal, J. (2001), 'A Beckett chronology: Samuel Beckett's work in images and words' Exhibit, New York University, B Level of Bobst Library, New York City (19 March–2 May).

Voigts-Virchow, E. (2001), 'Sarah Kane, a late modernist: Intertextuality and montage in the broken images of *Crave* (1998)', in B. Reitz and H. Stahl (eds), *CDE Studies 8: What Revels Are in Hand? Assessments of Contemporary Drama in English in Honour of Wolfgang Lippke* (Trier: Wissenschaftlicher Verlag Trier), pp. 205–20.

Wald, C. (2007), *Hysteria, Trauma and Melancholia. Performative Maladies in Contemporary Anglophone Drama* (Basingstoke: Palgrave).

Walker, D. A. (1995), *Outrage and Insight: Modern French Writers and the 'Fait Divers'* (Oxford: Berg Publishers).

Wallace, C. (2004), 'Dramas of radical alterity. Sarah Kane and codes of trauma for a postmodern age', in H.-U. Mohr and K. Mächler (eds), *CDE Volume 11: Extending the Code. New Forms of Dramatic and Theatrical Expression* (Trier: Wissenschaftlicher Verlag Trier), pp. 117–30.

Wandor, M. (2001), *Post-War British Drama: Looking Back in Gender* (London: Routledge).

Wattenberg, R. (2002), 'Duplicity abounds in the violent world of defunct theatre's *Phaedra's Love*', *Oregonian* (16 January).

Wengrow, A. (2000), 'The year in British drama', in *Dictionary of Literary Biography Yearbook 1999* (Detroit: Gale), pp. 111–19.

Williams, B. (2002), *Truth and Truthfulness: An Essay in Genealogy* (Princeton: Princeton University Press).

Wilson Knight, G. (1930), *The Wheel of Fire* (London: Methuen).

Worth, K. (1986), *The Irish Drama of Europe from Yeats to Beckett* (Athlone Press, London).

Wulf, C. (1987), 'Religion und Gewalt', in D. Kamper and C. Wulf (eds), *Das Heilige: Seine Spur in der Moderne* (Frankfurt am Main: Athenäum), pp. 245–54.

Zimmermann, H. (2001), 'Theatrical transgression in totalitarian and democratic societies: Shakespeare as a trojan horse and the scandal of Sarah Kane', in B. Reitz and A. v. Rothkirch (eds), *CDE Volume 8: Crossing Borders, Intercultural Drama and Theatre at the Turn of the Millennium* (Trier: Wissenschaftlicher Verlag Trier), pp. 173–82.

—— (2002), 'Martin Crimp, *Attempts on Her Life*. Postdramatic, postmodern, satiric?', in M. Rubik and E. Mettinger-Schartmann (eds), *CDE Vol. 9: (Dis)Continuities. Trends and Traditions in Contemporary Theatre and Drama in English* (Trier: Wissenschaftlicher Verlag Trier), pp. 105–24.

Websites

In-Yer-Face Theatre, www.inyerface-theatre.com.

Live Art Archive, www.ahds.ac.uk/ahdscollections/docroot/liveart/liveartsearch.jsp.

United Nations, 'Universal Declaration of Human Rights', www.un.org/en/documents/udhr.

Sphinx Theatre Company. Glass Ceiling 6, www.sphinxtheatre.co.uk/index.cfm?nid=EB95C1F5-3FCF-4A7F-9C00-156832242382.

Index

B.b. # 831063

822.91
KAN.S

Lightning Source UK Ltd.
Milton Keynes UK
UKOW05f100250414

230577UK00003B/22/P

9 780719 086458